ExamWise® Volume

CFA® 2015 Level I Certification

The Candidates Question And Answer Workbook For Chartered Financial Analyst Exam

Jane Vessey, CFA

With the CFA Certification Success Team

www.totalrecallpress.com

TotalRecall Publications, Inc.

All rights reserved. Printed in the United States of AmericA. Except as permitted under the United States Copyright Act of 1976, No part of this publication may be reproduced, stored in a retrieval system, or transmitted in any form or by any means electronic or mechanical or by photocopying, recording, or otherwise without the prior permission of the publisher.

Printed in United States of America, Australia, Canada, and United Kingdom.

Copyright © 2015 TotalRecall Publications, Inc.

ISBN: 978-1-59095-958-9

UPC: 6-43977-95582-1

To my two children, Adam and Julia

Jane Vessey

About the Author:

Jane Vessey, CFA, manages a training company in the United Kingdom specializing in financial analysis and investment. She has been a visiting lecturer at Cass Business School teaching classes in asset management and valuation and is a visiting lecturer at Cranfield Business School. She is an associate at a leading London financial training company where she teaches courses covering investment management and related topics. She has developed online training programs for students taking the CFA examinations and teaches CFA preparatory courses at a number of universities.

Jane graduated in Mathematics from Oxford University and is a CFA charterholder. She has some eighteen years' experience working in the investment industry; she started out as an equity analyst before becoming an investment manager. She was based in London and Tokyo and took responsibility for managing equity portfolios invested in the Japanese and other Asian markets. In 1990 Jane moved to Indonesia and established and ran an investment management operation on behalf of MeesPierson. She took responsibility for all areas of the business, including investment, operations, marketing and administration. Whilst in Asia, Jane was involved in providing training to capital market participants, state officials and teaching at courses provided by local universities

About the Book:

ExamWise For CFA Level I Volume 2 Concept Check Q&A Workbook is designed to give you plenty of practice questions to test your readiness for the CFA exam. It offers 550+ concept check questions based on 18 exam study sessions that cover the Learning Outcome Statements and their associated CFA Assigned Readings. For additional practice, there is an accompanying free download test engine that generates multiple mock exams similar in design and difficulty to the real CFA exam.

Use this workbook to test your understanding of the basic concepts covered in the CFA Readings and identify your strengths and weaknesses. Then you can move on to more advanced study materials to sharpen your weakest knowledge areas.

This book is divided into Study Sessions (1 – 18) that cover the Learning Outcome Statements and the associated 67 Assigned Readings.

The 18 2015 CFA Level I Study Sessions breakout is as follows:

Ethical and Professional Standards

Study Session 1: Ethical and Professional Standards

Investment Tools

Study Session 2. Quantitative Methods: Basic Concepts
Study Session 3. Quantitative Methods: Application
Study Session 4. Economics: Microeconomic Analysis
Study Session 5. Economics: Macroeconomic Analysis
Study Session 6. Economics: Global Context
Study Session 7. Financial Reporting & Analysis: Introduction
Study Session 8. FR&A: Income Statement, Balance Sheet, and Cash Flow Statements
Study Session 9. FR&A: Inventories, Long-Lived Assets, Income Taxes, and Liabilities
Study Session 10. FR&A: Evaluating Financial Reporting Quality and Other Applications
Study Session 11. Corporate Finance

Portfolio Management

Study Session 12. Portfolio Management

Asset Valuation

Study Session 13. Equity: Market Organizaion, Indices and Efficiency
Study Session 14. Equity: Analysis and Valuation
Study Session 15. Fixed Income: Basic Concepts
Study Session 16. Fixed Income: Analysis and Valuation
Study Session 17. Derivatives
Study Session 18. Alternative Investments

Link to a free financial glossary for CFA Candidates.

http://www.financialexams.com

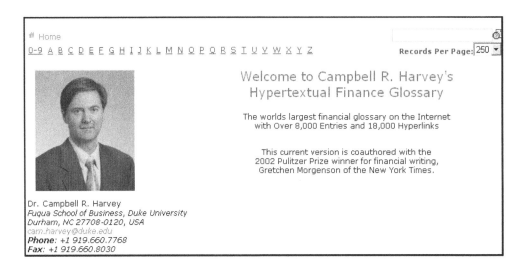

With the purchase of this book you get FREE Author Collaberation:

Now that you have purchased this product you have access to the Instructors/Authors that authored this book. **eMail your questions to us and we will answer them for you.**
In the subject use 2015 CFA Level I.
Bruce@financialexams.com

Table of Contents

Study Session 01:
Ethical and Professional Standards:

The readings in this study session present a framework for ethical conduct in the investment profession by focusing on the CFA Institute Code of Ethics and Standards of Professional Conduct as well as the Global Investment Performance Standards (GIPS®).

The principles and guidance presented in the CFA Institute Standards of Practice Handbook (SOPH) form the basis for the CFA Institute self-regulatory program to maintain the highest professional standards among investment practitioners. "Guidance" in the SOPH addresses the practical application of the Code of Ethics and Standards of Professional Conduct. The guidance reviews the purpose and scope of each standard, presents recommended procedures for compliance, and provides examples of the standard in practice.

The Global Investment Performance Standards (GIPS) facilitate efficient comparison of investment performance across investment managers and country borders by prescribing methodology and standards that are consistent with a clear and honest presentation of returns. Having a global standard for reporting investment performance minimizes the potential for ambiguous or misleading presentations.

1. Compliance with Global Investment Performance Standards (GIPS) can be claimed:

   A. only on a firm-wide basis.

   B. on an investment manager by investment manager basis.

   C. on an asset class by asset class basis.

2. Material nonpublic information, as a matter of course in business, circulates within an investment banking department. If the investment bank has an equity brokerage division, it may create considerable value by using the information in advising the brokerage clients. In order to help conform to the Code and Standards, which of the following is the *best* policy for the brokerage firm to follow?

   A. Ensure that all transactions executed by the brokerage division that result from access to material nonpublic information are fully documented.

   B. Prohibit buy and sell recommendations on the stocks of the investment banking clients until the transactions with the clients are officially completed and the material information becomes public.

   C. Prohibit purchase recommendations because of the unfair advantage that the information may create, but allow the sale of current holdings until transactions with the investment banking clients are officially completed and the material information becomes public.

1. Compliance with Global Investment Performance Standards (GIPS) can be claimed:

*A. only on a firm-wide basis.

    B. on an investment manager by investment manager basis.

    C. on an asset class by asset class basis.

Explanation: LOS: Reading 4-b

Compliance can only be claimed if all the firm's fee paying and discretionary accounts are include in composites, and all composites are GIPS compliant. Partial compliance is not permitted.

---

2. Material nonpublic information, as a matter of course in business, circulates within an investment banking department. If the investment bank has an equity brokerage division, it may create considerable value by using the information in advising the brokerage clients. In order to help conform to the Code and Standards, which of the following is the *best* policy for the brokerage firm to follow?

    A. Ensure that all transactions executed by the brokerage division that result from access to material nonpublic information are fully documented.

*B. Prohibit buy and sell recommendations on the stocks of the investment banking clients until the transactions with the clients are officially completed and the material information becomes public.

    C. Prohibit purchase recommendations because of the unfair advantage that the information may create, but allow the sale of current holdings until transactions with the investment banking clients are officially completed and the material information becomes public.

Explanation: LOS: Reading 2-c

The procedures in applying Standard II(A) are aimed to eliminate the possibility of dissemination of material nonpublic information. The most common ways are to establish a firewall and to create a restricted list of securities if a firm has access to material nonpublic information.

3. Marco Maggio, CFA, is scheduled to visit the corporate headquarters of Venus Industries. Maggio expects to use the information obtained there to complete his research report on Venus stock. The location of Venus Industries is within a 15-minute drive of a prestigious golf course. On arrival at the Venus premises, Marco Maggio learns that Venus is offering Maggio an extension of his stay that weekend and invites him for a day of golf with all expenses paid. Venus Industries also offers to pay for all the expenses for the trip, including the cost of meals, hotel room, and air transportation back to Venus Industries. The total cost for the weekend is about $2,000. Which of the following actions would be the *best* course for Maggio to take under the Code and Standards?

A. Pay for all travel expenses, including costs of meals and incidental items and politely reject the golf outing offer.

B. Reject the golf outing offer but accept the reimbursement of the travel expenses since they are legitimate business-related expenses.

C. Accept the expenses-paid trip and disclose the value of the trip in the report, but it is at Maggio's discretion to take the golf outing offer without disclosing it as it occurs outside working hours.

4. Which one of the following is *least likely* to be a reason why the Global Investment Performance Standards (GIPS) were created?

A. Many countries have not established comprehensive investment performance standards.

B. Investment management firms have operations in multiple countries.

C. GIPS were established to compete with the European-based mandatory global investment performance standards.

3. Marco Maggio, CFA, is scheduled to visit the corporate headquarters of Venus Industries. Maggio expects to use the information obtained there to complete his research report on Venus stock. The location of Venus Industries is within a 15-minute drive of a prestigious golf course. On arrival at the Venus premises, Marco Maggio learns that Venus is offering Maggio an extension of his stay that weekend and invites him for a day of golf with all expenses paid. Venus Industries also offers to pay for all the expenses for the trip, including the cost of meals, hotel room, and air transportation back to Venus Industries. The total cost for the weekend is about $2,000. Which of the following actions would be the *best* course for Maggio to take under the Code and Standards?

*A. Pay for all travel expenses, including costs of meals and incidental items and politely reject the golf outing offer.

  B. Reject the golf outing offer but accept the reimbursement of the travel expenses since they are legitimate business-related expenses.

  C. Accept the expenses-paid trip and disclose the value of the trip in the report, but it is at Maggio's discretion to take the golf outing offer without disclosing it as it occurs outside working hours.

Explanation: LOS: Reading 2-b

Maggio risks violating Standard I(B) Independence and Objectivity because accepting any significant gift may impede his independence and objectivity. He should pay, whenever possible, for his own travel expenses and not accept the golf outing.

---

4. Which one of the following is *least likely* to be a reason why the Global Investment Performance Standards (GIPS) were created?

  A. Many countries have not established comprehensive investment performance standards.

  B. Investment management firms have operations in multiple countries.

*C. GIPS were established to compete with the European-based mandatory global investment performance standards.

Explanation: LOS: Reading 3-a

GIPS were created to fill the void of a globally recognized investment performance standard, not to compete with European standards. There are no mandatory global standards.

5. Joshua Horne has just been awarded a CFA charter. His employer, AEB Investments, decides to change their marketing literature since they now employ three CFA charterholders in the company. Which of the following is an acceptable statement for the firm to include in its brochure?

A. The credibility of the firms' investments services is underlined by its employment of three CFAs.

B. The firm is committed to the highest ethical standards, supported by our three CFA charterholders.

C. We have decided to rename the firm AEB Chartered Financial Analysts Corp. to reflect our commitment to our employees studying for the CFA Designation.

6. Global Advisors runs advisory and discretionary accounts for clients domiciled in a number of different countries. Some of the client portfolios invest in single markets and some invest on a regional or global basis. Global Advisors has established a composite for their discretionary portfolios where the portfolio's strategy is to achieve capital growth through investment in global equity markets. The composite:

A. on the basis of the information given, is compliant with GIPS.

B. is not compliant with GIPS because it should also include advisory accounts.

C. is not compliant with GIPS because it should not state an investment objective in the composite description.

5. Joshua Horne has just been awarded a CFA charter. His employer, AEB Investments, decides to change their marketing literature since they now employ three CFA charterholders in the company. Which of the following is an acceptable statement for the firm to include in its brochure?

    A. The credibility of the firms' investments services is underlined by its employment of three CFAs.

*B. The firm is committed to the highest ethical standards, supported by our three CFA charterholders.

    C. We have decided to rename the firm AEB Chartered Financial Analysts Corp. to reflect our commitment to our employees studying for the CFA Designation.

Explanation: LOS: Reading 2-a

CFA is an adjective not a noun, a firm's name should not include the CFA Designation and the CFA Designation should not be used to claim superior investment skills. Statement "The firm is committed" is acceptable, CFA charterholders should be committed to the highest ethical standards.

---

6. Global Advisors runs advisory and discretionary accounts for clients domiciled in a number of different countries. Some of the client portfolios invest in single markets and some invest on a regional or global basis. Global Advisors has established a composite for their discretionary portfolios where the portfolio's strategy is to achieve capital growth through investment in global equity markets. The composite:

*A. on the basis of the information given, is compliant with GIPS.

    B. is not compliant with GIPS because it should also include advisory accounts.

    C. is not compliant with GIPS because it should not state an investment objective in the composite description.

Explanation: LOS: Reading 3-b

Composites should only include discretionary, and not advisory, accounts. They group together accounts based on strategy and style and are not restricted to a single market. There is no information in the question to suggest that it is not GIPS compliant.

7. Tamara Deneuve, CFA, is an investment manager in charge of Asian equity portfolios. Together with her colleagues, she has developed a new proprietary valuation model for emerging markets in AsiA. Back testing using 12-month earnings data, the valuation model produces favorable results particularly when applied to certain industries, but not to others. Deneuve has decided to implement the new model to those industries but use the usual model for the others. According to the Code and Standards:

A. Deneuve must inform her clients prior to implementing the model.

B. Deneuve has the sole right to any proprietary model she has developed.

C. Deneuve may implement the new model without informing her private clients since they would be unlikely to understand the model.

8. Martha Pierpont, CFA, works for the securities custody department of North Pole Trust Bank. She makes a reciprocal referral fee arrangement with Robert Underhill, CFA, an advisor at *Best*Advice.com. She does not disclose the referral arrangement but Underhill does so by inserting one clause in *Best*Advice.com's investment advisory agreement that includes "… from time to time referral fees may be arranged with a number of selected securities custodians." Clients of *Best*Advice regularly use North Pole's services and pay referral fees. Which of the following is *most accurate*?

A. Only Pierpont complies with the Code and Standards.

B. Only Underhill complies with the Code and Standards.

C. Neither Pierpont nor Underhill complies with the Code and Standards.

7. Tamara Deneuve, CFA, is an investment manager in charge of Asian equity portfolios. Together with her colleagues, she has developed a new proprietary valuation model for emerging markets in AsiA. Back testing using 12-month earnings data, the valuation model produces favorable results particularly when applied to certain industries, but not to others. Deneuve has decided to implement the new model to those industries but use the usual model for the others. According to the Code and Standards:

*A. Deneuve must inform her clients prior to implementing the model.

   B. Deneuve has the sole right to any proprietary model she has developed.

   C. Deneuve may implement the new model without informing her private clients since they would be unlikely to understand the model.

Explanation: LOS: Reading 2-b

The application of a new valuation model may constitute a significant change to the investment process. Her clients must be informed in advance and given sufficient time to evaluate and decide whether such changes have a significant impact to their situation. This falls under Standard V(B) Communication with Clients and Prospective Clients.

---

8. Martha Pierpont, CFA, works for the securities custody department of North Pole Trust Bank. She makes a reciprocal referral fee arrangement with Robert Underhill, CFA, an advisor at *Best*Advice.com. She does not disclose the referral arrangement but Underhill does so by inserting one clause in *Best*Advice.com's investment advisory agreement that includes "… from time to time referral fees may be arranged with a number of selected securities custodians." Clients of *Best*Advice regularly use North Pole's services and pay referral fees. Which of the following is *most accurate*?

   A. Only Pierpont complies with the Code and Standards.

   B. Only Underhill complies with the Code and Standards.

*C. Neither Pierpont nor Underhill complies with the Code and Standards.

Explanation: LOS: Reading 2-b

The best choice is "Neither" since any referral fee arrangement that a client ultimately pays must be disclosed in terms of the nature of the consideration or the benefit together with the estimated monetary value, by both the payer and recipient of the fee. See Standard VI (C) Referral Fees.

9. Simon Freud, CFA, is a private-client investment manager at Super Echo investment firm based in Vienna, AustriA. One of his clients in Monaco offers him a bonus as compensation beyond that provided by his firm if the portfolio performance exceeds the agreed benchmark. To make it more attractive to Freud, his client will send the bonus compensation to a tax-free account in a tax haven. Freud:

  A. should report the situation to the compliance officer of the CFA Institute according to Standard I(B) Independence and Objectivity.

  B. should turn down the additional compensation offer because it violates Standard IV(B) Additional Compensation Arrangements.

  C. may accept the additional compensation subject to the approval of his employer as required by Standard IV(B) Additional Compensation Arrangements.

10. Patricia Lualua, CFA, is a portfolio manager of Raven Asset Management. Recently she won a mandate from the Flemish Widows pension fund trustees to manage the investments of the fund. One of the Flemish Widows trustees privately mentions that Lualua should direct her trades to Churner Securities, which is owned by a relative of one of the trustees. Lualua, for fear of losing the account, directs 50% of the trades to Churner Securities. She is pleased to find that Churner's quality of execution is good and the emerging market research quality is excellent. Although Flemish Widows does not invest in emerging markets, Lualua finds the research useful for the other funds she manages. Lualua decides not to inform anyone regarding the situation. According to the Code and Standards:

  A. Lualua should stop trading with Churner Securities.

  B. Lualua may continue trading with Churners Securities.

  C. Lualua should disclose this arrangement to Flemish Widows.

9. Simon Freud, CFA, is a private-client investment manager at Super Echo investment firm based in Vienna, AustriA. One of his clients in Monaco offers him bonus compensation beyond that provided by his firm if the portfolio performance exceeds the agreed benchmark. To make it more attractive to Freud, his client will send the bonus compensation to a tax-free account in a tax haven. Freud:

    A. should report the situation to the compliance officer of the CFA Institute according to Standard I(B) Independence and Objectivity.

    B. should turn down the additional compensation offer because it violates Standard IV(B) Additional Compensation Arrangements.

*C. may accept the additional compensation subject to the approval of his employer as required by Standard IV(B) Additional Compensation Arrangements.

Explanation: LOS: Reading 2-b

Standard IV(B) Additional Compensation Arrangements does not prohibit the acceptance of additional compensation as long as approval from the employer is obtained.

---

10. Patricia Lualua, CFA, is a portfolio manager of Raven Asset Management. Recently she won a mandate from the Flemish Trust pension fund trustees to manage the investments of the fund. One of the Flemish Trust trustees privately mentions that Lualua should direct her trades to Churner Securities, which is owned by a relative of one of the trustees. Lualua, for fear of losing the account, directs 50% of the trades to Churner Securities. She is pleased to find that Churner's quality of execution is good and the quality of their emerging market research is excellent. Although Flemish Trust does not invest in emerging markets, Lualua finds the research useful for the other funds she manages. Lualua decides not to inform anyone regarding the situation. According to the Code and Standards:

    A. Lualua should stop trading with Churner Securities.

    B. Lualua may continue trading with Churners Securities.

*C. Lualua should disclose this arrangement to Flemish Trust.

Explanation: LOS: Reading 2-b

Under most securities laws this situation is acceptable but under Standard III(A), Loyalty, Prudence and Care, Lualua's trading relationship does not put her client's interest first.

Lualua should disclose the arrangement to the Board of Trustees of Flemish Trust and let the Board give direction.

11. Which of the following statements regarding the requirements of the nine main provisions of the Global Investment Performance Standards (GIPS) requirements is *least accurate*?

A. Firms must present performance results incorporating the following elements: input data, calculation methodology, composite construction, disclosures and presentation and reporting.

B. The composite return is an asset-weighted return of the performance of all the portfolios comprising the composite.

C. GIPS recommend disclosures about performance presentation and calculation methodology. Disclosures are always recommended, but not required.

12. Albert Wonghi, CFA, is a fund manager with Prospect Asset Management. At a lunch time party, hosted by a brokerage firm to whom he directs 50 percent of his transactions, Wonghi has too much to drink and behaves embarrassingly before returning to his office. Other fund managers attend the party. Wonghi's personal behavior at the party is *most likely* to violate Standard I(D) of the Code and Standards because:

A. Wonghi breaks the local laws regarding behavior in public.

B. Wonghi should not drink any alcohol during business hours.

C. Wonghi's behavior reflects poorly on him and the investment industry.

11. Which of the following statements regarding the requirements of the nine main provisions of the Global Investment Performance Standards (GIPS) requirements is *least accurate*?

  A. Firms must present performance results incorporating the following elements: input data, calculation methodology, composite construction, disclosures and presentation and reporting.

  B. The composite return is an asset-weighted return of the performance of all the portfolios comprising the composite.

*C. GIPS recommend disclosures about performance presentation and calculation methodology. Disclosures are always recommended, but not required.

Explanation: LOS: Reading 4-a

Disclosures, in some cases, are required. In other cases it is up to the firm to decide if additional disclosures would enhance the understanding of the performance data provided.

---

12. Albert Wonghi, CFA, is a fund manager with Prospect Asset Management. At a lunch time party, hosted by a brokerage firm to whom he directs 50 percent of his transactions, Wonghi has too much to drink and behaves embarrassingly before returning to his office. Other fund managers attend the party. Wonghi's personal behavior at the party is *most likely* to violate Standard I(D) of the Code and Standards because:

  A. Wonghi breaks the local laws regarding behavior in public.

  B. Wonghi should not drink any alcohol during business hours.

*C. Wonghi's behavior reflects poorly on him and the investment industry.

Explanation: LOS: Reading 2-a

With reference to Standard I(D) Misconduct, Wonghi's excessive drinking will inhibit his ability to work in the afternoon and reflects badly on the profession. The best choice is "Wonghi's behavior reflects poorly on him and the investment industry."

13. Joseph Morgon, CFA, is a research analyst covering the Bourgogne Vineyard Corporation. Morgon's parents bought $50 worth of Bourgogne Vineyard Corporation shares for his two-year old son on his birthday. Under Standard VI(A), Disclosure of Conflicts, Morgon:

A. must file a report with the SEC.

B. must disclose the ownership of the shares by a member of his immediate family.

C. does not need to disclose the fact that his son owns the shares of Bourgogne Vineyard Corporation.

14. Fiona Griffiths, CFA, is an equity sales manager at a London-based Tiger Securities branch in an emerging market. Initial public offerings are often oversubscribed making it difficult to ensure a fair allocation. Griffiths understands the local environment so she is able to influence the allocation process so that she can personally subscribe to the maximum she can afford and then allocate the rest to her clients. Her clients never complain because they have almost always profited from investing in the emerging market over the last couple of years. Which of the following describes Griffiths' situation?

A. Griffiths violates the Code and Standards due to the priority she gives to transactions.

B. Griffiths violates the Code and Standards since she does not maintain client, confidentiality.

C. Griffiths violates the Code and Standards since she lacks independence and objectivity.

13. Joseph Morgon, CFA, is a research analyst covering the Bourgogne Vineyard Corporation. Morgon's parents bought $50 worth of Bourgogne Vineyard Corporation shares for his two-year old son on his birthday. Under Standard VI(A), Disclosure of Conflicts, Morgon:

    A. must file a report with the SEC.

    B. must disclose the ownership of the shares by a member of his immediate family.

*C. does not need to disclose the fact that his son owns the shares of Bourgogne Vineyard Corporation.

Explanation: LOS: Reading 2-b

The share ownership is not likely to be material and therefore will not reasonably affect Morgon's ability to make unbiased and objective recommendation according to Standard VI(A) Disclosure of Conflicts.

---

14. Fiona Griffiths, CFA, is an equity sales manager at a London-based Tiger Securities branch in an emerging market. Initial public offerings are often oversubscribed making it difficult to ensure a fair allocation. Griffiths understands the local environment so she is able to influence the allocation process so that she can personally subscribe to the maximum she can afford and then allocate the rest to her clients. Her clients never complain because they have almost always profited from investing in the emerging market over the last couple of years. Which of the following describes Griffiths' situation?

    A. Griffiths violates the Code and Standards due to the priority she gives to transactions.

*B. Griffiths violates the Code and Standards since she does not maintain client, confidentiality.

    C. Griffiths violates the Code and Standards since she lacks independence and objectivity.

Explanation: LOS: Reading 2-b

Griffiths is in violation as Standard VI(B) Priority of Transactions, since she puts her personal investment ahead of her clients.

15. Joseph Luny, CFA, is a bank analyst with London Fog Securities. On a recent trip to see a bank that he covers, he was presented with a rosy outlook for the bank's earnings in the next two years which is above the consensus expectations. When probed further about the assumptions, the CFO inadvertently mentioned that serious discussions are taking place for a tender offer of a smaller well-managed bank that Luny also covers. This information has not been made publiC. Luny feels very lucky to receive this unexpected tip and rushes back to his office to revise his projections and advise his major clients to buy the smaller bank's stock. What should Luny have done instead?

    A. Luny is entitled to take advantage of the information as he did not misappropriate it.

    B. Luny should refrain from taking any action on the smaller bank's stock until the bank has made the tender offer information public.

    C. Luny should encourage the bank to disclose the tender offer information to the public but is free to take advantage of the information in the meantime.

16. Charles Chaplane, who is not a member of CFA Institute, is a senior partner of a small brokerage firm, Blue Moon Securities, which recently participated in a large stock offering. The offering company has been given an unfavorable recommendation by his research department in the past two quarters due to lacklustre performance. Chaplane immediately calls his junior analyst John Blumenberg, CFA, and instructs him to upgrade his recommendation. Blumenberg comes up with a more favorable recommendation within a short period of time. Blumenberg is *least likely* to have violated the Standards because he failed to:

    A. to avoid a conflict of interest.

    B. to maintain independence and objectivity.

    C. to make a fair statement of investment performance.

15. Joseph Luny, CFA, is a bank analyst with London Fog Securities. On a recent trip to see a bank that he covers, he was presented with a rosy outlook for the bank's earnings in the next two years which is above the consensus expectations. When probed further about the assumptions, the CFO inadvertently mentioned that serious discussions are taking place for a tender offer of a smaller well-managed bank that Luny also covers. This information has not been made publiC. Luny feels very lucky to receive this unexpected tip and rushes back to his office to revise his projections and advise his major clients to buy the smaller bank's stock. What should Luny have done instead?

   A. Luny is entitled to take advantage of the information as he did not misappropriate it.

*B. Luny should refrain from taking any action on the smaller bank's stock until the bank has made the tender offer information public.

   C. Luny should encourage the bank to disclose the tender offer information to the public but is free to take advantage of the information in the meantime.

Explanation: LOS: Reading 2-b

Under Standard II(A) Material Nonpublic Information Luny should not act or cause others to act on this information . If it is not appropriate to encourage public dissemination of the information he can only communicate the information to his supervisor or compliance department.

---

16. Charles Chaplane, who is not a member of CFA Institute, is a senior partner of a small brokerage firm, Blue Moon Securities, which recently participated in a large stock offering. The offering company has been given an unfavorable recommendation by his research department in the past two quarters due to lacklustre performance. Chaplane immediately calls his junior analyst John Blumenberg, CFA, and instructs him to upgrade his recommendation. Blumenberg comes up with a more favorable recommendation within a short period of time. Blumenberg is *least likely* to have violated the Standards because he failed:

   A. to avoid a conflict of interest.

   B. to maintain independence and objectivity.

*C. to make a fair statement of investment performance.

Explanation: LOS: Reading 2-b

To make a fair statement of investment performance is the best choice ", because there is no evidence to suggest that performance presentation is relevant to the question.

17. Marianne Warner, CFA, is a portfolio manager at Creative Investment Management and in charge of managing several discretionary portfolios. Her husband holds 25 percent of the shares of Gurita Corporation, a computer services company. In line with the high sector growth, Gurita Corporation went public earlier in the year. The share price skyrocketed and the value of her husband's holding went up from $1 million prior to the public offering to $8 million at the current market price. Warner believes that the current market price is too high and immediately advises her husband to sell half of his shares. She also recommends he put the proceeds into one of the discretionary portfolios she is currently managing. Is Warner violating the Code and Standards?

A. Warner does not appear to be violating the Code and Standards.

B. Warner violates the Code and Standards for failing to disclose the conflicts of interest.

C. Warner violates the Code and Standards for possessing material non-public information.

18. Which of the following is not one of the nine main sections of the Global Investment Performance Standards (GIPS)?

A. Input data.

B. Verification.

C. Calculation methodology.

17. Marianne Warner, CFA, is a portfolio manager at Creative Investment Management and in charge of managing several discretionary portfolios. Her husband holds 25 percent of the shares of Gurita Corporation, a computer services company. In line with the high sector growth, Gurita Corporation went public earlier in the year. The share price skyrocketed and the value of her husband's holding went up from $1 million prior to the public offering to $8 million at the current market price. Warner believes that the current market price is too high and immediately advises her husband to sell half of his shares. She also recommends he put the proceeds into one of the discretionary portfolios she is currently managing. Is Warner violating the Code and Standards?

*A. Warner does not appear to be violating the Code and Standards.

   B. Warner violates the Code and Standards for failing to disclose the conflicts of interest.

   C. Warner violates the Code and Standards for possessing material non-public information.

Explanation: LOS: Reading 2-b

Conflicts of interest" would apply if the advice was given when one or more of the portfolios contain Gurita shares and there is no information that she holds material non public information.

There is no mention of additional compensation so Warner has not violated any of the Standards.

---

18. Which of the following is not one of the nine main sections of the Global Investment Performance Standards (GIPS)?

   A. Input data.

*B. Verification.

   C. Calculation methodology.

Explanation: LOS: Reading 4-d

Verification is not one of the nine main sections, although strongly recommended. The nine sections are fundamentals of compliance, input data, calculation methodology, composite construction, disclosure, presentation and reporting, real estate, private equity and wrap fee/SMA portfolios.

19. The Code of Ethics requires members and candidates to act with integrity, competence, diligence, respect and in an ethical manner when dealing with:

    A. the public, clients and prospective clients only.

    B. clients and prospective clients only

    C. the public, clients and prospective clients, and employers, employees, and colleagues in the investment profession.

---

20. Which of the following statements is *most accurate*? A firm can claim compliance with the Global Investment Performance Standards (GIPS) standards

    A. without all of their composites meeting the GIPS requirements.

    B. with a "moving window" of 5-year compliant results.

    C. if it has been in existence less than 5 years, as long as any performance record is GIPS complaint.

19. The Code of Ethics requires members and candidates to act with integrity, competence, diligence, respect and in an ethical manner when dealing with:

   A. the public, clients and prospective clients only.

   B. clients and prospective clients only

*C. the public, clients and prospective clients, and employers, employees, and colleagues in the investment profession.

Explanation: LOS: Reading 1-b

The first component of the Code of Ethics is:

'Act with integrity, competence, diligence, respect and in an ethical manner with the public, clients, prospects, employers, employees, colleagues in the investment profession and other participants in the global capital markets'.

---

20. Which of the following statements is *most accurate*? A firm can claim compliance with the Global Investment Performance Standards (GIPS) standards

   A. without all of their composites meeting the GIPS requirements.

   B. with a "moving window" of 5-year compliant results.

*C. if it has been in existence less than 5 years, as long as any performance record is GIPS complaint.

Explanation: LOS: Reading 4-b

If the firm has been in existence for less than five years, it can claim compliance since its inception, but disclosure of the fact is required. Otherwise it needs a compliant track record of five years which must be built up to ten years as each year's results are added. All composites must be included.

21. The Professional Conduct staff under the direction of CFA Institute are *least likely* to make an enquiry into a member's conduct when:

A. they perform random checks on members' professional conduct.

B. members self-disclose on their Professional Conduct Statement that they are involved in litigation regarding their investment advice.

C. the media reports on a member whose professional conduct appears to have been unethical.

22. Johnson McCall, CFA, makes stock recommendations to clients after taking into account the findings of a third-party quantitatively based research service used by his firm. The firm he works for has performed due diligence to ensure the research is sound. Which of the following *best* describes McCall's position?

A. McCall is free to use the research.

B. McCall cannot use quantitatively based research, since it is often using selection criteria that may not be understood in detail by the client.

C. McCall should not use third-party research when making recommendations; he can only use his own firm's research.

21. The Professional Conduct staff under the direction of CFA Institute are *least likely* to make an enquiry into a member's conduct when:

*A. they perform random checks on members' professional conduct.

B. members self-disclose on their Professional Conduct Statement that they are involved in litigation regarding their investment advice.

C. the media reports on a member whose professional conduct appears to have been unethical.

Explanation: LOS: Reading 1-a

There is no mention of CFA Institute performing random checks on members' (or candidates') behavior. The circumstances that might prompt an enquiry are self-disclosure by a member, written complaints, media or other public sources providing information, or whenever a candidate is suspected of comprising their professional conduct during an examination.

---

22. Johnson McCall, CFA, makes stock recommendations to clients after taking into account the findings of a third-party quantitatively based research service used by his firm. The firm he works for has performed due diligence to ensure the research is sound. Which of the following *best* describes McCall's position?

*A. McCall is free to use the research.

B. McCall cannot use quantitatively based research, since it is often using selection criteria that may not be understood in detail by the client.

C. McCall should not use third-party research when making recommendations; he can only use his own firm's research.

Explanation: LOS: Reading 2-a

McCall can rely on his firms' due diligence unless he has grounds for suspecting the validity or the process of the due diligence. Using quantitative criteria to select stocks is acceptable as long as it is based on a sound process and the general principles of how selections are made are communicated to the clients.

23. Jonathan Seller, CFA, works for an investment bank that is acting as the principal underwriter for an issue of stock of a large tire manufacturer. Seller found out that the prospectus has concealed an impending product recall due to a quality control error. Since the number of items affected is relatively small, the product recall is planned to be a quiet affair. However Seller is aware that recently a competitor's product recall received a large amount of adverse publicity. The preliminary prospectus has been distributed. According to the Code and Standards:

A. Seller should do nothing as it may jeopardize the success of the issue.

B. Seller should revise the preliminary prospectus to include the omitted information to avoid any possible misrepresentation.

C. Seller should inform CFA Institute of the violation of the Code and Standards so he can clear himself of the possible misrepresentation.

24. Which of the following is a statement of a member's duty under the Code and Standards?

A. In the absence of a specific applicable law and other rules and regulations, the Code and Standards govern the member's actions.

B. When the applicable local law, rules and regulations do not adequately cover the use of material nonpublic information; a member is free to take advantage of the loophole.

C. When there is a conflict between the Code and Standards and local law, rules and regulations a member can use their discretion when deciding which rules or Standards to comply with.

23. Jonathan Seller, CFA, works for an investment bank that is acting as the principal underwriter for an issue of stock of a large tire manufacturer. Seller found out that the prospectus has concealed an impending product recall due to a quality control error. Since the number of items affected is relatively small, the product recall is planned to be a quiet affair. However Seller is aware that recently a competitor's product recall received a large amount of adverse publicity. The preliminary prospectus has been distributed. According to the Code and Standards:

A. Seller should do nothing as it may jeopardize the success of the issue.

*B. Seller should revise the preliminary prospectus to include the omitted information to avoid any possible misrepresentation.

C. Seller should inform CFA Institute of the violation of the Code and Standards so he can clear himself of the possible misrepresentation.

Explanation: LOS: Reading 2-b

Standard V requires that members shall make reasonable and diligent efforts to avoid any material misrepresentation in any research report or investment recommendation, is the best choice.

---

24. Which of the following is a statement of a member's duty under the Code and Standards?

*A. In the absence of a specific applicable law and other rules and regulations, the Code and Standards govern the member's actions.

B. When the applicable local law, rules and regulations do not adequately cover the use of material nonpublic information; a member is free to take advantage of the loophole.

C. When there is a conflict between the Code and Standards and local law, rules and regulations a member can use their discretion when deciding which rules or Standards to comply with.

Explanation: LOS: Reading 2-a

The rule of thumb is that if an applicable law is stricter than the requirements of the Code and Standards, members must adhere to the law; otherwise they must adhere to the Code and Standards. This relates to Standard I(A) Knowledge of the Law.

25. As an expression of gratitude, Tracy Blanc, CFA, a portfolio manager, is invited to spend a three-week vacation valued at $10,000 with her spouse in a luxurious resort owned by a wealthy private client after she skillfully protected the value of the client's capital during a severe market downturn. The private client is a fee-paying client of Blanc's firm. According to Standard IV(B) – Disclosure of Additional Compensation Arrangements:

    A. Blanc must refuse the invitation as it may jeopardize her investment judgment.

    B. Blanc is recommended to donate the monetary value of the vacation to a charity of her choice.

    C. Blanc may accept such an invitation as long as she reports it in writing to her employer and gains their approval.

---

26. Rachael Jocund, CFA, is an equity analyst following cigarette companies and a rising star in her firm. Her supervisor has been recommending Morass Tobacco as a 'buy' and asks Jocund to take over the coverage of the company. He tells Jocund that she can only change the recommendation with his approval. The Code and Standards say that:

    A. Jocund must be independent and objective in her analysis.

    B. Jocund should report the situation to CFA Institute and try to seek legal protection.

    C. Jocund should follow her supervisor's direction as she reports to him, although she should keep records of any information that would lead her to feel uncomfortable with the buy recommendation.

25. As an expression of gratitude, Tracy Blanc, CFA, a portfolio manager, is invited to spend a three-week vacation valued at $10,000 with her spouse in a luxurious resort owned by a wealthy private client after she skillfully protected the value of the client's capital during a severe market downturn. The private client is a fee-paying client of Blanc's firm. According to Standard IV(B) – Disclosure of Additional Compensation Arrangements:

A. Blanc must refuse the invitation as it may jeopardize her investment judgment.

B. Blanc is recommended to donate the monetary value of the vacation to a charity of her choice.

*C. Blanc may accept such an invitation as long as she reports it in writing to her employer and gains their approval.

Explanation: LOS: Reading 2-b

Blanc needs to report in writing the additional compensation so her supervisor and the firm can assess whether it is potentially a conflict of interest. If there is no objection she is free to accept the invitation.

---

26. Rachael Jocund, CFA, is an equity analyst following cigarette companies and a rising star in her firm. Her supervisor has been recommending Morass Tobacco as a 'buy' and asks Jocund to take over the coverage of the company. He tells Jocund that she can only change the recommendation with his approval. The Code and Standards say that:

*A. Jocund must be independent and objective in her analysis.

B. Jocund should report the situation to CFA Institute and try to seek legal protection.

C. Jocund should follow her supervisor's direction as she reports to him, although she should keep records of any information that would lead her to feel uncomfortable with the buy recommendation.

Explanation: LOS: Reading 2-a

As part of responsibilities to clients and prospects, members must personally maintain independence and objectivity so their clients will have the benefit of their work and opinions unaffected by any potential conflict of interest or other circumstance adversely affecting their judgment

27. Muhammad Taqdir, CFA, is an investment manager whose clients are high-net worth individuals. Taqdir is a member of a local charity organization that supports children with asthmA. During a meeting at the charity, Taqdir recommends that the organization sends a letter to Xara Corporation requesting they make a donation to the charity. Taqdir knows of Xara Corporation's involvement in this cause from previous discussions with a colleague in the office. The chief executive and owner of Xara Corporation is a client of the firm. The charity, citing Taqdir's recommendation, sent the letter and received a substantial donation. According to the CFA Institute Code and Standards:

   A. Taqdir should not have disclosed the identity of the chief executive without his prior approval.

   B. Taqdir should have requested the approval of his colleague before disclosing the name of the chief executive of Xara.

   C. Taqdir should have informed the chief executive of Xara that he is going to receive a letter from the organization.

28. Which of the following is not a concept covered by the CFA Institute Code of Ethics?

   A. Competence.

   B. Integrity and diligence.

   C. Remuneration levels of investment professionals.

27. Muhammad Taqdir, CFA, is an investment manager whose clients are high-net worth individuals. Taqdir is a member of a local charity organization that supports children with asthmA. During a meeting at the charity, Taqdir recommends that the organization sends a letter to Xara Corporation requesting they make a donation to the charity. Taqdir knows of Xara Corporation's involvement in this cause from previous discussions with a colleague in the office. The chief executive and owner of Xara Corporation is a client of the firm. The charity, citing Taqdir's recommendation, sent the letter and received a substantial donation. According to the CFA Institute Code and Standards:

*A. Taqdir should not have disclosed the identity of the chief executive without his prior approval.

    B. Taqdir should have requested the approval of his colleague before disclosing the name of the chief executive of Xara.

    C. Taqdir should have informed the chief executive of Xara that he is going to receive a letter from the organization.

Explanation: LOS: Reading 2-b

Regardless of the fact that that the organization finally received the substantial donation, Tariq has violated the preservation of confidentiality under Standard III(E), Preservation of Confidentiality, in disclosing the name of the chief executive and owner of Xara without prior knowledge of both the chief executive and his colleague.

---

28. Which of the following is not a concept covered by the CFA Institute Code of Ethics?

    A. Competence.

    B. Integrity and diligence.

*C. Remuneration levels of investment professionals.

Explanation: LOS: Reading 1-cb

Remuneration of investment professionals is not explicitly covered in the Code of Ethics. Disclosure of compensation is stipulated in Standard IV(B) Additional Compensation Arrangements and in Standard VI(C) Referral Fees.

29. Carlina Paparazzi, a fund manager with Abbotswood Advisors, has just been given the authority to manage a newly acquired client which has a retirement benefit plan; when she realizes that a US Government Bond belonging to the account matures the next day. The bond comprises 5% of the total assets. Abbotswood Advisors is still in the midst of a discussion with the client regarding the formulation of a new investment policy and portfolio objectives. Looking at what the current market has to offer, there are a number of attractive opportunities. One opportunity that stands out is a corporate bond of a major oil company that went out of favor due to an environmental accident that occurred the week before. She has followed the oil company for a number of years and knows that its fundamentals are sound. The prospect of an improved credit rating in the next six months is not yet reflected in the current price. Her supervisor asks Paparazzi to invest the proceeds in the corporate bond. Paparazzi prefers however to invest them in 3-month Treasury Bills, albeit with a much lower yield, until the new investment policy and objectives are formulated. What is the *best* course of action for Paparazzi?

A. I. Invest in the Treasury Bills until the new investment policy and objectives are established.

B. II. Split the investment between the corporate bond and the Treasury Bills to diversify the risk.

C. III. Follow her supervisor's direction as the corporate bond opportunity will benefit the overall performance of the fund.

---

30. Which one of the following requirements is *least likely* to help to ensure the establishment of an information barrier (fire wall)?

A. Physically separating departments and their files.

B. Monitor employees working for more than one department at any one time.

C. Limit proprietary trading when a firm has access to material nonpublic information.

29. Carlina Paparazzi, a fund manager with Abbotswood Advisors, has just been given the authority to manage a newly acquired client which has a retirement benefit plan; when she realizes that a US Government Bond belonging to the account matures the next day. The bond comprises 5% of the total assets. Abbotswood Advisors is still in the midst of a discussion with the client regarding the formulation of a new investment policy and portfolio objectives. Looking at what the current market has to offer, there are a number of attractive opportunities. One opportunity that stands out is a corporate bond of a major oil company that went out of favor due to an environmental accident that occurred the week before. She has followed the oil

company for a number of years and knows that its fundamentals are sound. The prospect of an improved credit rating in the next six months is not yet reflected in the current price. Her supervisor asks Paparazzi to invest the proceeds in the corporate bond. Paparazzi prefers however to invest them in 3-month Treasury Bills, albeit with a much lower yield, until the new investment policy and objectives are formulated. What is the *best* course of action for Paparazzi?

*A. I. Invest in the Treasury Bills until the new investment policy and objectives are established.

B. II. Split the investment between the corporate bond and the Treasury Bills to diversify the risk.

C. III. Follow her supervisor's direction as the corporate bond opportunity will benefit the overall performance of the fund.

Explanation: LOS: Reading 2-b

Regardless of whether it is the best investment decision, choices II and III. will violate Standard III(C), Suitability, because the overall investment policy and objectives are not yet established. So the best choice is I. , where the client's interest is protected, as a Treasury Bill is a cash equivalent and is risk-free, as are the maturing Treasury Bonds.

30. Which one of the following requirements is *least likely* to help to ensure the establishment of an information barrier (fire wall)?

    A. Physically separating departments and their files.

*B. Monitor employees working for more than one department at any one time.

    C. Limit proprietary trading when a firm has access to material nonpublic information.

Explanation: LOS: Reading 2-a

Firewalls are intended to block the dissemination of material nonpublic information. Ideally employees should only work for one department at any one time B so is the best answer.

Study Session 02: Quantitative Methods: Basic Concepts

This introductory study session presents the fundamentals of those quantitative techniques that are essential in almost any type of financial analysis, and which will be used throughout the remainder of the CFA curriculum. This session introduces two main building blocks of the quantitative analytical tool kit:

(1) the time value of money and

(2) statistics and probability theory.

The time value of money concept is one of the main principles of financial valuation. The calculations based on this principle (e.g., present value, future value, and internal rate of return) are the basic tools used to support corporate finance decisions and estimate the fair value of fixed income, equity, or any other type of security or investment.

Similarly, the basic concepts of statistics and probability theory constitute the essential tools used in describing the main statistical properties of a population and understanding and applying various probability concepts in practice.

Reading Assignments

Reading 5: The Time Value of Money"
Reading 6: Discounted Cash Flow Applications
Reading 7: Statistical Concepts and Market Returns
Reading 8: Probability Concepts
   Reference: *Quantitative Methods for Investment Analysis, Second Edition*,
   by Richard A. DeFusco, CFA, Dennis W. McLeavey, CFA, Jerald E. Pinto, CFA, and
   David E. Runkle, CFA

1. The probability of passing an eye test for people over 70 years old is 80% and failing is 20%, for people under 70 years old the rates are 95% and 5% respectively. 15% of the people tested are over 70 years old.

A report is found of someone failing the test, what is the probability that they are over 70 years old?

    A. 20.00%.

    B. 41.40%.

    C. 95.75%.

---

2. Which of the following statements regarding a data distribution is *most accurate*?

    A. A sample is all members of a specified group.

    B. A statistic is a characteristic of a population.

    C. A mean of a population is an example of a parameter.

1. The probability of passing an eye test for people over 70 years old is 80% and failing is 20%, for people under 70 years old the rates are 95% and 5% respectively. 15% of the people tested are over 70 years old.

A report is found of someone failing the test, what is the probability that they are over 70 years old?

    A. 20.00%.

*B. 41.40%.

    C. 95.75%.

Explanation: LOS: Reading 8-n

Bayes formula: $P(A_1 | B) = \dfrac{P(A_1)P(B | A_1)}{P(A_1)P(B | A_1) + P(A_2)P(B | A_2)}$

Define A1 is that they are over 70, and B is that the person fails the test.

$$P(A_1 | B) = \frac{0.15 \times 0.20}{0.15 \times 0.20 + 0.85 \times 0.05} = 0.414$$

Note that this is the joint probability that they are over 70 and fail, divided by the total probability of failure.

---

2. Which of the following statements regarding a data distribution is *most accurate*?

    A. A sample is all members of a specified group.

    B. A statistic is a characteristic of a population.

*C. A mean of a population is an example of a parameter.

Explanation: LOS: Reading 7-b

A parameter is a characteristic of a population and a statistic is a characteristic of a sample. A population, not a sample, is all members of a group.

3. An investment is attractive if:

   A. the IRR provides a positive net present value (NPV).

   B. the net internal rate of return (IRR) is positive.

   C. the internal rate of return (IRR) is *higher* than the cost of capital.

---

4. The following data is provided on the returns from a universe of mutual funds over the previous year.

	1st Quartile	2nd Quartile	3rd Quartile	4th Quartile
Return	8.0%	9.5%	9.8%	15.5%

Which of the following statements is supported by the data?

   A. The *average* fund return was between 9.5% and 9.8%.

   B. Three quarters of funds achieved returns less than or equal to 9.8%.

   C. One quarter of funds achieved returns that were less than or equal to 8%.

3. An investment is attractive if:

   A. the IRR provides a positive net present value (NPV).

   B. the net internal rate of return (IRR) is positive.

*C. the internal rate of return (IRR) is *higher* than the cost of capital.

Explanation: LOS: Reading 6-a

The IRR needs to be above the hurdle rate, which is the cost of capital, for it to be attractive.

The NPV needs to be positive. The IRR is the discount rate that makes the NPV equal to zero.

---

4. The following data is provided on the returns from a universe of mutual funds over the previous year.

	1st Quartile	2nd Quartile	3rd Quartile	4th Quartile
Return	8.0%	9.5%	9.8%	15.5%

Which of the following statements is supported by the data?

   A. The *average* fund return was between 9.5% and 9.8%.

   B. Three quarters of funds achieved returns more than or equal to 9.8%.

*C. One quarter of funds achieved returns that were less than or equal to 8%.

Explanation: LOS: Reading 7-f

The first quartile is 8% which means that 25% of funds had returns of 8% or below, the second quartile is 9.5% which means that 50% of funds had return of 9.5% and below and so on. We cannot conclude from the data the average returns for funds.

5. An analyst estimates that there is a 75% probability that the stock market will rise in the next quarter. In the case that the market rises, ABC Corp. shares will have a 90% probability of also rising, in the case that the market is flat or declines he estimates that ABC Corp. shares have a 60% probability of declining. The probability of ABC Corp. shares rising is *closest* to:

    A. 75.0%.

    B. 77.5%.

    C. 82.5%.

6. A stock market series is trading at 700 and is estimated to rise to 800 in one year's time. If the dividend payment on the stock market series over this period is 25 then the expected holding period return is *closest* to:

    A. 14.28%.

    B. 15.63%.

    C. 17.85%.

5. An analyst estimates that there is a 75% probability that the stock market will rise in the next quarter. In the case that the market rises, ABC Corp. shares will have a 90% probability of also rising, in the case that the market is flat or declines he estimates that ABC Corp. shares have a 60% probability of declining. The probability of ABC Corp. shares rising is *closest* to:

    A. 75.0%.

*B. 77.5%.

    C. 82.5%.

Explanation: LOS: Reading 8-h

Apply the total probability rule $P(A) = P(A\,|\,S_1)P(S_1) +\ P(A\,|\,S_2)P(S_2)$

where A is the case that ABC Corp. shares rise and

S_1 is that the market rises and S_2 is that the market falls.

$$P(A) = (0.90 \times 0.75) + (0.40 \times 0.25) = 0.675 + 0.1 = 0.775$$

---

6. A stock market series is trading at 700 and is estimated to rise to 800 in one year's time. If the dividend payment on the stock market series over this period is 25 then the expected holding period return is *closest* to:

    A. 14.28%.

    B. 15.63%.

*C. 17.85%.

Explanation: LOS: Reading 6-b

The expected return is given by E(R) where:

E(R) = (EV – BV + Div)/BV = 125/700 = 17.85%

and E(V) is end value, B(V) is beginning value, and Div is the dividend.

7. Which of the following statements is *most accurate* regarding a money-weighted rate of return for a portfolio?

　　A. I. It is the internal rate of return.

　　B. II. It is always lower than the time-weighted rate of return.

　　C. III. It is the geometric *average* of the periodic rates of return.

---

8. Conditional probability refers to the probability:

　　A. that one of two mutually exclusive events will occur.

　　B. that two or more events will occur concurrently.

　　C. of a particular event occurring given that another event has already occurred.

7. Which of the following statements is *most accurate* regarding a money-weighted rate of return for a portfolio?

*A. It is the internal rate of return.

   B. It is always lower than the time-weighted rate of return.

   C. It is the geometric *average* of the periodic rates of return.

Explanation: LOS: Reading 6-d

I. Internal rate of return (IRR)

Dollar-weighted rate of return. Discount rate at which net present value (NPV) investment is zero. The rate at which a bond's future cash_flow, discounted back to today, equal its price.

B. will not be true if there have been cash flows into the portfolio before superior performance.

C. refers to the geometric time-weighted rates of return.

---

8. Conditional probability refers to the probability:

   A. that one of two mutually exclusive events will occur.

   B. that two or more events will occur concurrently.

*C. of a particular event occurring given that another event has already occurred.

Explanation: LOS: Reading 8-d

Conditional probability is the probability of an event occurring given another event has already occurred. It is 'conditional' on the other event.

9. A perpetuity has a price of $1,500 and interest rates are 5% then the payments made per year are *closest* to:

    A. $33.33.

    B. $50.00.

    C. $75.00.

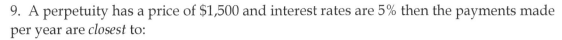

10. If a credit card company charges interest at a rate of 15% compounded monthly, then the effective annual rate of interest is *closest* to:

    A. 14.04%.

    B. 15.86%.

    C. 16.08%.

9. A perpetuity has a price of $1,500 and interest rates are 5% then the payments made per year are *closest* to:

    A. $33.33.

    B. $50.00.

*C. $75.00.

Explanation: LOS: Reading 5-e

$$PV = \frac{A}{r}$$

$$A = \$1,500 \times 0.05 = \$75$$

---

10. If a credit card company charges interest at a rate of 15% compounded monthly, then the effective annual rate of interest is *closest* to:

    A. 14.04%.

    B. 15.86%.

*C. 16.08%.

Explanation: LOS: Reading 5-c

$$EAR = \left(1 + \frac{r_S}{m}\right)^m - 1$$

$$= (1 + 0.0125)^{12} - 1$$

$$= 16.08\%$$

11. The probability of a customer purchasing US dollars is 40%, the probability of them purchasing Japanese Yen is 60% and the probability of them purchasing both is 10%. What is the probability of a customer, chosen at random, ordering neither US dollars nor Japanese Yen?

    A. 0.10.

    B. 0.14.

    C. 0.24.

---

12. Which of the following statements is *most accurate* with respect to the holding period return of an investment?

    A. The return cannot be negative.

    B. The return is an annual percentage yield.

    C. The return includes cash paid to the investor over the period.

11. The probability of a customer purchasing US dollars is 40%, the probability of them purchasing Japanese Yen is 60% and the probability of them purchasing both is 10%. What is the probability of a customer, chosen at random, ordering neither US dollars nor Japanese Yen?

*A. 0.10.

B. 0.14.

C. 0.24.

Explanation: LOS: Reading 8-e

Use the general rule of addition to calculate the probability that a customer purchases either dollars or Yen:

P(A or B) =   P(A) + P(B) - P(A and B

= 0.4 + 0.6 - 0.1   = 0.9

The probability of a customer purchasing neither is 1 - 0.9 = 0.1

---

12. Which of the following statements is *most accurate* with respect to the holding period return of an investment?

A. The return cannot be negative.

B. The return is an annual percentage yield.

*C. The return includes cash paid to the investor over the period.

Explanation: LOS: Reading 6-c

The holding period return is given by the equation below; it is the capital gain (or loss) plus income as a percentage of initial value.

R   = (EV – BV + Div)/BV

13. A portfolio of investments is initially worth $100 million. At the end of the first period the value rises to $120 million and then falls to $90 million at the end of the second period. If there are no cash flows the geometric mean rate of return is *closest* to:

    A. - 2.5%.

    B. -5.1%.

    C. -10.0%.

14. If the mean of a distribution is 6 and the standard deviation is 3 then Chebyshev's inequality states that the percentage of the observations that lie between 0 and 12 is at least:

    A. 40%.

    B. 75%.

    C. 94%.

13. A portfolio of investments is initially worth $100 million. At the end of the first period the value rises to $120 million and then falls to $90 million at the end of the second period. If there are no cash flows the geometric mean rate of return is *closest* to:

    A. - 2.5%.

*B. -5.1%.

    C. -10.0%.

Explanation: LOS: Reading 7-e

The geometric mean (GM) is given by:

The geometric mean (GM) is given by:

$$1 + R_G = \sqrt[n]{(1+R_1)(1+R_2).....(1+R_n)}$$

$$R_G = (1.2 \times 0.75)^{1/2} - 1 = -5.1\%$$

14. If the mean of a distribution is 6 and the standard deviation is 3 then Chebyshev's inequality states that the percentage of the observations that lie between 0 and 12 is at least:

    A. 40%.

*B. 75%.

    C. 94%.

Explanation: LOS: Reading 7-h

0 and 12 are 2 standard deviations away from the mean so using Chebyshev's inequality with k = 2, $1 - 1/k2$ or at least 75% of observations will lie within this range.

15. Which is the lowest yield on a 90-day Treasury bill?

   A. Bank discount yield.

   B. Effective annual yield.

   C. Money market yield.

---

16. If P(A | B) = P(A) then the events A and B are:

   A. independent.

   B. mutually exclusive.

   C. equally likely to occur.

15. Which is the lowest yield on a 90-day Treasury bill?

*A. Bank discount yield.

    B. Effective annual yield.

    C. Money market yield.

Explanation: LOS: Reading 6-e

The highest will be the effective annual yield, followed by the money market yield, followed by the bank discount yield. This is a result of the compounding in the effective annual yield calculation, and the money market yield being based on the purchase price, whereas the bank discount yield is based on the maturity value.

---

16. If $P(A \mid B) = P(A)$ then the events A and B are:

*A. independent.

    B. mutually exclusive.

    C. equally likely to occur.

Explanation: LOS: Reading 8-g

Two events are independent if the occurrence of one event does not affect the probability of the other event occurring.

17. A shop which sells matches knows that 14 out of 20 boxes of matches will contain 100 matches exactly; the remainder will contain more than 100 matches. The probability of a customer picking up a box of matches that contains more than 100 matches, and then picking up a second box containing more than 100 matches is *closest* to:

    A. 0.06.

    B. 0.08.

    C. 0.09.

18. An investor puts $50,000 into a mutual fund at the end of each quarter and his purchase prices are $20, $25, $28, $23. The *average* price that he pays per share is *closest* to:

    A. $23.12.

    B. $23.64.

    C. $24.00.

17. A shop which sells matches knows that 14 out of 20 boxes of matches will contain 100 matches exactly; the remainder will contain more than 100 matches. The probability of a customer picking up a box of matches that contains more than 100 matches, and then picking up a second box containing more than 100 matches is *closest* to:

   A. 0.06.

*B. 0.08.

   C. 0.09.

Explanation: LOS: Reading 8-f

Use the general rule of multiplication, which says that:

$$P(A \text{ and } B) \quad = P(A)\,P(B\,|\,A)$$
$$= 6/20 \;\; 5/19$$
$$= 0.08$$

---

18. An investor puts $50,000 into a mutual fund at the end of each quarter and his purchase prices are $20, $25, $28, $23. The *average* price that he pays per share is *closest* to:

   A. $23.12.

*B. $23.64.

   C. $24.00.

Explanation: LOS: Reading 7-e

The harmonic mean is the *average* price on a per share basis.

$$\overline{X}_H = \frac{n}{\sum\limits_{i=1}^{n}\left(\dfrac{1}{X_i}\right)} = \frac{4}{\left(\dfrac{1}{20}+\dfrac{1}{25}+\dfrac{1}{28}+\dfrac{1}{23}\right)} = \frac{4}{0.1692} = \$23.64$$

19. A mortgage has an annual quoted interest rate of 12 percent. If mortgage payments are made monthly, then the effective annual interest rate is *closest* to:

    A. 12.36%.

    B. 12.55%.

    C. 12.68%.

---

20. The value of a portfolio starts at $100 million, at the end of the first year it has fallen to $80 million, at the end of the second year it has risen to $105 million, and at the end of the third year it has risen to $115 million. The geometric mean rate of return is *closest* to:

    A. 4.1%.

    B. 4.8%.

    C. 6.7%.

19. A mortgage has an annual quoted interest rate of 12 percent. If mortgage payments are made monthly, then the effective annual interest rate is *closest* to:

    A. 12.36%.

    B. 12.55%.

*C. 12.68%.

Explanation: LOS: Reading 5-c

The effective annual rate (EAR) is given by:

$$EAR = \left(1 + \frac{r_s}{m}\right)^m - 1$$

where

m = number of compounding periods per year

r_s = quoted annual interest rate

EAR = $(1.01)^{12} - 1$

= 12.68%

---

20. The value of a portfolio starts at $100 million, at the end of the first year it has fallen to $80 million, at the end of the second year it has risen to $105 million, and at the end of the third year it has risen to $115 million. The geometric mean rate of return is *closest* to:

    A. 4.1%.

*B. 4.8%.

    C. 6.7%.

Explanation: LOS: Reading 7-e

$$
\begin{aligned}
R_G &= \sqrt[n]{(1 + R_1)(1 + R_2).....(1 + R_n)} - 1 \\
&= (0.80 \times 1.313 \times 1.095)^{1/3} - 1 \\
&= 0.0476
\end{aligned}
$$

21. Stock A has a coefficient of variation of 30% and stock B has a coefficient of variation of 60%. Which of the following statements is the *most accurate*?

A. I. The dispersion of returns relative to the mean is lower for stock A than stock B.

B. II. The standard deviation of stock A is double that of stock B, if the mean returns of both stocks are the same.

C. III. The variance of stock A is double that of stock B, if the mean returns of both stocks are the same.

22. An analyst states

" …. the odds against the company increasing its dividend are twelve to one".

This means that the analyst believes that the probability of it increasing the dividend is *closest* to:

A. 0.0769.

B. 0.0833.

C. 0.9166.

21. Stock A has a coefficient of variation of 30% and stock B has a coefficient of variation of 60%. Which of the following statements is the *most accurate*?

*A. I. **The dispersion of returns relative to the mean is lower for stock A than stock B.**

   B. II. The standard deviation of stock A is double that of stock B, if the mean returns of both stocks are the same.

   C. III. The variance of stock A is double that of stock B, if the mean returns of both stocks are the same.

Explanation: LOS: Reading 7-i

$$CV = \frac{S}{\overline{X}} \times 100$$

"The standard deviation of stock A is double that of stock B, if the mean returns of both stocks are the same" and "The variance of stock A is double that of stock B, if the mean returns of both stocks are the same" are incorrect since, if the mean return is the same the standard deviation of stock A is half that of B.

Therefore

   Answers II. and III. are incorrect since, if the mean return is the same the standard deviation of stock A is half that of stock B. The coefficient of variation measures the dispersion of returns relative to the mean return.

---

22. An analyst states

   " …. the odds against the company increasing its dividend are twelve to one".

This means that the analyst believes that the probability of it increasing the dividend is *closest* to:

*A. 0.0769.

   B. 0.0833.

   C. 0.9166.

Explanation: LOS: Reading 8-c

Odds against of twelve to one, means the probability is $1/(12 + 1) = 0.0769,$

there is a one in thirteen chance it will happen.

23. A shop buys pens from two manufacturers, 55% from Mountain Pens and 45% from Valley Pens. The shop knows that 3% of the pens supplied by Mountain Pens are defective and 5% of the pens supplied by Valley Pens are defective. The pens in the shops are mixed together. If a pen is chosen at random and found to be defective what is the probability that it was supplied by Mountain Pens?

    A. 42.3%.

    B. 55.0%.

    C. 60.0%.

---

24. There is a competition in which there are six contestants and you need to pick winners for 1st, 2nd and 3rd places, how many ways can they be selected?

    A. 36.

    B. 120.

    C. 720.

23. A shop buys pens from two manufacturers, 55% from Mountain Pens and 45% from Valley Pens. The shop knows that 3% of the pens supplied by Mountain Pens are defective and 5% of the pens supplied by Valley Pens are defective. The pens in the shops are mixed together. If a pen is chosen at random and found to be defective what is the probability that it was supplied by Mountain Pens?

*A. 42.3%.

   B. 55.0%.

   C. 60.0%.

Explanation: LOS: Reading 8-n

Apply Bayes' formula:

$$P(A_1 \mid B) = \frac{P(A_1)P(B \mid A_1)}{P(A_1)P(B \mid A_1) + P(A_2)P(B \mid A_2)}$$

define A_1 - Mountain Pens supply the pen

         A_2 - Valley Pens supply the pen

         B - the information that the pen is defective

$$P(A_1 \mid B) = \frac{0.55 \times 0.03}{(0.55 \times 0.03) + (0.45 \times 0.05)}$$

$$= 0.423$$

---

24. There is a competition in which there are six contestants and you need to pick winners for 1st, 2nd and 3rd places, how many ways can they be selected?

   A. 36.

*B. 120.

   C. 720.

Explanation: LOS: Reading 8-o

This requires the permutation formula since the order of the r objects matters, so apply:

Number of ways =

$$\text{Apply } \frac{n!}{(n-r)!} = 6!/(6-3)! = 120$$

25. A deposit of $1,000,000 earns a return of 5% compounded continuously for 8 years. The future value is *closest* to:

A. $1,477,000.

B. $1,492,000.

C. $1,500,000.

---

26. The following information was collected on the average numbers of days in a month hours that a currency appreciated against the US dollar:

| 5 | 5 | 8 | 4 | 4 | 6 | 7 | 6 |
| 6 | 5 | 4 | 2 | 7 | 7 | 5 | |

The mean, median and mode are *closest* to:

	Mean	Median	Mode
A.	5.0	6.0	5.0
B.	5.0	6.0	5.4
C.	5.4	5.0	5.0

25. A deposit of $1,000,000 earns a return of 5% compounded continuously for 8 years. The future value is *closest* to:

A. $1,477,000.

*B. $1,492,000.

C. $1,500,000.

Explanation: LOS: Reading 5-d

The future value is given by

$$FV_N = PVe^{\text{rs} \times N}$$
$$= \$1,000,000e^{0.05 \times 8}$$
$$= \$1,491,825$$

Note: to find the programmed value of e on your CFA Institute-approved financial calculator, use the keystrokes:

The future value is given by

HP-12C   1 g e^x **2.7183**

BA II Plus1 2nd [e^x]   **2.7183**

Note: to find the programmed value of e on your CFA Institute-approved financial calculator, use the keystrokes:

26. The following information was collected on the average numbers of days in a month hours that a currency appreciated against the US dollar:

5	5	8	4	4	6	7	6
6	5	4	2	7	7	5	

The mean, median and mode are *closest* to:

	Mean	Median	Mode
A.	5.0	6.0	5.0
B.	5.0	6.0	5.4
*C.	5.4	5.0	5.0

Explanation: LOS: Reading 7-e

$$\text{Mean} = \text{X} = \frac{\sum w_i X_i}{\sum w_i}$$
$$= [1(2) + 3(4) + 4(5) + 3(6) + 3(7) + 1(8)]/15 = 5.4$$

The median is the middle observation, which is 5.

The mode is the most frequently occurring observation, which is 5.

27. The following data is provided on the quarterly performance of a fund.

	1st Quarter	2nd Quarter	3rd Quarter	4th Quarter
Beginning value	$1,000,000	$1,200,000	$1,500,000	$1,500,000
Cash inflow at beginning of quarter	$100,000	$100,000	($200,000)	$300,000
Ending value	$1,200,000	$1,500,000	$1,500,000	$1,600,000

The time-weighted return for the year is *closest* to:

    A. 28.7%.

    B. 29.1%.

    C. 61.4%.

28. A sample of PEG (P/E divided by growth) ratios are taken for six shares and the ratios are 3, 3, 4, 5, 7, and 8.

The sample standard deviation is closest to:

   A. 1.9

   B. 2.1.

   C. 4.4.

27. The following data is provided on the quarterly performance of a fund.

	1st Quarter	2nd Quarter	3rd Quarter	4th Quarter
Beginning value	$1,000,000	$1,200,000	$1,500,000	$1,500,000
Cash inflow at beginning of quarter	$100,000	$100,000	($200,000)	$300,000
Ending value	$1,200,000	$1,500,000	$1,500,000	$1,600,000

The time-weighted return for the year is *closest* to:

   A. 28.7%.

*B. 29.1%.

   A. 61.4%.

Explanation: LOS: Reading 6-c

The first step is to calculate the returns for each quarter:

Q1, HPR = ($1,200,000 - $1,100,000)/$1,100,000 =   9.09%

Q2, HPR = ($1,500,000 - $1,300,000)/$1,300,000 = 15.38%

Q3, HPR = ($1,500,000 - $1,300,000)/$1,300,000 = 15.38%

Q4, HPR = ($1,600,000 - $1,800,000)/$1,800,000 = -11.11%

Then calculate the compounded return to get the time-weighted return:

$(1.0909) \times (1.1538) \times (1.1538) \times (0.8889) - 1 = 0.2909 = 29.1\%$

28. A sample of PEG (P/E divided by growth) ratios are taken for six shares and the ratios are 3, 3, 4, 5, 7, and 8.

The sample standard deviation is closest to:

    A. 1.9

*B. 2.1.

    C. 4.4.

Explanation:　　　　　　　　　　　　　　　　　　　　　　　　LOS: Reading 7-g

The mean, $\overline{X}$, is $(3 + 3 + 4 + 5 + 7 + 8)/6 = 5$

The sample standard deviation is given by s, where

The mean is $(3 + 3 + 4 + 5 + 7 + 8)/6 = 5$

$$s^2 = \frac{\sum_{i=1}^{n}(X_i - \overline{X})^2}{n-1}$$

$$= (4 + 4 + 1 + 4 + 9)/5 = 4.4$$

$s = 2.1$

Study Session 03:   Quantitative Methods: Application

This study session introduces the discrete and continuous probability distributions that are most commonly used to describe the behavior of random variables. Probability theory and calculations are widely applied in finance, for example, in the field of investment and project valuation and in financial risk management.

Furthermore, this session teaches how to estimate different parameters (e.g., mean and standard deviation) of a population if only a sample, rather than the whole population, can be observed. Hypothesis testing is a closely related topic. This session presents the techniques that can be applied to accept or reject an assumed hypothesis (null hypothesis) about various parameters of a population.

The last reading introduces the fundamentals of technical analysis and illustrates how it is used to analyze securities and securities markets.

Reading Assignments

Reading 9:   Common Probability Distributions
   Quantitative Methods for Investment Analysis, Second Edition, by Richard A. DeFusco, CFA, Dennis W. McLeavey, CFA, Jerald E. Pinto, CFA, and David E. Runkle, CFA
Reading 10: Sampling and Estimation
   Quantitative Methods for Investment Analysis, Second Edition, by Richard A. DeFusco, CFA, Dennis W. McLeavey, CFA, Jerald E. Pinto, CFA, and David E. Runkle, CFA
Reading 11: Hypothesis Testing
   Quantitative Methods for Investment Analysis, Second Edition, by Richard A. DeFusco, CFA, Dennis W. McLeavey, CFA, Jerald E.Pinto, CFA, and David E. Runkle, CFA
Reading 12: Technical Analysis
   By Barry M. Sine, CFA and Robert A. Strong, CFA

1. A confidence interval is:

   A. the probability that a population parameter will lie within a certain range.

   B. the probability that the point estimate as an estimate of the population parameter is correct.

   C. a range of values in which the population parameter falls with a specified probability.

---

2. A support level in technical analysis is a price at which an increase in:

   A. supply of stock will reverse a rising trend.

   B. supply of stock will reverse a declining trend.

   C. demand for a stock will reverse a declining trend.

1. A confidence interval is:

    A. the probability that a population parameter will lie within a certain range.

    B. the probability that the point estimate as an estimate of the population parameter is correct.

*C. a range of values in which the population parameter falls with a specified probability.

Explanation: LOS: Reading 10-f

A confidence interval is simply an interval or range where we expect to find, with a specified probability, the population parameter.

2. A support level in technical analysis is a price at which an increase in:

    A. supply of stock will reverse a rising trend.

    B. supply of stock will reverse a declining trend.

*C. demand for a stock will reverse a declining trend.

Explanation: LOS: Reading 12-c

A support level occurs when buyers come into the market and support the price of a stock. Often this happens when the price has previously risen then fallen back due to profit taking. At this point buyers, who perhaps missed earlier opportunities to buy, come back to the market leading to a surge in demand and the price increasing.

3. A dice is thrown four times, what is the probability of throwing exactly one six?
(Assume the dice has an equal chance of showing a 1, 2, 3, 4, 5 or 6.)

    A. 9.7%.

    B. 25.0%..

    C. 38.6%.

---

4. Which of the following describe lognormal distributions?

Skew	Often used to describe asset
A. positively skewed	prices
B. negatively skewed	returns
C. negatively skewed	prices

3. A dice is thrown four times, what is the probability of throwing exactly one six?
(Assume the dice has an equal chance of showing a 1, 2, 3, 4, 5 or 6.)

    A. 9.7%.

    B. 25.0%..

*C. 38.6%.

Explanation: LOS: Reading 9-F
This is a binomial probability distribution so to calculate the probability of x successes
from n trials, when the trials are independent and the probability of success across trials
is constant, use the formula:

$$p(x) = \frac{n!}{(n-x)! \times x!} p^x (1-p)^{n-x}$$

where

        n   =   number of trials
        x   =   number of observed successes
        p   =   probability of success

$$p(1) = \frac{4!}{1! \times 3!} 0.167^1 (1-0.167)^3 = 0.386$$

---

4. Which of the following describe lognormal distributions?

Skew	Often used to describe asset
*A. positively skewed	prices
B. negatively skewed	returns
C. negatively skewed	prices

Explanation: LOS: Reading 9-n
A lognormal distribution is bounded by zero on the left and has a long tail on the right
so it is positively skewed. The bound of zero means the distribution is often used to
model asset prices.

5. A manager is testing to see whether a *higher* number of widgets being manufactured per hour are faulty. Previously 5 widgets per hour were faulty. He takes a sample of 50 hours production and the mean number found faulty is 5.5, with a standard deviation of 1.25. Using the z-test he can conclude that:

A. at both the 1% and 5% significance levels there is evidence that a *higher* number of widgets are faulty.

B. at the 5% significance level, but not at the 1% significance level, there is evidence that a *higher* number of widgets are faulty.

C. at the 1% significance level, but not at the 5% significance level, there is evidence that a *higher* number of widgets are faulty.

6. A Type II error in hypothesis testing is:

A. using an incorrect test statistiC.

B. rejecting the null hypothesis when it is true.

C. not rejecting the null hypothesis when it is false.

5. A manager is testing to see whether a *higher* number of widgets being manufactured per hour are faulty. Previously 5 widgets per hour were faulty. He takes a sample of 50 hours production and the mean number found faulty is 5.5, with a standard deviation of 1.25. Using the z-test he can conclude that:

*A. at both the 1% and 5% significance levels there is evidence that a *higher* number of widgets are faulty.

B. at the 5% significance level, but not at the 1% significance level, there is evidence that a *higher* number of widgets are faulty.

C. at the 1% significance level, but not at the 5% significance level, there is evidence that a *higher* number of widgets are faulty.

Explanation: LOS: Reading 11-g
Set the null hypothesis as being that the mean is less than or equal to 5.0.

$$z = (5.5 - 5.0) \times \frac{7.07}{1.25} = 2.83$$

This is more than 2.33 (the critical value for the 1% significance level, for a one-tailed test) and more than 1.65 (the critical value for the 5% significance level). So reject the null hypothesis at both the 1% level and the 5% level.

---

6. A Type II error in hypothesis testing is:

A. using an incorrect test statistiC.

B. rejecting the null hypothesis when it is true.

*C. not rejecting the null hypothesis when it is false.

Explanation: LOS: Reading 11-c
A Type II error is when the null hypothesis is false but we do not reject it, possibly because we have selected a small significance level to reduce the occurrence of Type I errors.

7. An investment manager is managing a diversified portfolio of international equities and the performance benchmark is the MSCI World index. Shortfall risk for the portfolio refers to:

   A. the absolute deviation of returns relatives to the MSCI World Index.

   B. the risk that the value of the portfolio falls below a critical level.

   C. the standard deviation of returns relatives to the MSCI World Index.

8. The standard error of the sample mean is:

   A. the standard deviation of the sampling distribution of sample mean.

   B. the standard deviation of the sample divided by the standard deviation of the population.

   C. the standard deviation of the sample minus the standard deviation of the population.

7. An investment manager is managing a diversified portfolio of international equities and the performance benchmark is the MSCI World index. Shortfall risk for the portfolio refers to:

A. the absolute deviation of returns relatives to the MSCI World Index.

*B. the risk that the value of the portfolio falls below a critical level.

C. the standard deviation of returns relatives to the MSCI World Index.

Explanation: LOS: Reading 9-n

Shortfall risk is the risk that the value of a portfolio falls below a certain level, it can be reduced by minimizing the probability that the return falls below a certain minimum level.

---

8. The standard error of the sample mean is:

*A. the standard deviation of the sampling distribution of sample mean.

B. the standard deviation of the sample divided by the standard deviation of the population.

C. the standard deviation of the sample minus the standard deviation of the population.

Explanation: LOS: Reading 10-e

The standard deviation of a sample mean is the standard error. The central limit theorem says that this is equal to the population standard deviation divided by the square root of the sample size.

9. If a very large sample size is used it is *least likely* to lead to:

    A. a smaller standard error of the sample means.

    B. a larger dispersion in the distribution of the sample means.

    C. the sampling distribution of the sample mean being approximately a normal distribution.

10. When selecting a sample, a population is first divided into subpopulations and then random samples are taken from each subpopulation, the number taken proportional to the size of the subpopulation. This is an example of:

    A. structured sampling.

    B. stratified random sampling.

    C. simple random sampling.

9. If a very large sample size is used it is *least likely* to lead to:

    A. a smaller standard error of the sample means.

*B. a larger dispersion in the distribution of the sample means.

C. the sampling distribution of the sample mean being approximately a normal distribution.

Explanation: LOS: Reading 10-e

A large sample size will lead to a smaller standard error of the sample mean since the standard error is equal to the population standard deviation divided by the square root of the sample size. The central limit theorem says that the sampling distribution of the sample mean is close to a normal distribution if the sample size is large (greater than thirty).

However a large sample size will lead to sample means being close to the population mean and therefore less disperse, so "a larger dispersion " is the correct choice.

10. When selecting a sample, a population is first divided into subpopulations and then random samples are taken from each subpopulation, the number taken proportional to the size of the subpopulation. This is an example of:

    A. structured sampling.

*B. stratified random sampling.

    C. simple random sampling.

Explanation: LOS: Reading 10-b

Stratified random sampling ensures that different subdivisions within a population are represented in the sample.

11. An analyst is selecting a sample from the orders received from a firm's customers. The orders are time stamped and he decides to include in the sample every 5th order received by the firm. This is an example of:

    A. order random sampling.

    B. stratified random sampling.

    C. systematic random sampling.

---

12. Which of the following statements regarding normal distributions is *most accurate*?

    A. The normal distribution is a good model for the distribution of asset prices.

    B. The mean and standard deviation of the standard normal distribution are both 1.

    C. If the returns on individual securities in a portfolio are normally distributed, the returns of a portfolio containing these securities are normally distributed.

11. An analyst is selecting a sample from the orders received from a firm's customers. The orders are time stamped and he decides to include in the sample every 5th order received by the firm. This is an example of:

A. order random sampling.

B. stratified random sampling.

*C. systematic random sampling.

Explanation: LOS: Reading 10-b
Systematic random sampling is when we select every kth member of a population, often used when we cannot number or label the members of a population.

---

12. Which of the following statements regarding normal distributions is *most accurate*?

A. The normal distribution is a good model for the distribution of asset prices.

B. The mean and standard deviation of the standard normal distribution are both 1.

*C. If the returns on individual securities in a portfolio are normally distributed, the returns of a portfolio containing these securities are normally distributed.

Explanation: LOS: Reading 9-i
The normal distribution is a good model for many asset returns but not prices. By definition a standard normal distribution has a mean of 0 and standard deviation of 1.

13. A hypothesis is a statement about a:

A. population parameter.

B. sample parameter.

C. population statistic.

---

14. A company is analyzing the days that employees take off as sick leave each year and is concerned that the number of days that employees are taking off has risen above the past *average* number of 4.0 days. It is assumed that the population is approximately normally distributed. A sample of 20 employees is taken and the mean number of days taken is 4.5 with a standard deviation of 1.5 days. If the rejection point for a one-tailed test with 19 degrees of freedom is 1.729 at the 5% significance level we can conclude that:

A. using the t-statistic is not valid for a small sample.

B. the mean number of days is more than 4 days at the 5% significance level.

C. the mean number of days is still 4 days or less at the 5% significance level.

13. A hypothesis is a statement about a:

*A. population parameter.

   B. sample parameter.

   C. population statistic.

Explanation: LOS: Reading 11-a

A hypothesis is a statement about a population parameter. We use data from a sample to test whether we should accept or reject the hypothesis.

---

14. A manager is analyzing the volatility of a fund's returns and is concerned that the volatility has risen above the past *average* number of 0.40% per month. It is assumed that the population is approximately normally distributed. A sample of 20 months is taken and the mean volatility is 0.45% with a standard deviation of 0.15%. If the rejection point for a one-tailed test with 19 degrees of freedom is 1.729 at the 5% significance level we can conclude that:

   A. using the t-statistic is not valid for a small sample.

   B. the mean number of days is more than 4 days at the 5% significance level.

*C. the mean number of days is still 4 days or less at the 5% significance level.

Explanation: LOS: Reading 11-g

Set the null hypothesis as H0: $\mu \le 0.40\%$

We can use the t-test since we are assuming the population is normally distributed.

$$t_{19} = \frac{\overline{x} - \mu}{s / \sqrt{n}} = \frac{0.45 - 0.40}{0.15 / \sqrt{20}} = \frac{0.05}{0.0335} = 1.49$$

This is within the confidence interval so we do not reject the null hypothesis.

15. In hypothesis testing the probability of rejecting the null hypothesis when it is true is called the:

   A. decision rule.

   B. alternate hypothesis.

   C. level of significance.

---

16. Which of the following statements regarding lognormal distributions is *most accurate*?

   A. I. The mean of the distribution is zero.

   B. II. Y is a lognormal distribution if LnY is normally distributed.

   C. III. Lognormal distributions are frequently used to reflect the distribution of stock returns.

15. In hypothesis testing the probability of rejecting the null hypothesis when it is true is called the:

A. decision rule.

B. alternate hypothesis.

*C. level of significance.

Explanation: LOS: Reading 11-c

The level of significance is the probability of a Type I error, of rejecting the null hypothesis when it is true.

---

16. Which of the following statements regarding lognormal distributions is *most accurate*?

A. I. The mean of the distribution is zero.

*B. II. Y is a lognormal distribution if LnY is normally distributed.

C. III. Lognormal distributions are frequently used to reflect the distribution of stock returns.

Explanation: LOS: Reading 9-o

I. is not correct, they are frequently used to show the distribution of stock prices.

II. is not correct, the lower bound is zero.

17. A stock market rises by an *average* of 10% a year and the standard deviation of returns is 6%. The probability of the stock market falling by more than 2% in a year is *closest* to:

    A. 2.3%.

    B. 4.6%.

    C. 15.9%.

18. The Central Limit Theorem states that if the sampling distribution of the sample mean is calculated using samples of equal size from a population that is not normal, then:

    A. I. it is approximately a normal distribution.

    B. II. the standard error tends to one as the size of the samples increases.

    C. III. the mean of the distribution will be smaller than the population mean.

17. A stock market rises by an *average* of 10% a year and the standard deviation of returns is 6%. The probability of the stock market falling by more than 2% in a year is *closest* to:

*A. 2.3%.

   B. 4.6%.

   C. 15.9%.

Explanation: LOS: Reading 9-l

A fall of 2% is two standard deviations from the mean. 95.4% of observations fall between the mean plus or minus two standard deviations so 4.6% lie outside this range. Therefore 2.3% will be below -2% and 2.3% will be above 22%.

---

18. The Central Limit Theorem states that if the sampling distribution of the sample mean is calculated using samples of equal size from a population that is not normal, then:

*A. I. it is approximately a normal distribution.

   B. II. the standard error tends to one as the size of the samples increases.

   C. III. the mean of the distribution will be smaller than the population mean.

Explanation: LOS: Reading 10-f

I. is correct, the distribution will be approximately normal although the underlying population may not be normally distributed.

II. is not correct, the standard error tends to zero as the sample size increases.

III. is not correct, the mean of the distribution will be the same as the population mean.

19. The standard deviation of a population is 25 and a sample of 50 observations is taken from the population. The standard error of the sample mean is *closest* to:

    A. 0.28.

    B. 0.50.

    C. 3.54.

---

20. Large samples are taken from a normal population; the sample mean is 25 and the sample standard deviation is 5. The 95% confidence interval for the population mean is *closest* to:

    A. between 12.1 and 37.9.

    B. between 15.2 and 34.8.

    C. between 20.0 and 30.0.

19. The standard deviation of a population is 25 and a sample of 50 observations is taken from the population. The standard error of the sample mean is *closest* to:

   A. 0.28.

   B. 0.50.

*C. 3.54.

Explanation: LOS: Reading 10-e

The standard error of the sample mean is given by

$$\sigma_{\bar{x}} = \frac{\sigma}{\sqrt{n}}$$

= 25/7.07 = 3.54.

---

20. Large samples are taken from a normal population; the sample mean is 25 and the sample standard deviation is 5. The 95% confidence interval for the population mean is *closest* to:

   A. between 12.1 and 37.9.

*B. between 15.2 and 34.8.

   C. between 20.0 and 30.0.

Explanation: LOS: Reading 10-f

The 95% confidence interval is given by sample mean plus or minus 1.96 standard deviations.

This is which is between 15.2 and 34.8.

21. Historic analysis suggests that stocks trading on a low price/book value have tended to outperform the market. If the analysis has not included companies that have gone bankrupt then the analysis could be biased due to:

  A. data-snooping bias.

  B. data-mining bias.

  C. survivorship bias.

---

22. Hypothesis testing is used to determine the mean return of mutual funds in a single period. A sample of 25 funds is taken and the null hypothesis is defined as the mean is equal to 12%. Is this an example of a one or two-tailed test, and should the z-test or t-test be used?

Hypothesis test	Test statistic
A. a two-tailed test	z-test
B. a one-tailed test	z-test
C. a two-tailed test	t-test

21. Historic analysis suggests that stocks trading on a low price/book value have tended to outperform the market. If the analysis has not included companies that have gone bankrupt then the analysis could be biased due to:

   A. data-snooping bias.

   B. data-mining bias.

*C. survivorship bias.

Explanation: LOS: Reading 10-k

It has been argued that if all companies had been included, the companies that went bankrupt would have been trading on low price/book multiples, and this would have lowered the *average* performance of the low price/book value stocks.

---

22. Hypothesis testing is used to determine the mean return of mutual funds in a single period. A sample of 25 funds is taken and the null hypothesis is defined as the mean is equal to 12%. Is this an example of a one or two-tailed test, and should the z-test or t-test be used?

Hypothesis test	Test statistic
A. a two-tailed test	z-test
B. a one-tailed test	z-test
*C. a two-tailed test	**t-test**

Explanation: LOS: Reading 11-b and 11-g

If there is no direction (greater or less than) in the null hypothesis it is two-tailed. Give the sample size of less than 30 funds the t-test should be used. The z-test should only be used for large samples.

23. An analyst is studying the monthly income generated by a portfolio of investments. He is told that the mean income is $5,000 per month and he decided to look at a sample 100 months to see if this is correct. The sample mean is $5,018 with a standard deviation of 80. If he sets the null hypothesis as the population mean is $5,000 he should:

A. not reject the null hypothesis at both the 1% and 5% significance level.

B. not reject the null hypothesis at the 5% significance level but reject it at the 1% significance level.

C. not reject the null hypothesis at the 1% significance level but reject it at the 5% significance level.

24. In hypothesis tasting a p-value of 0.1 indicates that:

A. there is extremely strong evidence that H0 should be rejected.

B. there is a probability of 0.1 of observing a sample value at least as extreme as the value observed, assuming H0 is rejected.

C. there is a probability of 0.1 of observing a sample value at least as extreme as the value observed, assuming H0 is correct.

23. An analyst is studying the monthly income generated by a portfolio of investments. He is told that the mean income is $5,000 per month and he decided to look at a sample 100 months to see if this is correct. The sample mean is $5,018 with a standard deviation of 80. If he sets the null hypothesis as the population mean is $5,000 he should:

    A. not reject the null hypothesis at both the 1% and 5% significance level.

    B. not reject the null hypothesis at the 5% significance level but reject it at the 1% significance level.

*C. not reject the null hypothesis at the 1% significance level but reject it at the 5% significance level.

Explanation: LOS: Reading 11-g

$Z = (5018-5000)/80/\sqrt{100} = 2.25$. This is less than 2.58 (the critical value for the 1% significance level) so there is no evidence to reject the null hypothesis at the 1% level.. However it is more than 1.96 (the critical value for the 5% significance level) so we can reject the hypothesis at the 5% significance level.

---

24. In hypothesis tasting a p-value of 0.1 indicates that:

    A. there is extremely strong evidence that H0 should be rejected.

    B. there is a probability of 0.1 of observing a sample value at least as extreme as the value observed, assuming H0 is rejected.

*C. there is a probability of 0.1 of observing a sample value at least as extreme as the value observed, assuming H0 is correct.

Explanation: LOS: Reading 11-c

The p-value is the probability of observing a value as extreme or more extreme than the value observed, for it to be extremely strong evidence it would need to be 0.001 or less.

25. You are analyzing the monthly returns from a fund over the last year and calculate that the mean return was 1.25% with a sample standard deviation of 1.0%. You expected the fund to have achieved a return of 1.4% in line with the risk taken on by the fund and wish to decide at the 10% significance level whether the results are consistent with a population mean return of 1.4%. Given that t0.05,11= 1.796 you can conclude that:

A. the null hypothesis is not rejected and the results are not consistent with a mean of 1.4%

B. the null hypothesis is not rejected and the results are consistent with a mean of 1.4%.

C. the null hypothesis is rejected and the results are not consistent with a mean of 1.4%

26. A chi-square test statistic () could be used for hypothesis tests for

A. the variance for a single non-normally distributed population.

B. the variance for a single normally distributed population.

C. the mean for a single non-normally distributed population.

25. You are analyzing the monthly returns from a fund over the last year and calculate that the mean return was 1.25% with a sample standard deviation of 1.0%. You expected the fund to have achieved a return of 1.4% in line with the risk taken on by the fund and wish to decide at the 10% significance level whether the results are consistent with a population mean return of 1.4%. Given that t0.05,11= 1.796 you can conclude that:

    A. the null hypothesis is not rejected and the results are not consistent with

    a mean of 1.4%

***B. the null hypothesis is not rejected and the results are consistent with
a mean of 1.4%.**

    C. the null hypothesis is rejected and the results are not consistent with

    a mean of 1.4%

Explanation: LOS: Reading 11-e

Set the null hypothesis as H0: μ = 1.4%. We need to apply the t-test because it is a small sample.

$$t_{n-1} = \frac{\overline{x} - \mu}{s \big/ \sqrt{n}} = \frac{1.25 - 1.4}{1.0 \big/ \sqrt{12}} = -\frac{0.15}{0.29} = -0.52$$

This is within the confidence interval so the null hypothesis is not rejected and the results are consistent with the mean return being 1.4%.

---

26. A chi-square test statistic () could be used for hypothesis tests for

    A. the variance for a single non-normally distributed population.

*B. the variance for a single normally distributed population.

    C. the mean for a single non-normally distributed population.

Explanation: LOS: Reading 11-j

A chi-square test statistic is used to test for variance when we have a normally distributed population. It is always 0 or a positive number and has different distributions based on the number of degrees of freedom.

27. A sample of 100 observations is taken from a normally distributed population with a standard deviation of 2. The sample mean is 6. The 99% confidence level is *closest* to:

A. between 4.45 and 7.55.

B. between 5.48 and 6.52.

C. between 5.61 and 6.39.

28. A company is a clock manufacturer and the manager wishes to check that the *average* number of clocks produced has not fallen significantly below the mean of 100 clocks per day. The distribution is normal and the standard deviation is 5 clocks per day. If the manager looks at a sample of 100 days' production and finds that the mean production volume is 98, he should conclude using the z-test that:

A. the sample is not sufficiently large to arrive at a conclusion.

B. there is evidence that the production levels have declined at the 0.01 significance level.

C. there is no evidence that the production levels have declined at the 0.01 significance level.

29. If a distribution is normal:

A. approximately 68% of the observations will lie between the mean plus or minus one standard deviation.

B. approximately 99.7% of the observations will lie between the mean plus or minus one standard deviation.

C. approximately 99.7% of the observations will lie between the mean plus or minus two standard deviations.

27. A sample of 100 observations is taken from a normally distributed population with a standard deviation of 2. The sample mean is 6. The 99% confidence level is *closest* to:

    A. between 4.45 and 7.55.

*B. between 5.48 and 6.52.

    C. between 5.61 and 6.39.

Explanation: LOS: Reading 10-j

The confidence interval is given by $\overline{X} \pm Z_{\alpha/2} \dfrac{\sigma}{\sqrt{n}}$

where

$\overline{x}$ = sample mean, which is the point estimate of the population mean

σ = population standard deviation

n = sample size

$Z_{\alpha/2}$ = reliability factor, the point where $\alpha/2$ of the probability is in the right tail

The 99% confidence level is $6 \pm (2.58 \times 2)/10$ which is between 5.48 and 6.52

28. A company is a clock manufacturer and the manager wishes to check that the *average* number of clocks produced has not fallen significantly below the mean of 100 clocks per day. The distribution is normal and the standard deviation is 5 clocks per day. If the manager looks at a sample of 100 days' production and finds that the mean production volume is 98, he should conclude using the z-test that:

    A. the sample is not sufficiently large to arrive at a conclusion.

B. there is evidence that the production levels have declined at the 0.01 significance level.

    C. there is no evidence that the production levels have declined at the 0.01 significance level.

Explanation: LOS: Reading 11-g

define   H0 the mean production is greater than or equal to 100 clocks per day.

                         Ha: the mean production is less than 100 clocks per day

Calculate the z-value:

$$z = \frac{\overline{X} - \mu_0}{\sigma / \sqrt{n}} = -4$$

This is a one-tailed test so the critical value of z at the 0.01 significance level is -2.33. If the computed z value lies outside this range reject the null hypothesis and accept the alternative. In this case z falls outside the range at the 0.01 significance level.

---

29. If a distribution is normal:

*A. approximately 68% of the observations will lie between the mean plus or minus one standard deviation.

    B. approximately 99.7% of the observations will lie between the mean plus or minus one standard deviation.

    C. approximately 99.7% of the observations will lie between the mean plus or minus two standard deviations.

Explanation: LOS: Reading 9-j

68% will lie between the mean plus or minus one standard deviation, 95% will lie between the mean plus or minus two standard deviations, 99.7% will lie between the mean plus or minus three standard deviations.

Study Session 04:   Economics: Microeconomic Analysis

This study session focuses on the microeconomic principles used to describe the marketplace behavior of consumers and firms. The first reading explains the concepts and tools of demand and supply analysis—the study of how buyers and sellers interact to determine transaction prices and quantities. The second reading covers the theory of the consumer, which addresses the demand for goods and services by individuals who make decisions that maximize the satisfaction received from present and future consumption. The third reading deals with the theory of the firm, focusing on the supply of goods and services by profit-maximizing firms. That reading provides the basis for understanding the cost side of firms' profit equation. The fourth and final reading completes the picture by addressing revenue and explains the types of markets in which firms sell output. Overall, the study session provides the economic tools for understanding how product and resource markets function and the competitive characteristics of different industries.

Reading Assignments

Reading 13:   Demand and Supply Analysis: Introduction
    by Richard V. Eastin and Gary L. Arbogast, CFA
Reading 14:   Demand and Supply Analysis: Consumer Demand
    by Richard V. Eastin and Gary L. Arbogast, CFA
Reading 15:   Demand and Supply Analysis: The Firm
    by Gary L. Arbogast, CFA and Richard V. Eastin
Reading 16:   The Firm and Market Structures
    by Richard G. Fritz and Michele Gambera, CFA

1. If two goods are perfect substitutes, then the cross elasticity of demand will be:

   A. one.

   B. infinity.

   C. negative.

---

2. If the elasticity of supply and demand for a product both decrease, this will tend to lead to:

Consumer Surplus	Producer surplus
A. Increase	Increase
B. Increase	Decrease
C. Decrease	Increase

1. If two goods are perfect substitutes, then the cross elasticity of demand will be:

   A. one.

*B. infinity.

   C. negative.

Explanation: LOS: Reading 13-m

If they are perfect substitutes any increase in the price of one good will cause an infinitely large increase in demand for the other good so the cross elasticity of demand is infinite.

---

2. If the elasticity of supply and demand for a product both decrease, this will tend to lead to:

Consumer Surplus	**Producer surplus**
*A. Increase	**Increase**
B. Increase	Decrease
C. Decrease	Increase

Explanation: LOS: Reading 13-m

If elasticity of supply and demand both decrease it will lead to a steepening of the supply and demand curves which will expand the portion to the left of the equilibrium point. This portion represents the consumer and producer surpluses.

3. When a firm increases its output, its total production costs increase at an increasing rate. It is *likely* that the firm has:

   A. high fixed costs.

   B. economies of scale.

   C. diseconomies of scale.

4. Which of the following statements is *most accurate* regarding the behavior of monopolists?

   A. Monopolists will expand output until marginal revenue equals marginal cost.

   B. Monopolists do not need to advertise since they are not facing competition.

   C. Monopolists do not have any competition so they will charge the maximum possible price for their products.

3. When a firm increases its output, its total production costs increase at an increasing rate. It is likely that the firm has:

    A. high fixed costs.

    B. economies of scale.

*C. diseconomies of scale.

Explanation: LOS: Reading 15-d
When an increase in output leads to total costs increasing at an increasing rate it indicates that average total costs are increasing and there are diseconomies of scale.

---

4. Which of the following statements is *most accurate* regarding the behavior of monopolists?

*A. Monopolists will expand output until marginal revenue equals marginal cost.

    B. Monopolists do not need to advertise since they are not facing competition.

    C. Monopolists do not have any competition so they will charge the maximum possible price for their products.

Explanation: LOS: Reading 16-d
As is the case with other price searchers, monopolists will expand output until marginal revenue equals marginal cost. Monopolists still have a downward sloping demand curve and will need to attract demand (through advertising etc.) in order to make sales at a certain price level. Their concern is to achieve maximum profit rather than maximum price.

5. In the market economy, if a good has external benefits it is *least likely* to lead to:

    A. a social loss.

    B. a deadweight loss.

    C. overproduction of the good.

---

6. The efficient quantity produced of a good is *least likely* to:

    A. maximize the sum of the consumer and producer surpluses.

    B. be the point where the marginal society benefit equals the marginal society cost.

    C. disregard external benefits and external costs to the consumer and producer respectively.

5. In the market economy, if a good has external benefits it is *least likely* to lead to:

    A. a social loss.

    B. a deadweight loss.

*C. overproduction of the good.

Explanation: LOS: Reading 13-h
External benefits refer to benefits that accrue to people other than a consumer of a good so the demand curve for the good does not reflect all the benefits that accrue. This will lead to underproduction of the good, this inefficient production level leads to a deadweight loss. This is a loss to society as a whole, which is a social loss.

6. The efficient quantity produced of a good is *least likely* to:

    A. maximize the sum of the consumer and producer surpluses.

    B. be the point where the marginal society benefit equals the marginal society cost.

*C. disregard external benefits and external costs to the consumer and producer respectively.

Explanation: LOS: Reading 13-j
External costs and benefits will distort the quantity produced and consumed so the efficient quantity is unlikely to be produced if they are disregarded.

7. In a perfectly competitive market if prices fall below a firm's average total cost, the firm:

    A. should increase prices to marginal cost to reach breakeven.

    B. could temporarily shut down their operations to reduce losses.

    C. should increase prices to average total cost to reach breakeven.

---

8. If the price of a product rises then the substitution effect means that

    A. the slope of the budget constraint line will change.

    B. the budget constraint line will make a parallel shift upwards or downwards.

    C. the budget constraint line will move, but the point of tangency with the indiffference curves will be unchanged.

7. In a perfectly competitive market if prices fall below a firm's average total cost, the firm:

    A. should increase prices to marginal cost to reach breakeven.

*B. could temporarily shut down their operations to reduce losses.

    C. should increase prices to average total cost to reach breakeven.

Explanation: LOS: Reading 15-e

Shutting down the operations temporarily will eliminate variable costs and losses will be limited to fixed costs. If the owners expect a rise in prices in the future this would be probably preferable to going out of business. Increasing prices is not an option since the firm is a price taker, if they increase prices sales would fall to zero.

---

8. If the price of a product rises then the substitution effect means that

*A. the slope of the budget constraint line will change.

    B. the budget constraint line will make a parallel shift upwards or downwards.

    C. the budget constraint line will move, but the point of tangency with the indiffference curves will be unchanged.

Explanation: LOS: Reading 14-e

The budget constraint line will steepen or flatten, the income effect leads to a parallel shift.

9. The law of diminishing returns implies that

A. total profits diminish as output increases.

B. marginal product is initially upward sloping then downward sloping as quantities increase.

C. as more units of a variable resource are added marginal product eventually decreases.

---

10. The cross elasticity for two complementary products that are very *closely* related is a relatively:

A. small positive number.

B. arge negative number.

C. small negative number.

9. The law of diminishing returns implics that

   A. total profits diminish as output increases.

   B. marginal product is initially upward sloping then downward sloping as quantities increase.

*C. as more units of a variable resource are added marginal product eventually decreases.

Explanation: LOS: Reading 15-k

The law of diminishing returns sates that marginal product starts to decline as quantities increase due to constraints.

---

10. The cross elasticity for two complementary products that are very *closely* related is a relatively:

   A. small positive number.

*B. large negative number.

   C. small negative number.

Explanation: LOS: Reading 13-m

Cross elasticity measures the change in demand of one quantity for a percentage price move of the complementary product. If they are close complements this will be high. Cross elasticity is negative, if the price of one product rises, the demand for the other product falls and vice versa.

11. Which of the following are examples of implicit and explicit costs?

Implicit cost	Explicit cost
A. Interest foregone	Bank interest
B. Dividend payments	Salary costs
C. Depreciation	Capital expenditure

12. Points on a consumer indifference curve represent:

A. the consumption-opportunity constraint.

B. the demand for a product at different price levels.

C. combinations of goods that are equally preferred by the consumer.

11. Which of the following are examples of implicit and explicit costs?

Implicit cost	Explicit cost
*A. Interest foregone	Bank interest
B. Dividend payments	Salary costs
C. Depreciation	Capital expenditure

Explanation: LOS: Reading 15-a

Implicit costs are when there is no accounting cost incurred but another action has been foregone, these are often related to use of capital and use of owner's resources. Interest forgone and economic depreciation are both forms of implicit costs. Explicit costs include items such as bank interest, salaries, utilities, rental expense.

12. Points on a consumer indifference curve represent:

   A. the consumption-opportunity constraint.

   B. the demand for a product at different price levels.

*C. combinations of goods that are equally preferred by the consumer.

Explanation: LOS: Reading 14-b

Any point along an indifference curve represents a bundle of goods that have equal benefit to the consumer.

13. Which of the following curves is *least likely* to be U-shaped?

   A. The marginal cost curve.

   B. The average fixed cost curve.

   C. The average variable cost curve.

---

14. If a government puts a price ceiling on a service which is below the equilibrium price, which of the following is *least likely* to happen?

   A. Demand for the service will decline.

   B. There will be a shortage of supply of the service.

   C. The service providers' producer surplus will decline.

13. Which of the following curves is *least likely* to be U-shaped?

    A. The marginal cost curve.

*B. The average fixed cost curve.

    C. The average variable cost curve.

Explanation: LOS: Reading 15-d

The average total, marginal and variable costs decrease at low outputs and increase at high outputs, they are U-shaped. The average fixed cost decreases steadily as output increases.

---

14. If a government puts a price ceiling on a service which is below the equilibrium price, which of the following is *least likely* to happen?

*A. Demand for the service will decline.

    B. There will be a shortage of supply of the service.

    C. The service providers' producer surplus will decline.

Explanation: LOS: Reading 13-k

The price ceiling will lead to a drop in supply, reducing the producer surplus. Demand will be unchanged, or increase, so A is the correct answer.

15. A manufacturing company has sales of $1 million per annum and explicit costs of $700,000. The owner of the company, who also owns the factory, is charging an annual rent of only $25,000 for the factory whereas the rent he could receive in the open market is $75,000. He also does not charge for his time (wages would be $60,000 per annum). Interest forgone is $60,000 per annum. The owner could earn a normal annual profit of $50,000 in a similar business. The economic profit of the manufacturing company is closest to:

    A. $80,000

    B. $120,000.

    C. $130,000

---

16. A railway company provides low fares to travelers prepared to start their journey after 10:00 am. This is an example of:

    A. collusion.

    B. rent seeking.

    C. price discrimination.

15. A manufacturing company has sales of $1 million per annum and explicit costs of $700,000. The owner of the company, who also owns the factory, is charging an annual rent of only $25,000 for the factory whereas the rent he could receive in the open market is $75,000. He also does not charge for his time (wages would be $60,000 per annum). Interest forgone is $60,000 per annum. The owner could earn a normal annual profit of $50,000 in a similar business. The economic profit of the manufacturing company is closest to:

*A. $80,000

   B. $120,000.

   C. $130,000

Explanation: LOS: Reading 15-a

The economic profit is therefore $1,000,000 - $700,000 - $50,000 (additional implicit cost of rental) - $60,000 (wages foregone) - $60,000 - $50,000 (normal profit lost). This equals $80,000.

---

16. A railway company provides low fares to travelers prepared to start their journey after 10:00 am. This is an example of:

   A. collusion.

   B. rent seeking.

*C. **price discrimination.**

Explanation: LOS: Reading 16-d

Price discrimination is when a seller charges different customers different prices for the same product or service..

17. Which of the following is *likely* to lead to a change in demand for wine in the US?

   A. A decrease in the price of wine.

   B. An increase in the price of beer.

   C. A rapid increase in the volumes of wine being produced in Eastern Europe.

18. If two consumers have different preferences for two products it means their indifference curves will:

   A. intersect.

   B. convex and concave.

   C. be parallel to each other.

17. Which of the following is *likely* to lead to a change in demand for wine in the US?

    A. A decrease in the price of wine.

*B. An increase in the price of beer.

    C. A rapid increase in the volumes of wine being produced in Eastern Europe.

Explanation: LOS: Reading 13-b

A change in demand indicates a parallel shift in the demand curve, rather than a movement along the demand curve as a result of a price so A is not correct. C mainly affect the supply of wine so B is the correct answer.

18. If two consumers have different preferences for two products it means their indifference curves will:

*A. intersect.

    B. convex and concave.

    C. be parallel to each other.

Explanation: LOS: Reading 14-b

The consumers will have different marginal rates of substitution so their indifference curves will have different slopes and intersect.

26. The price of ABC Financial News is increased from \$2.00 to \$2.50, this leads to an increase in the sales of a competing financial magazine, XYZ Finance, which now sells 120,000 copies a week, up from 100,000 copies a week. The cross elasticity of demand is *closest* to:

*A. 0.81.

   B. 1.22.

   C. 1.25.

Explanation: LOS: Reading 13-m

$$\text{Cross elasticity of demand} = \frac{\%\,\Delta\,Q_{Dem}}{\%\,\Delta\,P_C}$$

where

QDem = quantity demanded

PC = price of substitute or complement

$\%\,\Delta\,Q_{Dem}$ = percentage change in quantity demanded.

The cross elasticity of demand is:

$$\frac{\%\,\Delta\,Q_{Dem}}{\%\,\Delta\,P_C} = \frac{20/110}{\$0.50/\$2.25} = \frac{0.1818}{0.2222} = 0.81$$

Study Session 05:   Economics:
Market Structure and Macroeconomic Analysis

This study session covers fundamental macroeconomic concepts. The first reading provides the building blocks of aggregate output and income measurement, aggregate demand and supply analysis, and the analysis of the factors affecting economic growth. The second reading explains fluctuations in economic activity, known as business cycles, which have important impacts on businesses and investment markets. Monetary and fiscal policy, the subject of the third reading, are the major approaches of governments and governmental agencies to mitigating the severity of economic fluctuations and achieving other policy goals.

Reading Assignments
Reading 17:   Aggregate Output, Prices, and Economic Growth
 by Paul R. Kutasovic, CFA and Richard G. Fritz
Reading 18:   Understanding Business Cycles
 by Michele Gambera, CFA, Milton Ezrati, and Bolong Cao, CFA
Reading 19:   Monetary and Fiscal Policy
 by Andrew Clare, PhD and Stephen Thomas, PhD

1. The demand for money is:

    A. the amount of money drawn out of cash and savings accounts over one year.

    B. the amount of money that people wish to hold in cash and highly liquid assets.

    C. a measure of consumers' willingness to increase productivity for additional remuneration.

---

2. The quantity theory of money says that an increase in money supply will lead to an increase in:

    A. prices.

    B. output.

    C. employment.

1. The demand for money is:

    A. the amount of money drawn out of cash and savings accounts over one year.

*B. the amount of money that people wish to hold in cash and highly liquid assets.

    C. a measure of consumers' willingness to increase productivity for additional remuneration.

Explanation: LOS: Reading 19-d

The demand for money is simply the amount of money that people wish to hold in cash and highly liquid assets.

---

2. The quantity theory of money says that an increase in money supply will lead to an increase in:

*A. prices.

    B. output.

    C. employment.

Explanation: LOS: Reading 17-f

The quantity theory of money says a change in money supply will lead to the same change in price levels, since velocity and output are unaffected by the quantity of money. This is derived from $MV = PY$.

3. Changes in unit labor costs are usually considered to be a

    A. leading economic indicator.

    B. lagging economic indicator.

    C. coincident economic indicator.

---

4. The demand for money curve shows that the quantity of money demanded is:

    A. positively related to GDP growth.

    B. inversely related to interest rates.

    C. inversely related to the price level.

3. Changes in unit labor costs are usually considered to be a

   A. leading economic indicator.

*B. lagging economic indicator.

   C. coincident economic indicator.

Explanation: LOS: Reading 18-i

It is late in an economic boom that upward wage pressure emerges and late in a recession companies reduce staff so unit labor costs are a lagging indicator.

4. The demand for money curve shows that the quantity of money demanded is:

   A. positively related to GDP growth.

*B. inversely related to interest rates.

   C. inversely related to the price level.

Explanation: LOS: Reading 19-d

Demand for money measures the relationship between interest rates and the amount of money that people want to hold. It is positively related to the price level.

5. When the Fed buys securities in an open market operation it usually has the effect of:

   A. reducing inflation.

   B. expanding real output.

   C. reducing quantity of money demanded.

---

6. An unanticipated increase in money supply in the short term will lead to:

   A. an expansion in real output.

   B. an increase in real interest rates.

   C. little or no change in real economic activity.

5. When the Fed buys securities in an open market operation it usually has the effect of:

   A. reducing inflation.

*B. expanding real output.

   C. reducing quantity of money demanded.

Explanation: LOS: Reading 19-o

The first impact will be to lower short-term interest rates and the quantity of money demanded increases. As the supply of bank loans increase, combined with lower interest rates, investment increases and aggregate demand increases.

---

6. An unanticipated increase in money supply in the short term will lead to:

*A. an expansion in real output.

   B. an increase in real interest rates.

   C. little or no change in real economic activity.

Explanation: LOS: Reading 19-h

An unanticipated increase in money supply will reduce real interest rates and make it easier to borrow, thus increasing demand pushing up product price ahead of costs.

7. If banks retain 5% of new deposits in reserves and lend out 95%, when a customer puts $100,000 on deposit with a bank, it will lead to a potential increase in loans and deposits of:

	Loans	Deposits
A.	$1,900,000	$2,000,000
B.	$2,000,000	$2,000,000
C.	$9,400,000	$9,500,000

---

8. Full employment occurs when:

A. equilibrium GDP is equal to potential GDP.

B. strong economic growth has eliminated structural unemployment.

C. strong economic growth has eliminated all forms of unemployment.

7. If banks retain 5% of new deposits in reserves and lend out 95%, when a customer puts $100,000 on deposit with a bank, it will lead to a potential increase in loans and deposits of:

	Loans	Deposits
*A.	$1,900,000	$2,000,000
B.	$2,000,000	$2,000,000
C.	$9,400,000	$9,500,000

Explanation: LOS: Reading 19-c

The bank keeps $5,000 as reserves and can lend out $95,000. This money is in turn placed on deposit at another bank (after being used as payment in a transaction) and the next bank keeps $4,750 as reserves and lends out $90,250. If we continue the exercise we can see that the total increase in deposits is $100,000(1/0.05) = $2,000,000

The potential deposit expansion multiplier is $1/0.05 = 20$.

The increase in loans will be $2,000,000, less the original $100,000.

---

8. Full employment occurs when:

*A. equilibrium GDP is equal to potential GDP.

  B. strong economic growth has eliminated structural unemployment.

  C. strong economic growth has eliminated all forms of unemployment.

Explanation: LOS: Reading 17-h

Full employment occurs when the AD curve intersects the SRAS curve at a point on the LRAS curve, so the economy is operating at potential GDP.

9. The crowding-out effect refers to:

A. financing high budget deficits pushes up interest rates which will reduce private investment.

B. individuals will spend more today if they think expenditure-related taxes will rise in the future.

C. the recognition by individuals that they must save more today to pay for higher taxes in the future if the government runs a budget deficit.

10. Which of the following is an automatic stabilizer?

A. Interest rates.

B. Exchange rates.

C. Progressive corporate tax.

9. The crowding-out effect refers to:

*A. financing high budget deficits pushes up interest rates which will reduce private investment.

    B. individuals will spend more today if they think expenditure-related taxes will rise in the future.

    C. the recognition by individuals that they must save more today to pay for higher taxes in the future if the government runs a budget deficit.

Explanation: LOS: Reading 19-r

The crowding-out effect refers to when a government tries to stimulate an economy by borrowing to finance a budget deficit. This will increase interest rates, which will reduce companies' and individuals' expenditure, particularly on investment, which will reduce the effectiveness of the government's policy.

---

10. Which of the following is an automatic stabilizer?

    A. Interest rates.

    B. Exchange rates.

*C. Progressive corporate tax.

Explanation: LOS: Reading 19-p

Automatic stabilizers will tend to expand a budget deficit during a recession and contract a budget deficit in a boom. They include unemployment benefits, progressive corporate and personal taxes.

11. In a fractional reserve banking system commercial banks:

A. must hold reserves equal to 100% of their loans.

B. are permitted to hold reserves of less than 100% of their loans.

C. are permitted to hold reserves of less than 100% of their deposits.

---

12. When a central bank purchases domestic securities this will tend to lead to:

	Monetary base	Money supply
A.	increase	increase
B.	increase	decrease
C.	decrease	increase

11. In a fractional reserve banking system commercial banks:

   A. must hold reserves equal to 100% of their loans.

   B. are permitted to hold reserves of less than 100% of their loans.

*C. are permitted to hold reserves of less than 100% of their deposits.

Explanation: LOS: Reading 19-h
A fractional reserve banking system means that banks only need to keep a fraction of their deposits as cash and other reserves. The rest are available to lend to customers.

---

12. When a central bank purchases domestic securities this will tend to lead to:

	Monetary base	Money supply
*A.	increase	increase
B.	increase	decrease
C.	decrease	increase

Explanation: LOS: Reading 19-f
When the central bank purchases securities it adds to currency in circulation or deposits with banks thereby increasing the monetary base. This will lead to an increase in the money supply.

13. Real money supply is usually considered to be a

   A. leading economic indicator.

   B. lagging economic indicator.

   C. coincident economic indicator.

---

14. If the first price rise in cost-push inflation is triggered by a jump in wage rates, the short-run aggregate supply curve:

   A. is unchanged.

   B. shifts to the left.

   C. shifts to the right.

13. Real money supply is usually considered to be a

*A. leading economic indicator.

    B. lagging economic indicator.

    C. coincident economic indicator.

Explanation: LOS: Reading 18-i

Easy money conditions are an indicator of future economic growth/recovery and restrictive money policy of a slowdown.

14. If the first price rise in cost-push inflation is triggered by a jump in wage rates, the short-run aggregate supply curve:

    A. is unchanged.

*B. shifts to the left.

    C. shifts to the right.

Explanation: LOS: Reading 18-h

Cost-put inflation is triggered by a rise in the price of labor or another resource; the first impact will be a move in the aggregate supply curve to the left as aggregate supply decreases.

15. The quantity theory of money says that if the quantity of money is increased then:

   A. output and prices will also both increase.

   B. the velocity of money will decrease, therefore output and prices are unchanged.

   C. the velocity of money is constant and real output is independent of monetary factors, so prices increase.

16. A major role of a central bank is usually to:

   A. implement fiscal policy.

   B. issue government securities.

   C. maintain a favorable monetary environment.

15. The quantity theory of money says that if the quantity of money is increased then:

   A. output and prices will also both increase.

   B. the velocity of money will decrease, therefore output and prices are unchanged.

*C. the velocity of money is constant and real output is independent of monetary factors, so prices increase.

Explanation: LOS: Reading 17-f

The quantity theory of money says that GDP can be expressed as price x output **or** quantity of money x velocity. The theory says output and velocity are unaffected by changes in the quantity of money so an increase in the supply of money will cause a proportionate increase in the price level.

16. A major role of a central bank is usually to:

   A. implement fiscal policy.

   B. issue government securities.

*C. maintain a favorable monetary environment.

Explanation: LOS: Reading 19-f

Central banks are responsible for implementing monetary policy and thereby providing a favorable economic climate.

17. The required reserve ratio is reduced to 15% giving a bank $1 billion of excess reserves. In the long term this will lead to a potential expansion in the money supply of:

    A. $0.15 billion.

    B. $0.87 billion.

    C. $6.67 billion.

18. An increase in the quantity of physical capital in an economy is likely to:

    A. shift only the long-run aggregate supply curve to the right.

    B. shift only the short-run aggregate supply curve to the right.

    C. shift both the short-run and long-run aggregate supply curves to the right.

17. The required reserve ratio is reduced to 15% giving a bank $1 billion of excess reserves. In the long term this will lead to a potential expansion in the money supply of:

   A. $0.15 billion.

   B. $0.87 billion.

*C. $6.67 billion.

Explanation: LOS: Reading 19-c

The money supply will potentially expand by the excess reserves multiplied by the reciprocal of the required reserve ratio, this is:

$1 billion x 1/0.15 = $6.67 billion.

18. An increase in the quantity of physical capital in an economy is likely to:

   A. shift only the long-run aggregate supply curve to the right.

   B. shift only the short-run aggregate supply curve to the right.

*C. shift both the short-run and long-run aggregate supply curves to the right.

Explanation: LOS: Reading 17-g

The larger the capital base, the higher the resource base shifting both supply curves to the right.

19. Demand-pull inflation is *least likely* to be accompanied by, in the short term:

A. an increase in money wage rates.

B. real GDP falling below potential GDP.

C. unemployment falling below its natural rate.

20. Monetarist economists believe:

A. money wage rates are slow to change in a recession.

B. governments should target stable money supply growth.

C. fiscal policy should be used to stimulate demand in a recession.

19. Demand-pull inflation is *least likely* to be accompanied by, in the short term:

    A. an increase in money wage rates.

*B. real GDP falling below potential GDP.

    C. unemployment falling below its natural rate.

Explanation: LOS: Reading 18-h

If the aggregate demand curve shifts to the right, without a move in the supply curve, then prices will rise. This will lead to:

       ⇒ unemployment falling below its natural rate.

       ⇒ money wage rates starting to rise.

       ⇒ the supply curve shifting to the left.

       ⇒ prices rising further.

       ⇒ real GDP starting to decrease which will push real GDP above potential GDP.

---

20. Monetarist economists believe:

    A. money wage rates are slow to change in a recession.

*B. governments should target stable money supply growth.

    C. fiscal policy should be used to stimulate demand in a recession.

Explanation: LOS: Reading 18-c

Monetarists believe government intervention is often ineffective and damaging and the economy can self-regulate. Stable and consistent government policies should be maintained.

21. If the CPI price index was 75 last year and 82 this year, then the annual inflation rate is *closest* to:

    A. 8.2%.

    B. 8.5%.

    C. 9.3%.

22. Which of the following statements is *least accurate* regarding the multiplier effect of a tax change?

    A. When the marginal propensity to consume falls the multiplier rises.

    B. The multiplier is a key factor in using fiscal policy to stabilize an economy.

    C. The magnitude of the tax multiplier is less than the government purchases multiplier.

21. If the CPI price index was 75 last year and 82 this year, then the annual inflation rate is *closest* to:

    A. 8.2%.

    B. 8.5%.

*C. 9.3%.

Explanation: LOS: Reading 18-f
The inflation rate is $[(82 - 75)/75] \times 100 = 9.33\%$

---

22. Which of the following statements is *least accurate* regarding the multiplier effect of a tax change?

*A. When the marginal propensity to consume falls the multiplier rises.

    B. The multiplier is a key factor in using fiscal policy to stabilize an economy.

    C. The magnitude of the tax multiplier is less than the government purchases multiplier.

Explanation: LOS: Reading 19-r
A is not correct – when the marginal propensity to consume falls people save more of the reduction in taxes, reducing the effect of the tax change.

23. Which of the following is *least likely* to be a major role of a central bank?

    A. Issuing currency.

    B. Managing the exchange rate.

    C. Regulating the banking system.

---

24. Which of the following groups of people is *least likely* to be included in the labor force?

    A. Retired workers.

    B. People looking for a job.

    C. People waiting to start a new job within two weeks.

23. Which of the following is *least likely* to be a major role of a central bank?

   A. Issuing currency.

*B. Managing the exchange rate.

   C. Regulating the banking system.

Explanation: LOS: Reading 19-f

Issuing the currency is usually a major role; an exception is the Federal Reserve which puts the money in circulation but the money is printed by the US Treasury. Regulating the banking system is frequently one of the major roles of a central bank.

Managing the exchange rate would not usually be a primary role of a central bank.

---

24. Which of the following groups of people is *least likely* to be included in the labor force?

*A. Retired workers.

   B. People looking for a job.

   C. People waiting to start a new job within two weeks.

Explanation: LOS: Reading 18-d

The labor force includes all the employed and unemployed; it does not include retired workers.

25. The supply of money in the US is dependent on:

   A. interest rates.

   B. the Federal Reserve's monetary policy.

   C. the net foreign investment into the country.

---

26. If a government believes in using fiscal policies to stabilize the economy, when there are signs that the economy is in an inflationary economic boom, the government is *most likely* to consider:

   A. raising personal tax rates.

   B. increasing defense spending.

   C. borrowing to finance a larger budget deficit.

25. The supply of money in the US is dependent on:

    A. interest rates.

*B. the Federal Reserve's monetary policy.

    C. the net foreign investment into the country.

Explanation: LOS: Reading 19-d

The role of a central bank, which is the Fed in the US, is to control money supply, through setting the reserve requirement, the discount rate and using open market operations.

26. If a government believes in using fiscal policies to stabilize the economy, when there are signs that the economy is in an inflationary economic boom, the government is *most likely* to consider:

*A. raising personal tax rates.

    B. increasing defense spending.

    C. borrowing to finance a larger budget deficit.

Explanation: LOS: Reading 19-p

The government is likely to adopt a restrictive fiscal policy which would involve increasing taxes and/or reducing government expenditure.

Study Session 06: Economics: Monetary and Fiscal Economics

This study session introduces economics in a global context. The first reading explains the flows of goods and services, physical capital, and financial capital across national borders. The reading explains how the different types of flows are linked and how trade may benefit trade partners. The accounting for these flows and the institutions that facilitate and regulate them are also covered. The payment system supporting trade and investment depends on world currency markets. Investment practitioners need to understand how these markets function in detail because of their importance in portfolio management as well as in economic analysis. The second reading provides an overview of currency market fundamentals.

Reading Assignments

Reading 20:. International Trade and Capital Flows
by Usha Nair-Reichert, PhD and Daniel Robert Witschi, PhD, CFA
Reading 21:. Currency Exchange Rates
by William A. Barker, CFA, Paul D. McNelis and Jerry Nickelsburg

1. A voluntary export restraint on a product will, in an importing country, increase:

    A. the producer surplus.

    B. the consumer surplus.

    C. government revenues.

---

2. Spot exchange transactions:

A. are usually settled within 48 hours.

B. must settle in the same business day.

C. are contracted today although settlement can be up to one month later.

1. A voluntary export restraint on a product will, in an importing country, increase:

*A. the producer surplus.

    B. the consumer surplus.

    C. government revenues.

Explanation: LOS: Reading 20-e

A voluntary export restraint means exporters agree to limit exports; this will not directly affect government revenues. It will lead to domestic producers being able to increase prices and/or volumes of sales and the consumer surplus being reduced.

---

2. Spot exchange transactions:

*A. are usually settled within 48 hours.

    B. must settle in the same business day.

    C. are contracted today although settlement can be up to one month later.

Explanation: LOS: Reading 21-a

Spot transactions are for immediate settlement which in practice usually means within 48 hours.

3. Which of the following is *least likely* to be a reason to impose a trade barrier?

   A. generating revenues for the government from tariffs.

   B. domestic producers often have strong political influence.

   C. they increase employment and keep wages artificially high.

---

4. The imposition of export subsidies on a product will in the exporting country increase:

   A. the producer surplus.

   B. the consumer surplus.

   C. government revenues.

3. Which of the following is *least likely* to be a reason to impose a trade barrier?

    A. generating revenues for the government from tariffs.

    B. domestic producers often have strong political influence.

*C. they increase employment and keep wages artificially high.

Explanation: LOS: Reading 20-e

Special interest groups representing producers and their workers have more political influence. If trade barriers are put in place to protect an industry it is often politically unacceptable to remove them later. Trade barriers will keep workers in inefficient industries rather than relocating them to industries that are efficient, therefore total output cannot grow as fast as if trade barriers were abolished and this will also lead to slower real wage growth.

---

4. The imposition of export subsidies on a product will in the exporting country increase:

*A. the producer surplus.

    B. the consumer surplus.

    C. government revenues.

Explanation: LOS: Reading 20-e

Producers will have the incentive to shift sales from the domestic market to the export market where they can receive the international price plus the subsidy. This increases the producer surplus and reduces the consumer surplus. The government will have to pay the subsidy reducing revenues.

5. The imposition of tariffs on a product will:

    A. benefit domestic and overseas producers of the product.

    B. benefit domestic producers and consumers of the product.

    C. benefit domestic producers of the product and the government.

---

6. If a country has a massive trade surplus and decides to let its currency appreciate in response international political pressure, which of the following is *most likely* to be necessary for the trade surplus to reduce?

    A. Local interest rates need to decline.

    B. Foreigners need to purchase assets in the country.

    C. Citizens of the country need to reduce their savings rate.

5. The imposition of tariffs on a product will:

    A. benefit domestic and overseas producers of the product.

    B. benefit domestic producers and consumers of the product.

*C. benefit domestic producers of the product and the government.

Explanation: LOS: Reading 20-e

Domestic producers will be able to expand output if they can sell at a higher price (world price plus the tariff) leading to higher profits. The government will collect extra revenue from the tariff being paid on imports. The loser is the consumer who pays a higher price for the product.

---

6. If a country has a massive trade surplus and decides to let its currency appreciate in response international political pressure, which of the following is *most likely* to be necessary for the trade surplus to reduce?

    A. Local interest rates need to decline.

*B. Foreigners need to purchase assets in the country.

    C. Citizens of the country need to reduce their savings rate.

Explanation: LOS: Reading 21-i

If reserves are unchanged then for the trade surplus to fall the capital account needs to increase. So foreigners need to buy assets from local investors.

7. A country is an importer of goods with an elasticity of 0.2 (in the domestic market) and exports goods with an elasticity of 0.5 (in the overseas market). If the country's domestic currency is dollars and the value of imports is $45 billion and exports is $55 billion a depreciation of the $ will:

  A. reduce the trade surplus.

  B. increase the trade surplus.

  C. have no impact on the surplus.

---

8. Pounds sterling is quoted at US$/£ = 1.6114-1.6152 and the Singapore dollar is quoted at US$/Sing $ = 0.5795-0.5830. What is the direct quote for pounds sterling in Singapore?

  A. S$ 0.9338 – 0.9417.

  B. S$ 2.7640 – 2.7872.

  C. S$ 2.7704 – 2.7807.

7. A country is an importer of goods with an elasticity of 0.2 (in the domestic market) and exports goods with an elasticity of 0.5 (in the overseas market). If the country's domestic currency is dollars and the value of imports is \$45 billion and exports is \$55 billion a depreciation of the \$ will:

*A. reduce the trade surplus.

   B. increase the trade surplus.

   C. have no impact on the surplus.

Explanation: LOS: Reading 21-i

We can apply the Marshall-Lerner condition to check if $w_x \varepsilon_x + w_M (\varepsilon_M - 1)$ is greater than zero. Since $55/100 \times 0.5 + 45/100 (1 - 0.2) = 0.28 + 0.36 < 0$

a depreciation of the currency will not increase the trade surplus.

---

8. Pounds sterling is quoted at US\$/£ = 1.6114-1.6152 and the Singapore dollar is quoted at US\$/Sing \$ = 0.5795-0.5830. What is the direct quote for pounds sterling in Singapore?

   A. S\$ 0.9338 – 0.9417.

*B. S\$ 2.7640 – 2.7872.

   C. S\$ 2.7704 – 2.7807.

Explanation: LOS: Reading 21-d

$$\left(FC_1/FC_2\right)_{ask} = \left(FC_1/DC\right)_{ask} \times \left(DC/FC_2\right)_{ask}$$
$$\left(FC_1/FC_2\right)_{bid} = \left(FC_1/DC\right)_{bid} \times \left(DC/FC_2\right)_{bid}$$

We are asked for the direct quote which is the Singapore dollar value of one pound so define FC_1 as Singapore dollars and FC_2 as pounds.

9. A manufacturer in Germany (with a euro cost base) sells machinery to a customer in the US and will receive in one month's time the payment of US$1,000,000. He is concerned that the dollar is going to depreciate against the euro in the short term. Which of the following strategies should he consider to reduce his foreign currency risk?

A. Go long of the dollar against the euro in the forward market.

B. Go short of the dollar against the euro in the forward market.

C. Borrow euros, exchange these into dollars and place on dollar deposit:

10. If the spot rate for US$/Japanese yen is 0.009345 and the 90-day forward US$/Japanese yen rate is 0.009460. The Japanese yen is selling at a forward annualized premium, or discount, of:

A. 1.23% premium.

B. 4.86% discount.

C. 4.92% premium.

9. A manufacturer in Germany (with a euro cost base) sells machinery to a customer in the US and will receive in one month's time the payment of US$1,000,000. He is concerned that the dollar is going to depreciate against the euro in the short term. Which of the following strategies should he consider to reduce his foreign currency risk?

   A. Go long of the dollar against the euro in the forward market.

*B. Go short of the dollar against the euro in the forward market.

   C. Borrow euros, exchange these into dollars and place on dollar deposit:

Explanation: LOS: Reading 21-g
He would consider entering into a one month forward contract to sell US$1,000,000 and buy euro at the forward rate. He will then offset the loss he makes, in euro terms, on the payment if the US$ depreciates, with a profit on the forward contract.

---

10. If the spot rate for US$/Japanese yen is 0.009345 and the 90-day forward US$/Japanese yen rate is 0.009460. The Japanese yen is selling at a forward annualized premium, or discount, of:

   A. 1.23% premium.

   B. 4.86% discount.

*C. 4.92% premium.

Explanation: LOS: Reading 21-g
Forward premium

$$
= \frac{(F-S)}{S} \times \frac{12}{N}
$$
$$
= \frac{(0.009460 - 0.009345)}{0.009345} \times \frac{12}{3}
$$
$$
= 0.492
$$

or a 4.92% premium

11. When a country adopts a passive crawling peg regime for their currency it means:

A. the currency is allowed to float against another currency within fixed bands.

B. the exchange rate will adjust frequently, usually based on inflation differentials between the currencies.

C. the central bank will automatically intervene in the currency market to ensure the currency stays at its target level.

_____

12. The balance of payments is:

A. made up of the current account, capital account and financial account.

B. the inflow into the country in terms of net investments and loans made to a country..

C. the difference between the value of merchandise exports and merchandise imports for a country.

11. When a country adopts a passive crawling peg regime for their currency it means:

A. the currency is allowed to float against another currency within fixed bands.

*B. the exchange rate will adjust frequently, usually based on inflation differentials between the currencies.

C. the central bank will automatically intervene in the currency market to ensure the currency stays at its target level.

Explanation: LOS: Reading 21-h

A is not correct, this is a target zone regime; C is not correct, this is a fixed rate regime. B describes a passive crawling peg.

---

12. The balance of payments is:

*A. made up of the current account, capital account and financial account.

B. the inflow into the country in terms of net investments and loans made to a country..

C. the difference between the value of merchandise exports and merchandise imports for a country.

Explanation: LOS: Reading 20-g

B describes the capital account.

C is the balance of merchandise trade and is just one component of the balance of payments.

13. The impact of depreciation of the currency will usually be most effective in improving a country's trade balance if they import and export goods:

    A. which are necessity products.

    B. for which there are good substitutes

    C. which represent only a small part of the users' total expenditures.

---

14. A customer requests a quote from a bank for the exchange rate between two currencies and he finds that the spread quoted is larger than the spread he was quoted on a previous quote (between the same two currencies). This is *most likely* to be because:

    A. it is a larger size of transaction.

    B. the currencies are now less widely traded.

    C. the bank is temporarily short of one of the currencies..

13. The impact of depreciation of the currency will usually be most effective in improving a country's trade balance if they import and export goods:

    A. which are necessity products.

*B. for which there are good substitutes

    C. which represent only a small part of the users' total expenditures.

Explanation: LOS: Reading 21-i

If a country trades in goods for which demand is very elastic it will be most effective in changing the trade balance. Demand is elastic for goods which have close substitutes, are traded in competitive markets, are luxuries and that represent a large portion of the user's expenditure.

---

14. A customer requests a quote from a bank for the exchange rate between two currencies and he finds that the spread quoted is larger than the spread he was quoted on a previous quote (between the same two currencies). This is *most likely* to be because:

    A. it is a larger size of transaction.

*B. the currencies are now less widely traded.

    C. the bank is temporarily short of one of the currencies..

Explanation: LOS: Reading 21-a

A is nor correct, larger transactions will usually have smaller spreads particularly if they are on the interbank market.

B is the *most likely* since the spread represents the liquidity in the market so currencies that are not widely traded will have wider spreads.

If a bank is short of one of the currencies they are likely to adjust the price spread up or down but this will not necessarily affect the size of the spread, so C is not correct.

15. In the Ricardian model of trade the main factor(s) of production:

A. is labor.

B. are capital and labor.

C. are raw materials and capital.

---

16. A current account deficit often indicates that:

A. the country is attracting large inflows of foreign capital.

B. the nation is producing more goods and services for foreigners than it is buying from them.

C. domestic investors have insufficient opportunities to invest domestically and are investing overseas.

15. In the Ricardian model of trade the main factor(s) of production:

*A. is labor.

    B. are capital and labor.

    C. are raw materials and capital.

Explanation: LOS: Reading 20-d

In the Ricardian model labor is the main factor of production and difference in labor productivity, driven by technology.

---

16. A current account deficit often indicates that:

*A. the country is attracting large inflows of foreign capital.

    B. the nation is producing more goods and services for foreigners than it is buying from them.

    C. domestic investors have insufficient opportunities to invest domestically and are investing overseas.

Explanation: LOS: Reading 20-h

A current account deficit indicates that a nation is buying more goods and services from foreigners than it is selling to them but a current account deficit can persist in the long term. It indicates that the capital account is in surplus and therefore the country is attracting foreign capital.

17. The imposition of quotas on a product is *likely* to:

   A. benefit domestic producers and consumers of the product.

   B. benefit domestic and some overseas producers of the product.

   C. benefit domestic producers of the product and the government.

18. A Swiss resident asks for a quotation for buying US dollars and is quoted SFR/$ = 1.5030 for delivery the following day. This is an example of:

   A. a direct quotation in the spot market.

   B. an indirect quotation in the spot market.

   C. a direct quotation in the forward market.

17. The imposition of quotas on a product is *likely* to:

A. benefit domestic producers and consumers of the product.

*B. benefit domestic and some overseas producers of the product.

C. benefit domestic producers of the product and the government.

Explanation: LOS: Reading 20-e

Domestic producers will be able to expand output if they can sell at a higher price (world price plus the tariff) leading to higher profits. Overseas producers who have a quota will be able to sell an amount of the product at an artificially high price. The loser is the consumer who pays a higher price for the product. The government does not collect additional revenue as in the case of tariffs.

---

18. A Swiss resident asks for a quotation for buying US dollars and is quoted SFR/$ = 1.5030 for delivery the following day. This is an example of:

*A. a direct quotation in the spot market.

B. an indirect quotation in the spot market.

C. a direct quotation in the forward market.

Explanation: LOS: Reading 21-a

In the spot market transactions are for immediate delivery, immediate usually means within two working days. Direct quotations give the price in the home currency of a certain quantity of the foreign currency.

19. The foreign exchange quotes for the Hong Kong dollar and Japanese Yen against £ are as follows:

HK$/£ = 12.30

Yen/£ = 170

The cross rate for HK$/Yen is *closest* to:
    A. 0.0478.
    B. 0.0724.
    C. 13.8211

---

20. When a country adopts a fixed parity regime for their currency it means
    A. the currency must be fixed against a single currency.
    B. the country can decide what level of reserves to hold.
    C. the government has committed to keep the fixed exchange rate indefinitely.

19. The foreign exchange quotes for the Hong Kong dollar and Japanese Yen against £ are as follows:

HK$/£ = 12.30
Yen/£ = 170

The cross rate for HK$/Yen is *closest* to:

A. 0.0478.
*B. 0.0724.
C. 13.8211

Explanation: LOS: Reading 21-d
The cross rate is given by

$$HK\$/Yen = HK\$/£ \times £/Yen = 12.30/170 = 0.07235$$

---

20. When a country adopts a fixed parity regime for their currency it means

A. the currency must be fixed against a single currency.
*B. the country can decide what level of reserves to hold.
C. the government has committed to keep the fixed exchange rate indefinitely.

Explanation: LOS: Reading 21-h
The currency can be fixed against a single currency or basket of currencies so A is not correct. A fixed parity regime differs form a currency board system is that there is no legislative commitment to continue with the parity level and the level of reserves is discretionary so B is correct and C is not correct.

21. If a country decides to fix its exchange rate to that of another currency whilst still maintaining convertibility of the currency it means that the country:

   A. will expect a rise in the inflation rate.

   B. must fix the currency at above the market rate.

   C. cannot follow an independent monetary policy.

22. An economic union:

   A. requires a common currency.

   B. requires common economic institutions.

   C. only allows free movement of goods, labor and capital between members.

21. If a country decides to fix its exchange rate to that of another currency whilst still maintaining convertibility of the currency it means that the country:

A. will expect a rise in the inflation rate.

B. must fix the currency at above the market rate.

*C. cannot follow an independent monetary policy.

Explanation: LOS: Reading 21-j

If the currency is fixed above the market rate then it will be difficult for citizens to find a counterparty from which to buy foreign exchange (unless the government can provide this function which will be difficult in the long run), this will lead to a fall in trade. Fixing the currency will generally be used as a measure to control inflation.

The country's monetary policy will reflect the monetary policy of the country that they have fixed their currency to.

---

22. An economic union:

A. requires a common currency.

*B. requires common economic institutions.

C. only allows free movement of goods, labor and capital between members.

Explanation: LOS: Reading 20-f

A refers to a monetary union. C refers to a common market where there is a free trade area with free movement of factors such as labor and capital. An economic union requires common economic institutions.

23. The gains from countries having comparative advantages in the production of goods imply that:

A. countries should focus on producing goods where they have low opportunity costs.

B. countries with an absolute advantage in the production of a good should export that good.

C. countries should put up trade barriers to protect the industries where they have a high opportunity cost.

---

24. The information below shows the daily output of workers in countries X and Y and the trade off in switching production from wine to cheese. It is assumed that other production costs are constant in each country and transportation costs are low.

COUNTRY X		COUNTRY Y	
Wine	Cheese	Wine	Cheese
1 unit	5 units	2 units	6 units
3 units	2 units	6 units	2 units

A. both countries would gain if X traded wine for Y's cheese.

B. both countries would gain if X traded cheese for Y's wine.

C. only Y can gain since it is a more efficient producer of both wine and cheese than X.

23. The gains from countries having comparative advantages in the production of goods imply that:

*A. countries should focus on producing goods where they have low opportunity costs.**

B. countries with an absolute advantage in the production of a good should export that good.

C. countries should put up trade barriers to protect the industries where they have a high opportunity cost.

Explanation: LOS: Reading 20-b

Trading partners can benefit if each specializes in the production of goods for which it has low production costs and trades those for goods where it has high opportunity costs. A country may have an absolute advantage in the production of many goods but they should only export a specific good if the *relative* cost of production of that good is low, therefore B is not necessarily true.

---

24. The information below shows the daily output of workers in countries X and Y and the trade off in switching production from wine to cheese. It is assumed that other production costs are constant in each country and transportation costs are low.

COUNTRY X		COUNTRY Y	
Wine	Cheese	Wine	Cheese
1 unit	5 units	2 units	6 units
3 units	2 units	6 units	2 units

A. both countries would gain if X traded wine for Y's cheese.

*B. both countries would gain if X traded cheese for Y's wine.**

C. only Y can gain since it's a more efficient producer of both wine & cheese than X.

Explanation: LOS: Reading 20-c

To make an extra 2 units of wine X has to give up 3 units of cheese whereas to make an extra 4 units of wine Y has to give up only 4 units of cheese. (or 1 to 1.5 and 1 to 1 respectively). So Y has a comparative advantage in producing wine.

25. The following data has been provided regarding the output per worker in Japan and the US

	Output per Worker per Day	
	Radios	Televisions
United States	4	1
Japan	7	2

It is assumed that other production costs are constant in each country and transportation costs are low. Which of the following statements *is most accurate*?

A. Japan has an absolute advantage in the production of both radios and televisions.

B. Both countries will gain if Japan focuses on the production of radios and the US on the production of televisions.

C. Both countries will gain if the US focuses on the production of televisions and Japan on the production of radios.

26. One year interest rates are 6% in the US and are 2% in Japan, and the spot rate is Yen/US$ = 110. If there is interest rate parity, the one year Yen/US$ forward rate is *closest* to:

A. 101.74.

B. 105.85.

C. 114.31.

25. The following data has been provided regarding the output per worker in Japan and the US

	Output per Worker per Day	
	Radios	Televisions
United States	4	1
Japan	7	2

It is assumed that other production costs are constant in each country and transportation costs are low. Which of the following statements *is most accurate*?

*A. Japan has an absolute advantage in the production of both radios and televisions.

B. Both countries will gain if Japan focuses on the production of radios and the US on the production of televisions.

C. Both countries will gain if the US focuses on the production of televisions and Japan on the production of radios.

Explanation: LOS: Reading 20-c

Although Japan has the absolute advantage in the production of both products (i.e. it can produce both products more cheaply in terms of man hours) the US has comparative advantage in the production of radios. If the US switched its workers to producing radios and Japan switched its workers to producing televisions there will be an expansion in total output and both countries would gain.

26. One year interest rates are 6% in the US and are 2% in Japan, and the spot rate is Yen/US$ = 110. If there is interest rate parity, the one year Yen/US$ forward rate is *closest* to:

    A. 101.74.

*B. 105.85.

    C. 114.31.

Explanation: LOS: Reading 21-g

Interest rate parity states:

$$\frac{F}{S} = \frac{(1 + r_{FC})}{(1 + r_{DC})}$$

$$\frac{1.06}{1.02} = \frac{F}{0.00909}$$

$$F = 0.09447$$

or Yen105.85 = US$1.

Study Session 07:   Financial Reporting and Analysis: An Introduction

The readings in this study session discuss the general principles of the financial reporting system, underscoring the critical role of the analysis of financial reports in investment decision making.

The first reading introduces the range of information that an analyst may use in analyzing the financial performance of a company, including the principal financial statements (the income statement, balance sheet, cash flow statement, and statement of changes in owners' equity), notes to those statements, and management discussion and analysis of results. A general framework for addressing most financial statement analysis tasks is also presented.

A company's financial statements are the end-products of a process for recording the business transactions of the company. The second reading illustrates this process, introducing such basic concepts as the accounting equation and accounting accruals.

The presentation of financial information to the public by a company must conform to the governing set of financial reporting standards applying in the jurisdiction in which the information is released. The final reading in this study explores the role of financial reporting standard-setting bodies worldwide and the International Financial Reporting Standards framework promulgated by one key body, the International Accounting Standards Board. The movement towards worldwide convergence of financial reporting standards is also introduced.

For the purpose of Level I questions on financial statement analysis, when a ratio is defined and calculated differently in various texts, candidates should use the definitions given in the **CFA Institute copyrighted readings by Robinson, et al. Variations in ratio definitions** are part of the nature of practical financial analysis.

Readings Assignments
Reading 22: Financial Statement Analysis: An Introduction
    by Elaine Henry, CFA and Thomas R. Robinson, CFA
Reading 23: Financial Reporting Mechanics
    International Financial Statement Analysis, by Thomas R. Robinson, CFA, Jan Hendrik van Greuning, CFA, Elaine Henry, CFA, and Michael A. Broihahn, CFA
Reading 24: Financial Reporting Standards
    by Elaine Henry, CFA, Jan Hendrik van Greuning, CFA, and Thomas R. Robinson, CFA

Note: New rulings and/or pronouncements issued after the publication of the readings in Study Sessions 7 through 10 in financial statement analysis may cause some of the information in these readings to become dated. Candidates are expected to be familiar with the overall analytical framework contained in the study session readings, as well as the implications of alternative accounting methods for financial analysis and valuation, as provided in the assigned readings. For the purpose of Level I questions on financial statement analysis, when a ratio is defined and calculated differently in various texts, candidates should use the definitions given in the CFA Institute copyrighted readings by Robinson, et al. Variations in ratio definitions are part of the nature of practical financial analysis.

1. Owners' equity is *least likely* to be described as:

    A. total assets.

    B. net book value.

    C. shareholders' equity

2. A qualified accountant's report indicates that the financial statements:

    A. are not prepared completely in accordance with accounting standards.

    B. the financial statements present a true and fair view of the company's performance and financial position.

    C. the financial statements are prepared in a manner which is materially out of line with accounting standards.

1. Owners' equity is *least likely* to be described as:

*A. total assets.

   B. net book value.

   C. shareholders' equity

Explanation: LOS: Reading 23-a

Owners' equity is total assets less total liabilities, so "total assets" is not correct.

---

2. A qualified accountant's report indicates that the financial statements:

*A. are not prepared completely in accordance with accounting standards.

   B. the financial statements present a true and fair view of the company's performance and financial position.

   C. the financial statements are prepared in a manner which is materially out of line with accounting standards.

Explanation: LOS: Reading 22-d

A qualified opinion indicates that there is some limitation or exception to accounting standards, details of which must be included in the audit report.

3. Which of the following is *least likely* to be included as a liability on the balance sheet?

    A. provisions.

    B. prepaid expenses.

    C. unearned revenue.

---

4. An auditor to a company is *least likely* to be responsible for which of the following?

    A. Preparing the financial statements.

    B. Examining a company's internal control systems.

    C. Ensuring the financial statements conform to generally accepted accounting principles.

3. Which of the following is *least likely* to be included as a liability on the balance sheet?

   A. provisions.

*B. prepaid expenses.

   C. unearned revenue.

Explanation: LOS: Reading 23-a

Prepaid expenses are payments made in advance of when they are due, so they are an asset rather than a liability.

---

4. An auditor to a company is *least likely* to be responsible for which of the following?

*A. Preparing the financial statements.

   B. Examining a company's internal control systems.

   C. Ensuring the financial statements conform to generally accepted accounting principles.

Explanation: LOS: Reading 22-d

It is the company's responsibility to prepare the financial statements.

5. Which of the following is *least likely* to be an obstacle to convergence in global financial reporting standards?

A. Differing objectives between the IASB and FASB.

B. Political lobbying including pressure from listed companies.

C. Regulators have different views on accounting standards to standard-setting bodies.

---

6. The Management Discussion and Analysis in a stockholder report is *least likely* to include:

A. the business outlook.

B. the background of the directors.

C. results of operations and sales trends.

5. Which of the following is *least likely* to be an obstacle to convergence in global financial reporting standards?

*A. Differing objectives between the IASB and FASB.

    B. Political lobbying including pressure from listed companies.

    C. Regulators have different views on accounting standards to standard-setting bodies.

Explanation: LOS: Reading 24-c

The IASB and FASB gave agreed that they are both committed to achieving convergence in standards, and to maintaining compatibility once it is achieved.

---

6. The Management Discussion and Analysis in a stockholder report is *least likely* to include:

    A. the business outlook.

*B. the background of the directors.

    C. results of operations and sales trends.

Explanation: LOS: Reading 22-c

Publicly traded securities are required to provide Management Discussion and Analysis. Information about the directors would normally be included in a stockholder report but not in the Management Discussion and Analysis.

7. Which of the following is *least likely* to be a constraint in preparing useful financial statements?

   A. The time taken to ensure information is accurate.

   B. The cost of providing information that is accurate and useful.

   C. The requirement to include information regardless of whether it is relevant or not.

---

8. The move towards a single accounting framework involves moving to an approach which is:

   A. Rules-based

   B. Principles-based

   C. Objectives-oriented

7. Which of the following is *least likely* to be a constraint in preparing useful financial statements?

    A. The time taken to ensure information is accurate.

    B. The cost of providing information that is accurate and useful.

*C. The requirement to include information regardless of whether it is relevant or not.

Explanation: LOS: Reading 24-d

Information that is not relevant, in terms of being out of date or would not influence decision makers, is not useful and does not automatically need to be included in financial statements. "The requirement" is the *best* choice.

---

8. The move towards a single accounting framework involves moving to an approach which is::

    A. Rules-based

    B. Principles-based

*C. Objectives-oriented

Explanation: LOS: Reading 24-f

IFRS historically adopted a principles–based approach which gives more flexibility on the preparation of financial reports. The FASB has been rules-based which means there are specific rules for each element or transaction. These are being combined in an objectives-oriented approach.

9. When a firm records an allowance for uncollectible receivables as a deduction against the receivables account this is:

  A. a contra account.

  B. an adjunct account.

  C. a non-recurring item.

---

10. A general journal records all:

  A. business transactions by account.

  B. business transactions in date order.

  C. account balances, usually prepared on a daily basis.

9. When a firm records an allowance for uncollectible receivables as a deduction against the receivables account this is:

*A. a contra account.

    B. an adjunct account.

    C. a non-recurring item.

Explanation: LOS: Reading 23-a

An account which reduces the value of an asset, to a new estimate of its net realizable value, is a contra account.

---

10. A general journal records all:

    A. business transactions by account.

*B. business transactions in date order.

    C. account balances, usually prepared on a daily basis.

Explanation: LOS: Reading 23-f

The general journal is the fist step in the flow of information through a financial reporting system. It is where all transactions are recorded showing which accounts they affect, they are recorded in date order.

11. Income that is independent of a firm's capital structure is:

   A. pre-tax income.

   B. operating income.

   C. comprehensive income.

---

12. Which of the following is *least likely* to be important to an analyst when using financial reports?

   A. Detail.

   B. Relevance.

   C. Materiality.

11. Income that is independent of a firm's capital structure is:

    A. pre-tax income.

*B. operating income.

    C. comprehensive income.

Explanation: LOS: Reading 22-b

Operating income is revenues less costs of goods sold, SGA, and research and development. Therefore it is prior to interest costs which reflect the cost of debt financing.

---

12. Which of the following is *least likely* to be important to an analyst when using financial reports?

*A. Detail.

    B. Relevance.

    C. Materiality.

Explanation: LOS: Reading 24-e

If the financial reports are to be relevant and timely it is not practical for them to include every detail of the financial data.

13. A company sells $50,000 of goods but under credit terms given to customers, payment will not be received for 30 days. The cost of the goods is recorded as $35,000. As a result of this transaction assets will:

    A. decrease by $50,000.

    B. increase by $15,000.

    C. increase by $50,000.

---

14. Two firms buy new photocopiers. The first firm is a retailer of office equipment and the photocopier will be resold, and the second firm is a bank planning to use the photocopier in its head office. How will the purchases be classified?

Retailer	Bank
A. investing activity	investing activity
B. operating activity	investing activity
C. operating activity	operating activity

13. A company sells $50,000 of goods but under credit terms given to customers, payment will not be received for 30 days. The cost of the goods is recorded as $35,000. As a result of this transaction assets will:

A. decrease by $50,000.

*B. increase by $15,000.

C. increase by $50,000.

Explanation: LOS: Reading 23-c

The accounting entries will be to increase accounts receivable (an asset) by $50,000 and decrease inventory by $35,000, a net increase in assets of $15,000. Additionally revenue of $50,000 and COGS of $35,000 are recorded.

---

14. Two firms buy new photocopiers. The first firm is a retailer of office equipment and the photocopier will be resold, and the second firm is a bank planning to use the photocopier in its head office. How will the purchases be classified?

	Retailer	Bank
A.	investing activity	investing activity
*B.	**operating activity**	**investing activity**
C.	operating activity	operating activity

Explanation: LOS: Reading 23-a

The purchase will be part of the day-to-day activity of the retailer so it will be classed as an operating activity. For the bank the photocopier will be a long-term asset to support its operations so it will be an investing activity.

15. When new accounting standards are issued which will be implemented in the future, which of the following *best* describes the requirements of a company under International Financial Reporting Standards (IFRS)?

A. The company must disclose whether the new standards will or will not apply to its financial statements.

B. At present a company is not obliged to comment on new standards until they are actually implemented.

C. The company must provide a discussion on whether there will be any impact from the new standards on the financial statements.

---

16. A manufacturing company receives dividends on a long-term investment it has made in another company's shares and pays a dividend to its own stockholders. These are likely to be classified as which types of activity?

Receives dividend	Pays dividend
A. Investing	Financing
B. Financing	Financing
C. Financing	Investing

15. When new accounting standards are issued which will be implemented in the future, which of the following *best* describes the requirements of a company under International Financial Reporting Standards (IFRS)?

A. The company must disclose whether the new standards will or will not apply to its financial statements.

B. At present a company is not obliged to comment on new standards until they are actually implemented.

*C. The company must provide a discussion on whether there will be any impact from the new standards on the financial statements.

Explanation: LOS: Reading 24-h
Companies are expected to provide a discussion on the impending regulations; the conclusions can be anything from 'does not apply' to 'management is still evaluating the impact' to 'the impact of adoption is discussed'.

---

16. A manufacturing company receives dividends on a long-term investment it has made in another company's shares and pays a dividend to its own stockholders. These are likely to be classified as which types of activity?

Receives dividend	Pays dividend
*A. Investing	**Financing**
B. Financing	Financing
C. Financing	Investing

Explanation: LOS: Reading 30-a
Receiving dividends from a long-term investment, if this is not the company's main business, will be an investing activity. Paying dividends to its own stockholders is a financing activity.

17. Under US GAAP minority interest appears in the:

    A. balance sheet as an asset.

    B. balance sheet as a liability.

    C. income statement as an expense.

---

18. A bank lends money and receives interest from the borrowers; it also takes deposits on which it pays interest. These activities are likely to be classified as which types of activity?

Receives interest	Pays interest
A. Financing	Operating
B. Financing	Financing
C. Operating	Operating

17. Under US GAAP minority interest appears in the:

A. balance sheet as an asset.

*B. balance sheet as a liability.

C. income statement as an expense.

Explanation: LOS: Reading 23-a

Minority interest refers to equity held by other investors in a subsidiary that is consolidated in the accounts; it is reported as a liability under US GAAP and is a balance sheet item.

---

18. A bank lends money and receives interest from the borrowers; it also takes deposits on which it pays interest. These activities are likely to be classified as which types of activity?

Receives interest	Pays interest
A. Financing	Operating
B. Financing	Financing
*C. Operating	**Operating**

Explanation: LOS: Reading 23-a

A bank's business is taking deposits and making loans so these are both operating activities.

19. Owners' equity is *least likely* to be referred to as:

    A. net book value.

    B. a residual claim.

    C. contributed capital less retained earnings.

---

20. The International Accounting Standards Board (IASB) is:

    A. a standard-setting body which was set up to harmonize accounting standards internationally.

    B. responsible for developing international financial reporting and accounting standards outside the US

    C. a regulatory body with responsibility for ensuring that companies adhere to International Financial Reporting Standards.

19. Owners' equity is *least likely* to be referred to as:

   A. net book value.

   B. a residual claim.

*C. contributed capital less retained earnings.

Explanation: LOS: Reading 23-b
Owners' equity is total assets less total liabilities, which is net book value. This is
equivalent to contributed capital plus retained earnings. Owners' equity is also referred
to as a residual claim since it is what remains after all the liabilities are settled.

---

20. The International Accounting Standards Board (IASB) is:

***A. a standard-setting body which was set up to harmonize accounting standards
internationally.**

   B. responsible for developing international financial reporting and accounting
   standards outside the US

   C. a regulatory body with responsibility for ensuring that companies adhere to
   International Financial Reporting Standards.

Explanation: LOS: Reading 24-b
The IASB is a standard-setting organization responsible for developing international
financial reporting and accounting standards in major countries including the US One of
its objectives is to achieve convergence in accounting standards, so "a standard-setting
body" is the *best* choice.

21. Information about directors' compensation is *most likely* to be included in a firm's

    A. auditor's report.

    B. proxy statement.

    C. Management's Discussion and Analysis.

---

22. Which of the following statements is *most accurate* in describing the measurement of assets and liabilities?

    A. Whenever possible fair values of assets should be used.

    B. Assets should generally be stated at historical cost and liabilities at present value.

    C. A company is permitted to use a number of different methods to calculate asset and liability values.

21. Information about directors' compensation is *most likely* to be included in a firm's

   A. auditor's report.

*B. proxy statement.

   C. Management's Discussion and Analysis.

Explanation: LOS: Reading 22-e

Proxy statements relate to shareholder meetings. They provide information on board members and management, executive compensation, stock options and major stockholders.

---

22. Which of the following statements is *most accurate* in describing the measurement of assets and liabilities?

   A. Whenever possible fair values of assets should be used.

   B. Assets should generally be stated at historical cost and liabilities at present value.

*C. A company is permitted to use a number of different methods to calculate asset and liability values.

Explanation: LOS: Reading 24-d

Companies can use different combinations of historical cost, current cost, realizable value, present vale and fair value, so "A company is permitted to use a number of different methods to calculate asset and liability values." is the *best* choice.

23. Which of the following statements is *least accurate* regarding US GAAP?

A. US GAAP has a hierarchical structure with standards issued by the FASB holding the highest position.

B. US GAAP includes standards established by a number of different organizations.

C. The target is to replace US GAAP by International Financial Reporting Standards by 2012.

24. A manufacturing company records a depreciation expense associated with the purchase of machinery and the company pays income tax. These are likely to be classified as which types of activity?

Depreciation	ncome tax
A. Investing	Financing
B. Operating	Financing
C. Operating	Operating

23. Which of the following statements is *least accurate* regarding US GAAP?

A. US GAAP has a hierarchical structure with standards issued by the FASB holding the highest position.

B. US GAAP includes standards established by a number of different organizations.

*C. The target is to replace US GAAP by International Financial Reporting Standards by 2012.

Explanation: LOS: Reading 24-c
The objective is to harmonize US GAAP and IFRS, not to replace one with the other.

---

24. A manufacturing company records a depreciation expense associated with the purchase of machinery and the company pays income tax. These are likely to be classified as which types of activity?

Depreciation	ncome tax
A. Investing	Financing
B. Operating	Financing
C. Operating	Operating

Explanation: LOS: Reading 23-a
Depreciation is a cost of using machinery which is likely to be used to manufacture goods for sale; therefore it is an operating item. Paying income tax is an operating item, since it results from the operations of the company.

25. The following information is provided on a company

Retained earnings at end of previous year	$28 million
Net income over year	$ 6 million
Contributed capital at year-end	$35 million
Dividends paid over year	$ 2 million
Expenses over year	$ 3 million

Owners' equity at year end will be:
   A. $32 million.
   B. $64 million.
   C. $67 million.

26. When a company has incurred salary costs that have not been paid by the end of the accounting period this gives rise to:

Expense	Asset/liability
A. accrued expense	liability
B. deferred expense	asset
C. deferred expense	liability

25. The following information is provided on a company

Retained earnings at end of previous year	$28 million
Net income over year	$ 6 million
Contributed capital at year-end	$35 million
Dividends paid over year	$ 2 million
Expenses over year	$ 3 million

Owners' equity at year end will be:

    A. $32 million.

    B. $64 million.

*C. $67 million.

Explanation: LOS: Reading 23-b

Owners' equity = contributed capital + retained earnings

= $35 million + $28 million + ($6 million – $2 million) = $67 million

26. When a company has incurred salary costs that have not been paid by the end of the accounting period this gives rise to:

Expense	Asset/liability
*A. **accrued expense**	**liability**
B. deferred expense	asset
C. deferred expense	liability

Explanation: LOS: Reading 23-d
This is an example of an expense which has been incurred but not yet paid, this is an accrued expense and a liability since it must be paid in the future.

Study Session 08: Financial Reporting and Analysis: The Income Statement, Balance Sheet, and Cash Flow Statement

The first three readings in this study session focus on the three major financial statements: the balance sheet, the income statement, and the statement of cash flows. For each financial statement, the reading describes its purpose, construction, pertinent ratios, and common-size analysis. These readings provide a background for evaluating trends in a company's performance over several measurement periods and for comparing the performance of different companies over a given period. The final reading covers in greater depth financial analysis techniques based on the financial reports.

Note: New rulings and/or pronouncements issued after the publication of the readings in financial reporting and analysis may cause some of the information in these readings to become dated. Candidates are expected to be familiar with the overall analytical framework contained in the study session readings, as well as the implications of alternative accounting methods for financial analysis and valuation, as provided in the assigned readings. Candidates are not responsible for changes that

Reading Assignments

Reading 25: Understanding Income Statements
Reading 26: Understanding Balance Sheets
    by Elaine Henry, CFA and Thomas R. Robinson, CFA
Reading 27: Understanding Cash Flow Statements
Reading 28: Financial Analysis Techniques
    by Elaine Henry, CFA, Thomas R. Robinson, CFA, Jan Hendrik van Greuning, CFA, and Michael A. Broihahn, CFA

1. A company has 2,000,000 common shares outstanding throughout the last year. Total dividends of $1,000,000 were paid to common stockholders and dividends of $400,000 were paid to preferred stockholders. Net income was $6,000,000 and the tax rate was 40%. The company also had 100,000 options on common stock outstanding throughout the period; the exercise price is $20.00. The *average* share price over the year was $27.00 and the end year price was $35.00. The diluted earnings per share was *closest* to:

   A. $2.74.

   B. $2.76.

   C. $2.96.

2. Under US accounting standards a brand name is:

   A. never reported in the balance sheet.

   B. only reported in the balance sheet when it is internally created.

   C. only reported in the balance sheet when purchased from another party.

1. A company has 2,000,000 common shares outstanding throughout the last year. Total dividends of $1,000,000 were paid to common stockholders and dividends of $400,000 were paid to preferred stockholders. Net income was $6,000,000 and the tax rate was 40%. The company also had 100,000 options on common stock outstanding throughout the period; the exercise price is $20.00. The *average* share price over the year was $27.00 and the end year price was $35.00. The diluted earnings per share was *closest* to:

   A. $2.74.

*B. $2.76.

   C. $2.96.

Explanation: LOS: Reading 25-g

diluted earnings per share

$$= \frac{\text{net income} - \text{preferred dividends}}{\text{common shares} + \text{additional shares}}$$

$$= \frac{\$6,000,000 - \$400,000}{2,000,000 + 100,000 - 74,074}$$

denominator adjusts for buying back shares with option proceeds at average price for the year

$$= \frac{\$5,600,000}{2,025,926} = \$2.76 \text{ (versus basic \$2.80)}$$

---

2. Under US accounting standards a brand name is:

   A. never reported in the balance sheet.

   B. only reported in the balance sheet when it is internally created.

*C. only reported in the balance sheet when purchased from another party.

Explanation: LOS: Reading 26-e

In the US if a brand name is internally created it is not included in the balance sheet. When it is acquired from another company it is included in the assets in the balance sheet.

3. If the interest payable decreased over an accounting period, under US GAAP, it will:

   A. increase financing cash flow.

   B. decrease financing cash flow.

   C. decrease operating cash flow.

---

4. A company reports a negative free cash flow to equity shareholders. This could be explained by the company having:

   A. raised funds by issuing new debt.

   B. increased dividends payments to equity shareholders.

   C. finished a major replacement project of their machinery.

3. If the interest payable decreased over an accounting period, under US GAAP, it will:

    A. increase financing cash flow.

    B. decrease financing cash flow.

*C. decrease operating cash flow.

Explanation: LOS: Reading 27-a
Interest expense is included in operating cash flows and if interest payable decreased it means that the cash paid out in interest was more than the interest expense accrued during the period.

---

4. A company reports a negative free cash flow to equity shareholders. This could be explained by the company having:

    A. raised funds by issuing new debt.

    B. increased dividends payments to equity shareholders.

*C. finished a major replacement project of their machinery.

Explanation: LOS: Reading 27-f
Free cash flow to equity is the cash generated by the company available for discretionary spending; this is often measured as operating cash flow less capital expenditure adjusted for payments to or from debt holders, so heavy expenditure on new machinery would reduce free cash flow. Increasing dividends would not affect free cash flow; they are part of cash flow from financing. Raising funds by issuing debt would increase free cash flow to equity.

5. A company had 500,000 common shares and $2,500,000 of a 7% convertible bond issue outstanding throughout the last accounting period. The convertible bond is convertible into six shares per $1,000. If the company's net income was $5,500,000 and the tax rate was 30% the diluted earnings per share was *closest* to:

   A. $10.68.

   B. $10.92.

   C. $11.25.

6. A US consultancy company discovers that a transaction that took place last year was incorrectly recorded and in fact a client paid an additional $10,000 of fees over that recorded as a bonus based on the benefits he received from the consultancy provided in that period. The company should:

   A. increase the income received in the current year's accounts.

   B. adjust the retained earnings in the previous year's balance sheet.

   C. recognize the $10,000 as an extraordinary profit in the current year.

5. A company had 500,000 common shares and $2,500,000 of a 7% convertible bond issue outstanding throughout the last accounting period. The convertible bond is convertible into six shares per $1,000. If the company's net income was $5,500,000 and the tax rate was 30% the diluted earnings per share was *closest* to:

   A. $10.68.

*B. $10.92.

   C. $11.25.

Explanation: LOS: Reading 25-g

Diluted earnings per share
$$= \frac{\text{net income} + \text{net interest saving if convertible converted}}{\text{average common shares} + \text{additional shares from convertible}}$$

$$\frac{\$5,500,000 + \$122,500}{500,000 + 15,000} = \$10.92$$

basic EPS = $11.00

6. A US consultancy company discovers that a transaction that took place last year was incorrectly recorded and in fact a client paid an additional $10,000 of fees over that recorded as a bonus based on the benefits he received from the consultancy provided in that period. The company should:

*A. increase the income received in the current year's accounts.

   B. adjust the retained earnings in the previous year's balance sheet.

   C. recognize the $10,000 as an extraordinary profit in the current year.

Explanation: LOS: Reading 25-f
Adjustments to prior years' accounts through adjustment to the retained earnings is only to be used for accounting errors. The adjustment should be reported in the current year's income statement. Although it is a non-recurring item it is not an extraordinary item.

7. A manufacturing company acquires a smaller competitor. The acquirer combines the inventory of the two companies which will be sold to generate future sales. This is *most likely* to have the following effect on the acquiring company's cash flows:

Operating cash flow	Financing cash flow
A. No effect	Understated.
B. Overstated	No effect.
C. Understated	No effect..

8. If a firm's quick ratio is above the industry *average* but the cash ratio is below the industry *average* this might be explained by:

A. the firm has *higher* inventory levels compared with the rest of the industry.

B. the firm has a large number of 'other short-term assets' in the balance sheet.

C. the firm has extended to their customers more favorable credit terms than their competitors.

7. A manufacturing company acquires a smaller competitor. The acquirer combines the inventory of the two companies which will be sold to generate future sales. This is *most likely* to have the following effect on the acquiring company's cash flows:

Operating cash flow	Financing cash flow
A. No effect	Understated.
*B. Overstated	No effect.
C. Understated	No effect..

Explanation: LOS: Reading 27-a

The acquirer will not be recognizing the cost of the inventory as an operating cash outflow; it will be recorded as an investment activity. Therefore cash flow from operations will be overstated. There is no direct impact on cash flow from financing activities.

---

8. If a firm's quick ratio is above the industry *average* but the cash ratio is below the industry *average* this might be explained by:

   A. the firm has *higher* inventory levels compared with the rest of the industry.

   B. the firm has a large number of 'other short-term assets' in the balance sheet.

*C. the firm has extended to their customers more favorable credit terms than their competitors.

Explanation: LOS: Reading 26-h

The quick ratio includes cash, marketable securities and receivables in the numerator whereas the cash ratio only includes cash and marketable securities. The relatively high quick ratio therefore indicates high levels of receivables, or customers owing money.

9. Which of the following ratios are correctly described as liquidity and solvency ratios?

Liquidity	Solvency
A. Cash	Current
B. Current	Debt To Equity
C. Debt To Equity	Financial Leverage

10. Under US GAAP which of the following is the *least accurate* statement concerning extraordinary items? An extraordinary item IS:

A. reported net of tax.

B. not part of operating income.

C. included in comprehensive income.

9. Which of the following ratios are correctly described as liquidity and solvency ratios?

    Liquidity   **Solvency**

    A. Cash   Current

*B. Current   Debt To Equity

    C. Debt To Equity   Financial Leverage

Explanation: LOS: Reading 26-h

Liquidity ratios measure a company's ability to meet its short-term obligations; solvency ratios measure the ability to meet long-term and other obligations.

---

10. Under US GAAP which of the following is the *least accurate* statement concerning extraordinary items? An extraordinary item IS:

    A. reported net of tax.

    B. not part of operating income.

*C. included in comprehensive income.

Explanation: LOS: Reading 25-f

An extraordinary item will be reported separately on the income statement, below discontinued operations, and net of tax. Therefore it will impact on net income and is not reported separately in comprehensive income.

11. If a company decides to change from a policy of leasing plant and equipment through operating leases to purchasing its own plant and equipment this will:

   A. increase investing cash flows.

   B. increase operating cash flows.

   C. decrease operating cash flows.

---

12. Which inventory accounting method usually gives a valuation of inventory that is *closest* to its economic value?

   A. FIFO.

   B. LIFO.

   C. Lower of cost or market.

11. If a company decides to change from a policy of leasing plant and equipment through operating leases to purchasing its own plant and equipment this will:

    A. increase investing cash flows.

*B. increase operating cash flows.

    C. decrease operating cash flows.

Explanation: LOS: Reading 27-a

Lease rentals are classified as an operating cash flow and the purchase of equipment is classified as an investing cash flow. The decision to switch from leasing to purchasing plant and equipment will increase operating cash flows but decrease investing cash flows.

---

12. Which inventory accounting method usually gives a valuation of inventory that is *closest* to its economic value?

*A. FIFO.

    B. LIFO.

    C. Lower of cost or market.

Explanation: LOS: Reading 25-d

Since FIFO leaves the most recently purchased goods in inventory the valuation will usually be the *closest* to current values.

13. Using common-size statement analysis of the balance sheet of a company will help identify changes in:

A. total assets.

B. financial leverage.

C. efficiency of use of assets

14. When a company recognizes a warranty expense in the same accounting period as the sale of a good this is an application of:

A. accrual accounting.

B. the matching principle.

C. the cost recovery method.

13. Using common-size statement analysis of the balance sheet of a company will help identify changes in:

   A. total assets.

*B. financial leverage.

   C. efficiency of use of assets

Explanation: LOS: Reading 26-g

Common-size statement analysis of the balance sheet will help identify changes in ratios which use balance sheet items; this includes financial leverage which is assets/equity. Total assets will also be read off the balance sheet, but in common-size statements assets will always be 100%.

---

14. When a company recognizes a warranty expense in the same accounting period as the sale of a good this is an application of:

   A. accrual accounting.

*B. the matching principle.

   C. the cost recovery method.

Explanation: LOS: Reading 25-d

Under matching principles expenses should be recognized in the same period as the associated revenues, so the company should recognize estimated warranty expenses in the same period as the sale.

15. The sale of a property which cost $3,000,000 is agreed. The purchaser makes a down payment of $1,500,000 and agrees to pay further installments of $600,000 per year at the end of each of the next five years. The profit that will be recognized as a result of the down payment, using the installment method and cost recovery method is *closest* to:

Installment Method	Cost Recovery Method
A. $ 0	$ 0
B. $750,000	$ 0
C. $750,000	$ 750,000

16. The Comprehensive Income Statement contains:

A. details of income from subsidiaries.

B. information on changes in stockholders' equity.

C. a detailed breakdown of cost of goods sold and other expenses.

15. The sale of a property which cost $3,000,000 is agreed. The purchaser makes a down payment of $1,500,000 and agrees to pay further installments of $600,000 per year at the end of each of the next five years. The profit that will be recognized as a result of the down payment, using the installment method and cost recovery method is *closest* to:

Installment	Cost Recovery
Method	Method
A. $ 0	$ 0
*B. $750,000	$ 0
C. $750,000	$ 750,000

Explanation: LOS: Reading 25-b

Installment method: the profit to sales ratio is ($4,500,000 - $3,000,000)/$3,000,000 equals 50%.

The profit recognized from the down payment is 50% x $1,500,000, equals $750,000.

Cost recovery method: no profit is recognized until the costs have been recovered.

---

16. The Comprehensive Income Statement contains:

A. details of income from subsidiaries.
B. information on changes in stockholders' equity.
C. a detailed breakdown of cost of goods sold and other expenses.

Explanation: LOS: Reading 25-l

Comprehensive income is the change in stockholders' equity as a result of net income and other revenue and expense items that have been excluded from the income statement. These items include foreign currency translation adjustments, pension liability adjustments, unrealized gains and losses on derivatives contracts and investments.

17. I.W.S. Inc. uses US GAAP and supplied the following financial data:

	$ million
Cash payment for salaries	23
Purchase of land	15
Cash payment for interest	3
Retirement of common stock	12
Cash collection from customers	115
Cash payment to suppliers	43
Depreciation expense	10
Dividend payment	8
Sale of equipment	6

Cash flow from operating activities was:

A. $39 million.

B. $46 million.

C. $49 million.

17. I.W.S. Inc. uses US GAAP and supplied the following financial data:

	$ million
Cash payment for salaries	23
Purchase of land	15
Cash payment for interest	3
Retirement of common stock	12
Cash collection from customers	115
Cash payment to suppliers	43
Depreciation expense	10
Dividend payment	8
Sale of equipment	6

Cash flow from operating activities was:

　A. $39 million.

*B. $46 million.

　C. $49 million.

Explanation: LOS: Reading 27-f

	$million
Cash flow from operating activities	
Cash collection from customers	115
Cash payment to suppliers	(43)
Cash payment for salaries	(23)
Cash payment for interest	(3)
	46

18. I.W.S. Inc uses US GAAP and supplied the following financial data:

	$ million
Cash payment for salaries	23
Purchase of land	15
Cash payment for interest	3
Retirement of common stock	12
Cash collection from customers	115
Cash payment to suppliers	43
Depreciation expense	10
Dividend payment	8
Sale of equipment	6

	$million
Cash flow from operating activities	
Cash collection from customers	115
Cash payment to suppliers	(43)
Cash payment for salaries	(23)
Cash payment for interest	(3)
	46

I.W.S. Inc.'s cash flow from investing was (ref. Question 41):

   A. ($12 million).

   B. ($9 million).

   C. ($6 million).

18. I.W.S. Inc uses US GAAP and supplied the following financial data:

	$ million
Cash payment for salaries	23
Purchase of land	15
Cash payment for interest	3
Retirement of common stock	12
Cash collection from customers	115
Cash payment to suppliers	43
Depreciation expense	10
Dividend payment	8
Sale of equipment	6

	$million
Cash flow from operating activities	
Cash collection from customers	115
Cash payment to suppliers	(43)
Cash payment for salaries	(23)
Cash payment for interest	(3)
	46

I.W.S. Inc.'s cash flow from investing was:

   A. ($12 million).

*B. ($9 million).

   C. ($6 million).

Explanation:

Cash flow from
investing activities

Purchase of land	(15 million)
Sale of equipment	6 million
	_____
	(9 million)

LOS: Reading 27-f

19. I.W.S. Inc.'s cash flow from financing was

	$ million
Cash payment for salaries	23
Purchase of land	15
Cash payment for interest	3
Retirement of common stock	12
Cash collection from customers	115
Cash payment to suppliers	43
Depreciation expense	10
Dividend payment	8
Sale of equipment	6

	$million
Cash flow from operating activities	
Cash collection from customers	115
Cash payment to suppliers	(43)
Cash payment for salaries	(23)
Cash payment for interest	(3)
	46

I.W.S. Inc.'s cash flow from financing was :

A. ($23 million).

B. ($20 million).

C. ($12 million).

19.

	$ million
Cash payment for salaries	23
Purchase of land	15
Cash payment for interest	3
Retirement of common stock	12
Cash collection from customers	115
Cash payment to suppliers	43
Depreciation expense	10
Dividend payment	8
Sale of equipment	6

	$million
Cash flow from operating activities	
Cash collection from customers	115
Cash payment to suppliers	(43)
Cash payment for salaries	(23)
Cash payment for interest	(3)
	46

I.W.S. Inc.'s cash flow from financing was:

A. ($23 million).

*B. ($20 million).

C. ($12 million).

Explanation: LOS: Reading 27-f

Cash flow from financing activities

Retirement of common stock	(12 million)
Dividend payment	(8 million)
	_____
	(20 million)

20. Bishop Steel Manufacturing reported little change in net income whereas the operating cash flows rose sharply. This might be explained by the company:

A. I. extending the payment period for customers.

B. II. selling land that was not being used for a substantial sum of money.

C. III. using inventory to meet their customers' orders and minimizing raw material purchases.

---

21. The costs of long-lived assets are usually allocated:

A. over 5 years.

B. over a period that is chosen by the firm.

C. when the impairment of the assets takes place.

20. Bishop Steel Manufacturing reported little change in net income whereas the operating cash flows rose sharply. This might be explained by the company:

   A. I. extending the payment period for customers.

   B. II. selling land that was not being used for a substantial sum of money.

*C. III. using inventory to meet their customers' orders and minimizing raw material purchases.

Explanation: LOS: Reading 27-h

I. is not correct since this would increase receivables and reduce operating cash flow.

II. is not correct since the sale of land would be classified as an investment cash flow.

III. is correct since this would raise cash from the sale of inventory.

---

21. The costs of long-lived assets are usually allocated:

   A. over 5 years.

*B. over a period that is chosen by the firm.

   C. when the impairment of the assets takes place.

Explanation: LOS: Reading 25-d

Usually the management has discretion over the period, or useful life, that assets are depreciated.

22. The indirect method of reporting cash flows calculates operating cash flow by which of the following methods?

A. Start with net income for the period and adjust for all non cash expenses/revenues and adjust for non-operating items included in net income.

B. Start with cash collections for the period and deduct cash outflows incurred in collecting this cash, and then adjust for changes in the balance of operating asset and liability accounts.

C. Start with net income for the period, adjust for all non cash expenses/revenues, adjust for non-operating items included in net income and then adjust for changes in the balance of operating asset and liability accounts.

---

23. Which of the following is *least likely* to be included in the Statement of Stockholders' Equity?

A. Capital leases.

B. Retained earnings.

C. Cumulative foreign exchange adjustments.

22. The indirect method of reporting cash flows calculates operating cash flow by which of the following methods?

   A. Start with net income for the period and adjust for all non cash expenses / revenues and adjust for non-operating items included in net income.

   B. Start with cash collections for the period and deduct cash outflows incurred in collecting this cash, and then adjust for changes in the balance of operating asset and liability accounts.

*C. Start with net income for the period, adjust for all non cash expenses/revenues, adjust for non-operating items included in net income and then adjust for changes in the balance of operating asset and liability accounts.

Explanation: LOS: Reading 34-d
The indirect method starts at the net income figure and makes adjustments whereas the direct method works through the cash items staring with cash collections.

---

23. Which of the following is *least likely* to be included in the Statement of Stockholders' Equity?

*A. Capital leases.

   B. Retained earnings.

   C. Cumulative foreign exchange adjustments.

Explanation: LOS: Reading 26-f
Capital leases are reported in the assets and liabilities section of the balance sheet. The other two items appear as part of shareholders' equity.

24. North Company uses US GAAP and provides the following financial statements.

Year Income Statement (in $'000)

Sales	5,400
COGS	(4,600)
Depreciation	(200)
Interest	(55)
Gain on sale of old machinery	30
Income before taxes	575
Income tax expense	(175)
Net income after taxes	400

Balance Sheet (in $'000)

	end Year	beg. Year
Assets:		
Cash	895	100
Accounts receivable	260	200
Inventory	500	800
Property, plant & equip.	300	00
less acc. depreciation		
Total Assets	1,955	1,600
Liabilities:		
Accounts payable	370	350
Bank notes	0	100
Deferred taxes	90	40
Common stock	1,000	1,000
Retained Earnings	495	110
Total Liabilities	1,955	1,600

- Total dividends of $15,000 were paid.

- Old machinery was sold; the machinery had already been fully depreciated.

The cash flow from operations in the begin year is:

A. $830,000.

B. $880,000.

C. $910,000.

24. North Company uses US GAAP and provides the following financial statements.

Year Income Statement (in $'000)	
Sales	5,400
COGS	(4,600)
Depreciation	(200)
Interest	(55)
Gain on sale of old machinery	30
Income before taxes	575
Income tax expense	(175)
Net income after taxes	400

Balance Sheet (in $'000)	end Year	beg. Year
Assets:		
Cash	895	100
Accounts receivable	260	200
Inventory	500	800
Property, plant & equip.	300	00
less acc. depreciation		
Total Assets	1,955	1,600
Liabilities:		
Accounts payable	370	350
Bank notes	0	100
Deferred taxes	90	40
Common stock	1,000	1,000
Retained Earnings	495	110
Total Liabilities	1,955	1,600

- Total dividends of $15,000 were paid.

- Old machinery was sold; the machinery had already been fully depreciated.

The cash flow from operations is:

　　A. $830,000.

*B. $880,000.

　　C. $910,000.

Explanation: LOS: Reading 27-f

Cash flow from operations:

Net income	400
Adjust for	
Depreciation	200
Deferred taxes	50
Gain on sale of machinery	(30)
Change in accounts receivable	(60)
Decrease in inventory	300
Change in accounts payable	20

Net from operations 880

25. North Company uses US GAAP and provides the following financial statements.

Year Income Statement (in $'000)	
Sales	5,400
COGS	(4,600)
Depreciation	(200)
Interest	(55)
Gain on sale of old machinery	30
Income before taxes	575
Income tax expense	(175)
Net income after taxes	400

Balance Sheet (in $'000)	end Year	beg. Year
Assets:		
Cash	895	100
Accounts receivable	260	200
Inventory	500	800
Property, plant & equip. less acc. depreciation	300	00
Total Assets	1,955	1,600
Liabilities:		
Accounts payable	370	350
Bank notes	0	100
Deferred taxes	90	40
Common stock	1,000	1,000
Retained Earnings	495	110
Total Liabilities	1,955	1,600

- Total dividends of $15,000 were paid.

- Old machinery was sold; the machinery had already been fully depreciated.

The cash flow from investments in 2013 for North Company is:

A. ($70,000).

B. $ 30,000.

C. $230,000.

26. North Company uses US GAAP and provides the following financial statements.

Year Income Statement (in $'000)

Sales	5,400
COGS	(4,600)
Depreciation	(200)
Interest	(55)
Gain on sale of old machinery	30
Income before taxes	575
Income tax expense	(175)
Net income after taxes	400

Balance Sheet (in $'000)

	end Year	beg. Year
Assets:		
Cash	895	100
Accounts receivable	260	200
Inventory	500	800
Property, plant & equip.	300	00
less acc. depreciation		
Total Assets	1,955	1,600
Liabilities:		
Accounts payable	370	350
Bank notes	0	100
Deferred taxes	90	40
Common stock	1,000	1,000
Retained Earnings	495	110
Total Liabilities	1,955	1,600

- Total dividends of $15,000 were paid.

- Old machinery was sold; the machinery had already been fully depreciated.

The cash flow from financing in 2014 for North Company is:

A. ($115,000).

B. ($100,000).

C. ($15,000).

25. North Company uses US GAAP and provides the following financial statements.

Year Income Statement (in $'000)

Sales	5,400
COGS	(4,600)
Depreciation	(200)
Interest	(55)
Gain on sale of old machinery	30
Income before taxes	575
Income tax expense	(175)
Net income after taxes	400

Balance Sheet (in $'000)

	end Year	beg. Year
Assets:		
Cash	895	100
Accounts receivable	260	200
Inventory	500	800
Property, plant & equip. less acc. depreciation	300	00
Total Assets	1,955	1,600
Liabilities:		
Accounts payable	370	350
Bank notes	0	100
Deferred taxes	90	40
Common stock	1,000	1,000
Retained Earnings	495	110
Total Liabilities	1,955	1,600

- Total dividends of $15,000 were paid.

- Old machinery was sold; the machinery had already been fully depreciated.

The cash flow from investments in 2014 for North Company is:

A. ($70,000).

*B. $ 30,000.

C. $230,000.

Explanation: LOS: Reading 27-f

Investing cash flows

    Sale of old machine 30

    Net from investment 30

The cash flow from investments is

  -\$470,000 = -\$300,000 increase in net property - \$200,000 depreciation + \$30,000 gain.

The cash flow from operations in 2014 is: \$880,000.

Cash flow from operations:

Net income	400
<u>Adjust for</u>	
Depreciation	200
Deferred taxes	50
Gain on sale of machinery	(30)
Change in accounts receivable	(60)
Decrease in inventory	300
Change in accounts payable	20
Net from operations 880	

26. North Company uses US GAAP and provides the following financial statements.

Year Income Statement (in $'000)

Sales	5,400
COGS	(4,600)
Depreciation	(200)
Interest	(55)
Gain on sale of old machinery	30
Income before taxes	575
Income tax expense	(175)
Net income after taxes	400

Balance Sheet (in $'000)

	end Year	beg. Year
Assets:		
Cash	895	100
Accounts receivable	260	200
Inventory	500	800
Property, plant & equip.	300	00
less acc. depreciation		
Total Assets	1,955	1,600
Liabilities:		
Accounts payable	370	350
Bank notes	0	100
Deferred taxes	90	40
Common stock	1,000	1,000
Retained Earnings	495	110
Total Liabilities	1,955	1,600

- Total dividends of $15,000 were paid.

- Old machinery was sold; the machinery had already been fully depreciated.

The cash flow from financing in 2012 for North Company is:

*A. ($115,000).

   B. ($100,000).

   C. ($15,000).

Explanation: LOS: Reading 27-f

Financing cash flows:

Bank note	(100)
Dividends paid	(15)
Net from financing	(115)

The cash flow from operations in 2014 is: $880,000.

Cash flow from operations:

Net income	400
Adjust for	
Depreciation	200
Deferred taxes	50
Gain on sale of machinery	(30)
Change in accounts receivable	(60)
Decrease in inventory	300
Change in accounts payable	20
Net from operations	**880**

Study Session 09: Financial Reporting and Analysis: Inventories, Long-Lived Assets, Income Taxes, and Non-Current Liabilities

The readings in this study session examine the financial reporting for specific categories of assets and liabilities. Analysts must understand the effects of alternative financial reporting policies on financial statements and ratios and be able to execute appropriate adjustments to enhance comparability between companies. In addition, analysts must be alert to differences between a company's reported financial statements and economic reality.

The description and measurement of inventories require careful attention because investment in inventories is frequently the largest current asset for merchandising and manufacturing companies. For these companies, the measurement of inventory cost (i.e., cost of goods sold) is a critical factor in determining gross profit and other measures of profitability. Long-lived operating assets are often the largest category of assets on a company's balance sheet. The analyst needs to scrutinize management's choices with respect to recognizing expenses associated with these operating assets because of the potentially large impact such choices can have on reported earnings and the opportunities for financial statement manipulation.

A company's accounting policies (such as depreciation choices) can cause differences in taxes reported in financial statements and taxes reported on tax returns. The reading "Income Taxes" discusses several issues relating to deferred taxes.

Non-current liabilities affect a company's liquidity and solvency and have consequences for its long-term growth and viability. The notes to the financial statements must be carefully reviewed to ensure that all potential liabilities (e.g., leasing arrangements and other contractual commitments) are appropriately evaluated for their conformity to economic reality. Adjustments to the financial statements may be required to achieve comparability when evaluating several companies.

Reading Assignments

Reading 29: Inventories
   by Michael A. Broihahn, CFA
Reading 30: Long-lived Assets
   by Elaine Henry, CFA and Elizabeth A. Gordon
Reading 31: Income Taxes
   International Financial Statement Analysis, by Thomas R. Robinson, CFA, Jan Hendrik van Greuning, CFA, Elaine Henry, CFA, and Michael A. Broihahn, CFA
Reading 32: Non-current (Long-term) Liabilities
   by Elizabeth A. Gordon and Elaine Henry, CFA

1. Under IFRS the treatment of research and development costs, when they arise from internal spending, is:

A. both research and development costs are normally expensed.

B. both research and development costs are normally capitalized.

C. research costs are normally expensed and development costs can be capitalized.

2. When a bond issuer makes a coupon payment for a bond that was issued at a premium it will be reported in the company's financial statements as a:

A. cash flow from financing.

B. cash flow from operations.

C. partly as a cash flow from operations and partly as a cash flow from financing.

1. Under IFRS the treatment of research and development costs, when they arise from internal spending, is:

    A. both research and development costs are normally expensed.

    B. both research and development costs are normally capitalized.

*C. research costs are normally expensed and development costs can be capitalized.

Explanation: LOS: Reading 30-a

Research costs are usually expensed but development costs can be capitalized if certain criteria are met, so "research costs are normally expensed and development costs can be capitalized" is the *best* choice.

---

2. When a bond issuer makes a coupon payment for a bond that was issued at a premium it will be reported in the company's financial statements (under US GAAP) as a:

    A. cash flow from financing.

*B. cash flow from operations.

    C. partly as a cash flow from operations and partly as a cash flow from financing.

Explanation: LOS: Reading 32-a

The coupon payment will be counted as a cash flow from operations although it can be argued that the interest component should be seen as a cash flow from operations and the reduction in principal as cash flow from financing.

3. A company manufactures a machine and agrees to lease the machine under a sales-type capital lease agreement. The company will record the gross investment in the machine as:

   A. the sum of the present values of the minimum lease payments.

   B. the sum of the minimum lease payments plus the residual value of the machine.

   C. the sum of the present values of the minimum lease payments plus the present value of the residual value of the machine.

4. When a bond is issued at a discount and the issuer uses the effective interest rate method, rather than the straight-line method, to amortize the discount it will lead to the issuer reporting:

   A. a lower interest expense in the first year.

   B. a higher interest expense in the first year.

   C. a higher total interest expense over the life of the bond.

3. A company manufactures a machine and agrees to lease the machine under a sales-type capital lease agreement. The company will record the gross investment in the machine as:

   A. the sum of the present values of the minimum lease payments.

*B. the sum of the minimum lease payments plus the residual value of the machine.

   C. the sum of the present values of the minimum lease payments plus the present value of the residual value of the machine.

Explanation: LOS: Reading 32-g
Net investment looks at the present value of the payments, the difference between the gross investment and net investment is the interest component of the revenue represented by unearned income.

---

4. When a bond is issued at a discount and the issuer uses the effective interest rate method, rather than the straight-line method, to amortize the discount it will lead to the issuer reporting:

*A. a lower interest expense in the first year.

   B. a higher interest expense in the first year.

   C. a higher total interest expense over the life of the bond.

Explanation: LOS: Reading 32-b
Under the straight-line method the interest expense will be spread equally over the life of the bond, using the effective rate method it will be lower in the early years when the carrying amount of the bond is lower. The total interest expense is the same with both methods.

5. If a company uses straight-line methods to depreciate assets, then classifying a lease as an operating lease rather than a capital lease will lead to:

A. lower operating income throughout the lease period.

B. *higher* operating income throughout the lease period.

C. lower operating income at the beginning of the lease period and then *higher* operating income.

6. If a company makes write downs due to impairments of long-lived assets, which are not recognized for tax purposes until the asset is disposed of, this will:

Deferred tax Assets	Debt to equity ratio
A. increase	increase
B. increase	decrease
C. decrease	increase

5. If a company uses straight-line methods to depreciate assets, then classifying a lease as an operating lease rather than a capital lease will lead to:

*A. lower operating income throughout the lease period.

B. *higher* operating income throughout the lease period.

C. lower operating income at the beginning of the lease period and then *higher* operating income.

Explanation: LOS: Reading 32-q

Using an operating lease will lead to *higher* operating costs since the lease payment will always be *higher* than the depreciation cost (remember interest costs will appear after the operating income level).

---

6. If a company makes write downs due to impairments of long-lived assets, which are not recognized for tax purposes until the asset is disposed of, this will:

Deferred tax Assets	Debt to equity ratio
*A. increase	**increase**
B. increase	decrease
C. decrease	increase

Explanation: LOS: Reading 30-h and 31-b

If impairment losses are not recognized for tax purposes until the asset is disposed of then net deferred tax assets will be recorded Impairment write-downs will lead to reduction in asset values and equity values and therefore an increase in the debt to equity ratio.

7. The financial ratios for a company, which uses operating leases compared to a company that uses capital leases, will be as follows:

Interest cover	Return on assets
A. lower	lower
B. higher	lower
C. higher	higher

8. An analyst notices that a company's net deferred tax liability has declined; this is *most likely* to be explained by:

A. I. the company has made a profit.

B. II. a new tax law has increased tax rates.

C. III. it is a company with declining capital expenditure.

7. The financial ratios for a company, which uses operating leases compared to a company that uses capital leases, will be as follows:

Interest cover	Return on assets
A. lower	lower
B. higher	lower
*C. higher	higher

Explanation: LOS: Reading 32-l

Interest cover will be *higher* as interest payments will be lower.

Return on assets will be *higher* since assets will be lower.

---

8. An analyst notices that a company's net deferred tax liability has declined; this is *most likely* to be explained by:

   A. I. the company has made a profit.

   B. II. a new tax law has increased tax rates.

***C. III. it is a company with declining capital expenditure.**

Explanation: LOS: Reading 31-a

I. would not reduce deferred tax liabilities

II. is not correct since this would increase deferred tax liabilities

III. is correct since this would to lead to decreasing deferred tax liabilities if accelerated tax depreciation methods are used for tax reporting.

9. Which of the following statements is most accurate? Under IFRS:

   A. the use of FIFO Is not permitted.

   B. inventory is recorded at the lower of cost and market value.

   C. a reversal in the write-down of inventory values is permitted.

---

10. A company decides to reduce the valuation allowance on a deferred tax asset resulting from tax loss carry forwards. This will:

   A. increase asset turnover.

   B. increase financial leverage.

   C. increase net profit margins.

9. Which of the following statements is most accurate? Under IFRS:

    A. the use of FIFO Is not permitted.

    B. inventory is recorded at the lower of cost and market value.

*C. a reversal in the write-down of inventory values is permitted.

Explanation: LOS: Reading 29-g

Under IFRS the use of LIFO is not permitted. Inventory is rerecorded at the lower of cost and net realizable value. Reversals of write-downs are permitted (but not under US GAAP)

---

10. A company decides to reduce the valuation allowance on a deferred tax asset resulting from tax loss carry forwards. This will:

    A. increase asset turnover.

    B. increase financial leverage.

*C. increase net profit margins.

Explanation: LOS: Reading 31-q

Reducing the valuation allowance will increase income from continuing operations and increase the value of assets and stockholders' equity, thereby reducing leverage and asset turnover.

11. A US company changes from reporting inventory under LIFO to reporting under FIFO and inventory balances recorded on the balance sheet increase significantly. Which of the following statements is *most accurate*?

    A. Inventory balances are closer to current value.

    B. The unit cost of the company's inventory has been decreasing.

    C. Only prospective changes are recorded on a company's balance sheet when it switches to FIFO.

12. A company will derecognize an asset if:

    A. the asset is fully depreciated.

    B. the asset has no further use or disposal value.

    C. it is impossible to reliably estimate the fair value of the asset.

11. A US company changes from reporting inventory under LIFO to reporting under FIFO and inventory balances recorded on the balance sheet increase significantly. Which of the following statements is *most accurate*?

*A. Inventory balances are closer to current value.

B. The unit cost of the company's inventory has been decreasing.

C. Only prospective changes are recorded on a company's balance sheet when it switches to FIFO.

Explanation: LOS: Reading 29-g

Under FIFO inventory balances are closer to current value so A is correct. A decrease in inventory unit costs would lead to a higher inventory balances under LIFO so B is not correct. A switch to FIFO would lead to a retrospective change in inventory balances so C is not correct.

---

12. A company will derecognize an asset if:

A. the asset is fully depreciated.

*B. the asset has no further use or disposal value.

C. it is impossible to reliably estimate the fair value of the asset.

Explanation: LOS: Reading 30-i

Derecognition occurs when an asset is not expected to provide any future benefits through use or disposal so B is the best answer.

13. A company has just bought a machine and wants to maximize the depreciation expense in the first year; they would consider:

   A. using an accelerated depreciation method.

   B. overestimating the useful life of the machine.

   C. overestimating the salvage value of the machine.

14. A US company reviews the value of its fixed assets and finds that an asset that had been written down due to impairment in the previous accounting period now has a carrying value less than the future cash flows expected to be received from the use of the asset. The company should, under US GAAP:

   A. revise the value of the asset and record the gain as 'other income'.

   B. revise the value of the asset and record the gain as an extraordinary income.

   C. not do anything, an increase in the value of assets cannot be recognized until they are sold.

13. A company has just bought a machine and wants to maximize the depreciation expense in the first year; they would consider:

*A. using an accelerated depreciation method.

   B. overestimating the useful life of the machine.

   C. overestimating the salvage value of the machine.

Explanation: LOS: Reading 30-c

Overestimating the salvage value or life of the machine would reduce the depreciation charges.

---

14. A US company reviews the value of its fixed assets and finds that an asset that had been written down due to impairment in the previous accounting period now has a carrying value less than the future cash flows expected to be received from the use of the asset. The company should, under US GAAP:

   A. revise the value of the asset and record the gain as 'other income'.

   B. revise the value of the asset and record the gain as an extraordinary income.

*C. not do anything, an increase in the value of assets cannot be recognized until they are sold.

Explanation: LOS: Reading 30-h

Under US GAAP an increase in the value of a held for use asset cannot be recognized until sale and also previous impairments cannot be restored.

15. A company who buys a patent and a copyright from another party should:

A. expense the costs of both purchases.

B. capitalize the cost of both purchases.

C. expense the cost of the patent but capitalize the cost of the copyright.

16. A company purchases an asset and then at the next valuation date finds the fair value has increased, under the revaluation model for the reporting of long-lived assets the company will report the gain as:

A. a revaluation surplus.

B. a component of net income.

C. a reduction in the depreciation expense.

15. A company who buys a patent and a copyright from another party should:

    A. expense the costs of both purchases.

*B. capitalize the cost of both purchases.

    C. expense the cost of the patent but capitalize the cost of the copyright.

Explanation: LOS: Reading 30-a

The costs should be capitalized; if they were developed internally they would be expensed.

---

16. A company purchases an asset and then at the next valuation date finds the fair value has increased, under the revaluation model for the reporting of long-lived assets the company will report the gain as:

*A. a revaluation surplus.

    B. a component of net income.

    C. a reduction in the depreciation expense.

Explanation: LOS: Reading 30-g

Since the increase in value is not a reversal of a previous decrease it will not be reported in net income but will go straight to equity as a revaluation surplus.

17. Under US GAAP if the market value of inventory held by a retailer has increased then:

    A. the gain is recorded in the current year's income statement.

    B. the value of inventory cannot be increased in balance sheet.

    C. the value of inventory can be increased in the balance sheet if it has been previously written down.

18. Tax rates are reduced at the beginning of a company's financial year. In the company's financial statements the tax rate reduction will lead to:

    A. a restatement of prior years' accounts.

    B. a reduction in the value of deferred tax assets.

    C. an extraordinary gain which is stated net of tax on the income statement.

17. Under US GAAP if the market value of inventory held by a retailer has increased then:

    A. the gain is recorded in the current year's income statement.

*B. the value of inventory cannot be increased in balance sheet.

    C. the value of inventory can be increased in the balance sheet if it has been previously written down.

Explanation: LOS: Reading 29-f

Under US GAAP inventory can not be increased in value, even if it has written down (unlike under IFRS) except for in the case of commodity-related firms.

---

18. Tax rates are reduced at the beginning of a company's financial year. In the company's financial statements the tax rate reduction will lead to:

    A. a restatement of prior years' accounts.

*B. a reduction in the value of deferred tax assets.

    C. an extraordinary gain which is stated net of tax on the income statement.

Explanation: LOS: Reading 31-e

The lower tax rate reduces the value of the tax benefit when the deferred tax asset is realized.

19. Market rates are 5% per annum and a 6% semi annual coupon bond is issued at $1,100 with a face value of $1,000. If an investor buys 1,000 bonds at issue and receives a coupon payment after six months how much of this coupon payment will be recorded as principal repayment by the issuer using the effective interest rate method to amortize the discount or premium?

A. $2,500.

B. $5,000.

C. $30,000.

20. A company enters into an agreement to lease equipment (treated as a capital lease) over two years and will pay lease payments of $50,000 at the end of each year. If the discount rate used is 8% the closing liability at the end of the first year is *closest* to:

A. $44,582.

B. $46,296.

C. $58,000.

19. Market rates are 5% per annum and a 6% semi annual coupon bond is issued at $1,100 with a face value of $1,000. If an investor buys 1,000 bonds at issue and receives a coupon payment after six months how much of this coupon payment will be recorded as principal repayment by the issuer using the effective interest rate method to amortize the discount or premium?

*A. $2,500.

   B. $5,000.

   C. $30,000.

Explanation: LOS: Reading 32-a
The coupon paid will be 3% multiplied by $1,000,000, which is $30,000. The interest the investor earns is 2.5% multiplied by $1,100,000, which is $27,500, so the remainder is principal repayment of $2,500.

---

20. A company enters into an agreement to lease equipment (treated as a capital lease) over two years and will pay lease payments of $50,000 at the end of each year. If the discount rate used is 8% the closing liability at the end of the first year is *closest* to:

   A. $44,582.

*B. $46,296.

   C. $58,000.

Explanation: LOS: Reading 32-q
At the beginning of the lease period the liability will be the present value of the lease payments, which is $89,163. The first lease payment is divided between interest (8% x $89,163 = $7,133) and principal repayment. Therefore the liability is reduced by $42,867 to $46,296.

21. Which of the following would be *most likely* to increase the reported pension expense for a company with a defined benefit pension plan? An increase in

A. the retirement age for employees.

B. compensation rates for employees.

C. the expected return on plan assets.

22. If a deferred tax liability is very unlikely to be paid then it should be treated by an analyst as:

A. a long-term liability.

B. stockholders' equity.

C. an extraordinary item.

21. Which of the following would be *most likely* to increase the reported pension expense for a company with a defined benefit pension plan? An increase in

    A. the retirement age for employees.

*B. compensation rates for employees.

    C. the expected return on plan assets.

LOS: Reading 32-j

An increase in the expected return on plan assets would reduce the pension expense, as would an increase in retirement age.

---

22. If a deferred tax liability is very unlikely to be paid then it should be treated by an analyst as:

    A. a long-term liability.

*B. stockholders' equity.

    C. an extraordinary item.

Explanation: LOS: Reading 31-b

If the factors that created the deferred tax liability are unlikely to be reversed, than it is considered part of stockholders' equity.

23. In a direct financing lease the sale value reported at the beginning of the lease on the lessor's financial statements is:

A. the present value of lease payments.

B. zero, there is no sale value reported.

C. the present value of lease payments plus the present value of the residual value.

24. If a company using US GAAP actively uses operating leases, which of the following statements is *least accurate*?

A. Total cash flow is understated.

B. Off-balance-sheet financing is significant.

C. Minimum lease payments for the next five years must be disclosed in the company's accounts.

23. In a direct financing lease the sale value reported at the beginning of the lease on the lessor's financial statements is:

   A. the present value of lease payments.

*B. zero, there is no sale value reported.

   C. the present value of lease payments plus the present value of the residual value.

Explanation: LOS: Reading 32-g

With a direct financing lease only financing or interest income is reported. There is no 'manufacturing' profit and no sale is recorded.

---

24. If a company using US GAAP actively uses operating leases, which of the following statements is *least accurate*?

*A. Total cash flow is understated.

   B. Off-balance-sheet financing is significant.

   C. Minimum lease payments for the next five years must be disclosed in the company's accounts.

Explanation: LOS: Reading 32-g

Total cash flow is not understated but cash flow from operations is lower than if the lease were capitalized.

25. When a company reports a large LIFO reserve, has it

(1) been using LIFO or FIFO to calculate inventory balances and has it

(2) overstated or understated the value of inventory compared with the current market value?

Inventory balances	Overstated/understated
A. LIFO	overstated
B. FIFO	overstated
C. LIFO	understated

26. A mining company is required by regulation to restore land to its original state when mining has finished. Under SFAS 143 the company is required to:

A. I. calculate the present value of restoring the land to its original state and deduct this from the carrying value of the assets.

B. II. calculate the present value of restoring the land to its original state and recognize this as an expense in the first year of operation of the mine.

C. III. calculate the present value of restoring the land to its original state at the end of each year and recognize the difference from the previous year is an accretion expense.

25. When a company reports a large LIFO reserve, has it

(1) been using LIFO or FIFO to calculate inventory balances and has it

(2) overstated or understated the value of inventory compared with the current market value?

Inventory balances	Overstated/understated
A. LIFO	overstated
B. FIFO	overstated
*C. LIFO	**understated**

Explanation: LOS: Reading 32-g

The LIFO reserve is reported by companies using LIFO. Accounting using LIFO usually leads to an understatement of the inventory balance compared with current values, so information on the LIFO reserve is provided.

---

26. A mining company is required by regulation to restore land to its original state when mining has finished. Under SFAS 143 the company is required to:

A. I. calculate the present value of restoring the land to its original state and deduct this from the carrying value of the assets.

B. II. calculate the present value of restoring the land to its original state and recognize this as an expense in the first year of operation of the mine.

*C. III. calculate the present value of restoring the land to its original state at the end of each year and recognize the difference from the previous year is an accretion expense.

Explanation: LOS: Reading 32-g

I. is not correct, present value should be added to the asset value.

II. is not correct, the cost should be added to the asset value and be depreciated over the useful life of the mine.

27. If a company decided to change the estimated life of an asset that is already owned by the company it must:

   A. restate prior years' accounts.

   B. not make any retroactive adjustment.

   C. calculate the cumulative effect of the change and report net of taxes.

28. If the Cost of Goods Sold under LIFO is $20 million, the increase in LIFO reserve over the same period is $5 million, and the closing inventory under LIFO is $80 million, then the Cost of Goods Sold under FIFO is:

   A. $15 million.

   B. $25 million.

   C. $75 million.

27. If a company decided to change the estimated life of an asset that is already owned by the company it must:

   A. restate prior years' accounts.

*B. not make any retroactive adjustment.

   C. calculate the cumulative effect of the change and report net of taxes.

Explanation: LOS: Reading 32-e

Since this is only a change in accounting estimate there is no need to make retroactive adjustments, only current and future depreciation expense will be affected.

The other choices are not correct since changing an estimate of life of an asset is not a change in accounting principle.

28. If the Cost of Goods Sold under LIFO is $20 million, the increase in LIFO reserve over the same period is $5 million, and the closing inventory under LIFO is $80 million, then the Cost of Goods Sold under FIFO is:

*A. $15 million.

   B. $25 million.

   C. $75 million.

Explanation: LOS: Reading 35-e

COGS under FIFO = COGS under LIFO – increase in LIFO reserve.

COGS under FIFO = $20 million - $5 million = $15 million

29. Which of the following is an example of a take-or-pay contract?

A. A firm agrees to buy a certain amount of oil from an oil producer at the market price each year for the next five years.

B. A firm has the option to buy a certain amount of oil from an oil producer at the market price each year for the next five years.

C. An oil producer has the option to sell a certain amount of oil to another firm at a fixed price each year for the next five years.

30. When market interest rates decline, a company that has fixed-rate debt outstanding will, under US GAAP:

A. lose in economic terms.

B. gain in economic terms.

C. the debt on the balance sheet is automatically adjusted to current market value so the economic loss will be reflected as an accounting loss.

29. Which of the following is an example of a take-or-pay contract?

*A. A firm agrees to buy a certain amount of oil from an oil producer at the market price each year for the next five years.

 B. A firm has the option to buy a certain amount of oil from an oil producer at the market price each year for the next five years.

 C. An oil producer has the option to sell a certain amount of oil to another firm at a fixed price each year for the next five years.

Explanation: LOS: Reading 38-i

A take-or-pay contract is a firm commitment, not an option, at either a fixed or market price, and can provide security of supply of a raw material for the buyer and security of income for the seller. These contracts are an example of off-balance-sheet financing since future commitments are not treated as debt.

---

30. When market interest rates decline, a company that has fixed-rate debt outstanding will, under US GAAP:

*A. lose in economic terms.

 B. gain in economic terms.

 C. the debt on the balance sheet is automatically adjusted to current market value so the economic loss will be reflected as an accounting loss.

Explanation: LOS: Reading 38-d

The debt on the balance sheet reflects the market rate at issuance and therefore if market interest rates decline the market value of the debt will increase which leads to an economic loss.

31. The following information is given regarding a company's activities:

- Tax rate is 30%.
- The only expense is depreciation.
- A new machine is purchased at a cost of $10,000.
- Annual revenues of $40,000 are generated from the new machine.
- The company, in its financial reports, depreciates the machine by using the straight-line method over four years and the salvage value is estimated to be $2,000.
- For tax purposes the machine is depreciated using the straight-line method over two years with the same salvage value.

The deferred tax expense in year 2 will be:

A. $ 600.

B. $ 1,200.

C. $10,800.

31. The following information is given regarding a company's activities:
    - Tax rate is 30%.
    - The only expense is depreciation.
    - A new machine is purchased at a cost of $10,000.
    - Annual revenues of $40,000 are generated from the new machine.
    - The company, in its financial reports, depreciates the machine by using the straight-line method over four years and the salvage value is estimated to be $2,000.
    - For tax purposes the machine is depreciated using the straight-line method over two years with the same salvage value.

The deferred tax expense in year 2 will be:

*A. $ 600.

  B. $ 1,200.

  C. $10,800.

Explanation: LOS: Reading 31-b

Tax reporting – straight-line depreciation over two years

	Year 1	Year 2
Revenue	$40,000	$40,000
Depreciation	$ 4,000	$ 4,000
Taxable income	$36,000	$36,000
Taxes payable	$10,800	$10,800

Financial statement reporting - straight-line depreciation over 4 years

	Year 1	Year 2
Revenue	$40,000	$40,000
Depreciation	$ 2,000	$ 2,000
Pre tax income	$38,000	$38,000
Tax expense	$11,400	$11,400
of which		
Taxes payable	$10,800	$10,800
Deferred tax expense	$ 600	$ 600

32. A company has just issued a bond with covenants. Which of the following clauses is *least likely* to be included in the bond covenants?

   A. A requirement that return on capital should exceed a specified percentage.

   B. A restriction on dividend payments to shareholders if they would reduce stockholders' equity below a specified level.

   C. A requirement that no future debt can be issued that ranks *higher* than the original bonds giving the holders a prior claim on assets.

---

33. The following financial data is provided by Sportswear Corporation:

$ million (using LIFO)	2011	2012
Inventory	105	125
Current assets	300	350
LIFO reserve	45	55
Current liabilities	110	160
COGS	1450	1700

The current ratios using FIFO are *closest* to:

	2011	2012
A.	2.32	1.84
B.	2.73	2.19
C.	3.14	2.53

32. A company has just issued a bond with covenants. Which of the following clauses is *least likely* to be included in the bond covenants?

*A. A requirement that return on capital should exceed a specified percentage.

   B. A restriction on dividend payments to shareholders if they would reduce stockholders' equity below a specified level.

   C. A requirement that no future debt can be issued that ranks *higher* than the original bonds giving the holders a prior claim on assets.

Explanation: LOS: Reading 32-b

Covenants tend to focus on clauses that restrict leverage, issuance of new debt or spending (on dividends or investment) that would limit the funds available to repay bond holders. Therefore a return on capital requirement is least likely to be specified.

---

33. The following financial data is provided by Sportswear Corporation:

$ million (using LIFO)	2011	2012
Inventory	105	125
Current assets	300	350
LIFO reserve	45	55
Current liabilities	110	160
COGS	1450	1700

The current ratios using FIFO are *closest* to:

2011	2012
A. 2.32	1.84
B. 2.73	2.19
*C. 3.14	**2.53**

Explanation: LOS: Reading 35-f

Adjust current assets by adding the LIFO reserve to get current assets under FIFO of 345 in 2011 and 405 in 2012.

Current ratio is current assets /current liabilities = 345/110 and 405/160 respectively which equal 3.14 and 2.53 respectively.

34. Top Radios Inc. provided the following data regarding its radio purchases and sales over last year.

1st January	Beginning inventory of 1,000 radios at cost of $300 each
1st March	Purchase of 1,000 radios at cost of $320 each
1st July	Purchase of 500 radios at cost of $325 each
31st December	Ending inventory of 1,200 radios

The reported value of inventory using LIFO (periodic method) and FIFO respectively at 31st December was:

	LIFO	FIFO
A.	$364,000	$375,600
B.	$364,000	$386,500
C.	$386,500	$364,000

35. The Cost of Goods Sold for Top Radios InC. was

1st January	Beginning inventory of 1,000 radios at cost of $300 each
1st March	Purchase of 1,000 radios at cost of $320 each
1st July	Purchase of 500 radios at cost of $325 each
31st December	Ending inventory of 1,200 radios

The reported value of inventory using LIFO (periodic method) and FIFO respectively at 31st December is as follows.

LIFO: ending inventory = $364,000

FIFO: ending inventory = $386,500

The Cost of Goods Sold for Top Radios InC. was:

A. *higher* under FIFO than using LIFO.

B. *higher* using the weighted *average* cost method than under LIFO.

C. *higher* under LIFO than using the weighted *average* cost method.

34. Top Radios Inc. provided the following data regarding its radio purchases and sales over last year.

1st January	Beginning inventory of 1,000 radios at cost of	$300 each
1st March	Purchase of 1,000 radios at cost of	$320 each
1st July	Purchase of 500 radios at cost of	$325 each
31st December	Ending inventory of	1,200 radios

The reported value of inventory using LIFO (periodic method) and FIFO respectively at 31st December was:

	LIFO	FIFO
A.	$364,000	$375,600
*B.	$364,000	$386,500
C.	$386,500	$364,000

Explanation: LOS: Reading 29-c

LIFO:

ending inventory 1,200 radios, 1,000 @ $300 and 200 @ $320   = $364,000

FIFO:

ending inventory 1,200 radios, 500 @ $325 and 700 @ $320   = $386,500

35. The Cost of Goods Sold for Top Radios Inc. was

1st January	Beginning inventory of 1,000 radios at cost of	$300 each
1st March	Purchase of 1,000 radios at cost of	$320 each
1st July	Purchase of 500 radios at cost of	$325 each
31st December	Ending inventory of	1,200 radios

The reported value of inventory using LIFO (periodic method) and FIFO respectively at 31st December is as follows.

LIFO: ending inventory = $364,000

FIFO: ending inventory = $386,500

The Cost of Goods Sold for Top Radios InC. was:

A. *higher* under FIFO than using LIFO.

B. *higher* using the weighted *average* cost method than under LIFO.

*C. **higher** under LIFO than using the weighted *average* cost method.**

Explanation: LOS: Reading 29-c

LIFO:

COGS 1,300 radios, 500 @ $ 325 and 800 @ $320   = $418,500

FIFO:

COGS 1,300 radios, 1,000 @ $300 and 300 @ $320   = $396,000

Weighted *average*:

cost of goods available was $782,500/2,500   = $313,000

COGS = 1,300 radios @ $313   = $406,900

Study Session 10: Financial Reporting and Analysis: Techniques, Applications, and International Standards Convergence

This study session covers evaluating financial reporting quality and shows the application of financial statement analysis to debt and equity investments. The most frequently used tools and techniques to evaluate companies include common-size analysis, cross-sectional analysis, trend analysis, and ratio analysis. Beyond mere knowledge of these tools, however, the analyst must recognize the implications of accounting choices on the quality of a company's reported financial results. Then the analyst can apply financial analysis techniques to analytical tasks including the evaluation of past and future financial performance, credit risk, and the screening of potential equity investments. The readings also explain analyst adjustments to reported financials. Such adjustments are often needed to put companies' reported results on a comparable basis.

Reading Assignments
Reading 33   Financial Reporting Quality:
   by Jack Ciesiklski, CFA, Elaine Henry, CFA, and Thomas I. Selling, PhD
Reading 34:   Financial Statement Analysis: Applications
   International Financial Statement Analysis, by Thomas R. Robinson, CFA, Jan Hendrik van
   Greuning, CFA, R. Elaine Henry, CFA, and Michael A. Broihahn, CFA

---

1. A company might be motivated to use conservative accounting standards in order to:

   A.   reduce the present value of tax payments.

   B.   ensure financial statements are not biased.

   C.   provide analysts with better quality information on the company.

---

2. When a company uses operating leases and an analyst makes adjustments to the financial statements to adjust for these leases, the effect will usually be to reduce:

   A. asset turnover.

   B. the debt-to-assets ratio.

   C. the depreciation expense.

1. A company might be motivated to use conservative accounting standards in order to:

*A.   **reduce the present value of tax payments.**

   B.   ensure financial statements are not biased.

   C.   provide analysts with better quality information on the company.

Explanation: LOS: Reading 33-e

Delaying recognizing profits until future years can delay tax payments and therefore reduce the present value of the payments. Conservative financial statements are biased and generally less useful to analysts so B and C are not correct.

---

2. When a company uses operating leases and an analyst makes adjustments to the financial statements to adjust for these leases, the effect will usually be to reduce:

*A. **asset turnover.**

   B. the debt-to-assets ratio.

   C. the depreciation expense.

Explanation: LOS: Reading 34-e

Asset turnover (sales/assets) will be reduced as the asset base will be larger.

The debts-to-assets ratio will increase as the increase in debt is usually proportionately more than the increase in assets. Depreciation of the leased assets will be recorded increasing depreciation expense.

3. Data is provided on two companies as shown below:

	Company ABC	Company XYZ
Market capitalization	$137 million	$28 million
Shareholder's equity	$86 million	$15 million
Goodwill	$22 million	$3 million
Other intangible assets	$35 million	$4 million

The price/tangible book value ratios for both companies are *closest* to

Company ABC	Company XYZ
A. 2.14	2.33
B. 2.40	4.00
C. 4.72	3.50

4. A company has been underestimating the useful life of its equipment, this will

A. reduced net income.

B. increased taxes payable.

C. have increased the asset base.

3. Data is provided on two companies as shown below:

	Company ABC	Company XYZ
Market capitalization	$137 million	$28 million
Shareholder's equity	$86 million	$15 million
Goodwill	$22 million	$3 million
Other intangible assets	$35 million	$4 million

The price/tangible book value ratios for both companies are *closest* to

	Company ABC	Company XYZ
A.	2.14	2.33
B.	2.40	4.00
*C.	4.72	3.50

Explanation: LOS: Reading 34-e
The tangible book value for Company ABC is ($86 - $22 - $35) million =$29 million
Price/tangible book value ratio for Company ABC is 137/29 = 4.72

The tangible book value for Company XYZ is ($15 - $3 - $4) million =$8 million
Price/tangible book value ratio for Company ABC is 28/8 = 3.50

4. A company has been underestimating the useful life of its equipment, this will
*A. reduced net income.
B. increased taxes payable.
C. have increased the asset base.

Explanation: LOS: Reading 34-e
Underestimating the useful life of equipment will have increased the depreciation
charge will have reduced asset values and reduced income so A is correct

5. When an analyst uses historic stock data for a screening program they find that their database includes financial data which has been updated to reflect subsequent changes in accounting principles. This is referred to as:

    A. selection bias.

    B. look-ahead bias.

    C. data-snooping bias.

---

6. Which of the following provides motivation for a company to prepare low quality financial statements?

    A.   Weak accounting standards.

    B.   Ineffective external directors.

    C.   High earnings expectations from investors.

5. When an analyst uses historic stock data for a screening program they find that their database includes financial data which has been updated to reflect subsequent changes in accounting principles. This is referred to as:

    A. selection bias.

*B. look-ahead bias.

    C. data-snooping bias.

Explanation: LOS: Reading 35-d

Look-ahead bias refers to databases which have a mismatch between what investors would have seen at the time and the information used in the screening.

---

6. Which of the following provides motivation for a company to prepare low quality financial statements?

    A.   Weak accounting standards.

    B.   Ineffective external directors.

*C.   High earnings expectations from investors.

Explanation: LOS: Reading 33-e

A and B would provide an opportunity whereas pressure from investors can provide the motivation.

7. Expensing research costs is an example of which type of accounting method?

    A.   Unbiased.

    B.   Aggressive.

    C.   Conservative.

---

8. Using back testing to test a model that discovers that stocks with specified characteristics have generated superior returns might have limited value due to data-snooping bias. This bias refers to:

    A. adjusting the financial data to ensure that the model is valid.

    B. only including stocks in the back testing that support the findings.

    C. using the same database for back testing as the database used by the analysts who built the original model.

7. Expensing research costs is an example of which type of accounting method?

   A.   Unbiased.

   B.   Aggressive.

*C.   **Conservative.**

Explanation: LOS: Reading 33-c

As the future benefit of research is uncertain it is usually expensed, however this is conservative in assuming research will not benefit future earnings of the company.

---

8. Using back testing to test a model that discovers that stocks with specified characteristics have generated superior returns might have limited value due to data-snooping bias. This bias refers to:

   A. adjusting the financial data to ensure that the model is valid.

   B. only including stocks in the back testing that support the findings.

***C. using the same database for back testing as the database used by the analysts who built the original model.**

Explanation: LOS: Reading 34-d

Data-snooping bias refers to using the same database to test a model as the original researchers used.

9. A company runs down their inventory towards the end of the financial year. In an inflationary environment, if the company uses LIFO, this is likely to result in an:

A. increase in net income

B. increase in financing cash flow.

C. increase in operating cash flow.

---

10. An analyst notices that the LIFO reserve for a company has risen over the last reporting period. This is *likely* to be a result of:

A. the company has switched to using FIFO.

B. the company has been reducing the size of its inventory.

C. the price of units of inventory purchased have been rising.

9. A company runs down their inventory towards the end of the financial year. In an inflationary environment, if the company uses LIFO, this is likely to result in an:

*A. increase in net income

    B. increase in financing cash flow.

    C. increase in operating cash flow.

Explanation: LOS: Reading 33-h

This is referred to as LIFO liquidation and the company can increase income if they sell inventory recorded at a low historic cost. Cash flows will only be affected by the increase in tax which will reduce operating cash flows.

---

10. An analyst notices that the LIFO reserve for a company has risen over the last reporting period. This is *likely* to be a result of:

    A. the company has switched to using FIFO.

    B. the company has been reducing the size of its inventory.

*C. the price of units of inventory purchased have been rising.

Explanation: LOS: Reading 34-e

The LIFO reserve is the difference between inventories calculated using LIFO and calculated using FIFO. A rise in prices would increase the difference between the value using LIFO and FIFO so C is the correct answer. Reducing the size of the inventory would reduce the LIFO reserve and companies using FIFO do not have a LIFO reserve.

11. A company reports the following data on its fixed assets; it uses the straight-line depreciation method:

Gross property, plant and equipment	$1,050,000
Net property, plant and equipment	$420,000
Depreciation expense	$70,000

The remaining useful life of the property, plant and equipment is expected to be:

  A. 6 years.

  B. 9 years.

  C. 15 years.

12. Which of the following factors does Moody's *usually* give the greatest weighting to when assigning credit ratings to companies?

  A. Financial policies.

  B. Operational efficiency.

  C. Scale and diversification.

11. A company reports the following data on its fixed assets; it uses the straight-line depreciation method:

Gross property, plant and equipment	$1,050,000
Net property, plant and equipment	$420,000
Depreciation expense	$70,000

The remaining useful life of the property, plant and equipment is expected to be:

*A. 6 years.

   B. 9 years.

   C. 15 years.

Explanation: LOS: Reading 34-e

Remaining useful life is the net PPE divided by the depreciation expense

= $420,000/$70,000 = 6 years

12. Which of the following factors does Moody's *usually* give the greatest weighting to when assigning credit ratings to companies?

*A. Financial policies.

   B. Operational efficiency.

   C. Scale and diversification.

Explanation: LOS: Reading 34-c

In the example in the text financial policies account for 55% of the total weighting; they look at the ability of the company to service and repay its debt.

13. Moody's analyses 'scale and diversification' as a component of their credit rating analysis. One of the reasons for this is:

   A. diversification of products or markets reduces risk.

   B. larger companies generally have stable cash flows.

   C. larger companies usually have a lower requirement for debt financing.

---

14. When an analyst is looking at the interest coverage of a company that is using operating leases it is *most likely* that the analyst making adjustments by capitalizing the lease expense will:

   A. reduce interest cover.

   B. increase interest cover.

   C. not affect interest cover.

13. Moody's analyses 'scale and diversification' as a component of their credit rating analysis. One of the reasons for this is:

*A. diversification of products or markets reduces risk.

B. larger companies generally have stable cash flows.

C. larger companies usually have a lower requirement for debt financing.

Explanation: LOS: Reading 34-c

Scale and diversification suggest lower risk; another reason is that they indicate potentially greater power over suppliers leading to lower costs.

---

14. When an analyst is looking at the interest coverage of a company that is using operating leases it is *most likely* that the analyst making adjustments by capitalizing the lease expense will:

*A. reduce interest cover.

B. increase interest cover.

C. not affect interest cover.

Explanation: LOS: Reading 34-e

Part of the operating lease payment represents interest. If the value of the lease obligations is capitalized by the analyst, this will *usually* lead to a decline in interest cover since the impact on interest expense is usually proportionately greater than a potential increase in EBIT. (Note: interest cover is EBIT/interest expense).

15. The revenue recognition accounting standards for oil exploration companies is usually considered to be an example of which type of accounting method?

    A.   Unbiased.

    B.   Aggressive.

    C.   Conservative.

---

16. If a firm's ratio of operating cash flow to net income has decreased each year this might be explained by the company:

    A.   increasing the valuation allowances on deferred tax assets.

    B.   increasing the estimates of the non-collection rate for sales.

    C.   using accrual accounting to move expenses to future years.

15. The revenue recognition accounting standards for oil exploration companies is usually considered to be an example of which type of accounting method?

    A.   Unbiased.

    B.   Aggressive.

*C.   **Conservative.**

Explanation: LOS: Reading 33-c

Revenue can only be recognized when the oil is shipped, not when it is discovered which is regarded as conservative (and extraction costs are recorded when they are incurred).

16. If a firm's ratio of operating cash flow to net income has decreased each year this might be explained by the company:

    A.   increasing the valuation allowances on deferred tax assets.

    B.   increasing the estimates of the non-collection rate for sales.

*C.   **using accrual accounting to move expenses to future years.**

Explanation: LOS: Reading 33-i

Shifting expenses to future years will increase net income in proportion to cash flows so C is a possible explanation. Increasing estimated non-collection rates and increasing valuation allowances will both reduce net income and not immediately affect cash flows

17. A company reports the following data on its fixed assets; it uses the straight-line depreciation method:

Gross property, plant and equipment	$1,800,000
Net property, plant and equipment	$1,200,000
Depreciation expense	$120,000

The average useful life of the property, plant and equipment at installation was *likely* to be:

A. 5 years.

B. 10 years.

C. 15 years.

18. When Moody's calculates that a firm's retained cash flow to debt is 0.25, this is *most likely* to mean that:

A. the firm could pay off its debt from retained cash flow in about three months.

B. unless the firm has a heavy capital expenditure program it could pay off its debt from retained cash flow in about four years.

C. the firm could increase debt financing by a factor of four times and still have sufficient cash flow to cover interest payments on the debt.

17. A company reports the following data on its fixed assets; it uses the straight-line depreciation method:

Gross property, plant and equipment	$1,800,000
Net property, plant and equipment	$1,200,000
Depreciation expense	$120,000

The average useful life of the property, plant and equipment at installation was *likely* to be:

    A. 5 years.

    B. 10 years.

*C. 15 years.

Explanation: LOS: Reading 35-e

Average useful life is the gross PPE divided by the depreciation expense

= $1,800,000/$120,000 = 15 years

18. When Moody's calculates that a firm's retained cash flow to debt is 0.25, this is *most likely* to mean that:

    A. the firm could pay off its debt from retained cash flow in about three months.

*B. unless the firm has a heavy capital expenditure program it could pay off its debt from retained cash flow in about four years.

    C. the firm could increase debt financing by a factor of four times and still have sufficient cash flow to cover interest payments on the debt.

Explanation: LOS: Reading 35-c

Retained cash flow is defined as operating cash flow before working capital changes, less dividends. If cash flows and debt remains stable and there were no capital expenditures then the company could pay off its debt from retained cash flow in 1/0.25, or 4 years.

19. Bill-and-hold sales arrangements refer to when a company records:

    A. a sale before the customer is invoiced for a sale.

    B. a sale before the goods are shipped to a customer.

    C. revenues in a different accounting period to the associated costs.

20. If a company wishes to overstate net income in the current financial year they might, for recently purchased fixed assets:

    A. use short useful lives.

    B. overestimate salvage values.

    C. use accelerated depreciation methods.

19. Bill-and-hold sales arrangements refer to when a company records:

   A. a sale before the customer is invoiced for a sale.

*B. a sale before the goods are shipped to a customer.

   C. revenues in a different accounting period to the associated costs.

Explanation: LOS: Reading 33-d

Bill-and-hold refers to invoicing a customer and recording a sale before the goods are shipped.

---

20. If a company wishes to overstate net income in the current financial year they might, for recently purchased fixed assets:

   A. use short useful lives.

*B. overestimate salvage values.

   C. use accelerated depreciation methods.

Explanation: LOS: Reading 35-e

Using short useful lives and accelerated depreciation methods will lead to a higher depreciation expense in the early years after a fixed asset purchase. A high salvage value will reduce depreciation expense.

21. Under US GAAP unrealized gains on which type of marketable securities are recorded in the income statement?

    A. Held-for-trading securities only.

    B. Available-for-sale securities only.

    C. Held-for-trading securities and available-for-sale securities only.

---

22. A company starts using a financial institution to finance its payables; this will have the effect of:

    A. decreasing the total cash outflows associated with payments to suppliers.

    B. converting the company's financing cash outflows to operating cash outflows.

    C. allowing the company to manage when payments are made representing payable to suppliers.

21. Under US GAAP unrealized gains on which type of marketable securities are recorded in the income statement?

*A. Held-for-trading securities only.

   B. Available-for-sale securities only.

   C. Held-for-trading securities and available-for-sale securities only.

Explanation: LOS: Reading 35-e

Available-for- sale securities are recorded at market value but any unrealized gains flow straight through to shareholders' equity. Only unrealized gains on held-for-trading securities are recorded in the income statement. Under IFRS exchange rate gains and losses on available-for-sale debt securities are recognized in the income statement.

---

22. A company starts using a financial institution to finance its payables; this will have the effect of:

   A. decreasing the total cash outflows associated with payments to suppliers.

   B. converting the company's financing cash outflows to operating cash outflows.

*C. allowing the company to manage when payments are made representing payable to suppliers.

Explanation: LOS: Reading 34-a

Using a financial institution to finance payables means that the supplier is paid by the financial institution, and the company will pay the financial institution the amount plus interest at a later date. This allows the company to manage the timing of cash outflows and classify payments as a repayment of a loan (financing cash flow).

23. If a company has used the FIFO method for inventory accounting in an inflationary environment, compared to a company using LIFO, it would lead to

	Asset turnover	Financial leverage
A.	increase	decrease
B.	decrease	increase
C.	decrease	decrease

---

24. If a company has grown internally and is being compared against one which has grown by acquisition, the company which has grown internally would tend to have:

A. lower leverage.

B. lower return on assets.

C. higher price/book value.

23. If a company has used the FIFO method for inventory accounting in an inflationary environment, compared to a company using LIFO, it would lead to

	Asset turnover	Financial leverage
A.	increase	decrease
B.	decrease	increase
*C.	**decrease**	**decrease**

Explanation: LOS: Reading 35-e

Using FIFO will lead to higher inventory balances (closer to current value) which will increase the asset base and reduce asset turnover (sales/assets). It will reduce financial leverage (assets/equity) since equity increases proportionately by more than assets.

---

24. If a company has grown internally and is being compared against one which has grown by acquisition, the company which has grown internally would tend to have:

A. lower leverage.

B. lower return on assets.

*C. **higher price/book value.**

Explanation: LOS: Reading 35-e

If a company has grown by acquisition it will report assets on its balance sheet reflecting the purchase of staff expertise, brand names, research, and probably goodwill (assuming they have not been written off). If a company has grown internally it will have expensed similar items and therefore will have a smaller asset base. Other things being equal this will lead to higher return on assets or equity, higher leverage (since equity falls proportionately more than assets), lower book value per share so higher price/book value, so C is correct.

25. An analyst is screening the characteristics of companies whose share prices outperformed the market using historic financial data. If the analysis was subject to look-ahead bias it means that:

A. investment decisions were being made using forecast rather than actual financial data.

B. some of the financial data was not available to investors at the time that they made decisions.

C. the data base being used is the same one as other analysts used so the screening is not adding new information or testing new outcomes.

26. Under US GAAP a company which has grown by acquisition and not recognized impairment of goodwill will, compared to a similar company that has grown internally, tend to report:

A. lower net income.

B. higher net income.

C. identical net income.

25. An analyst is screening the characteristics of companies whose share prices outperformed the market using historic financial data. If the analysis was subject to look-ahead bias it means that:

A. investment decisions were being made using forecast rather than actual financial data.

*B. some of the financial data was not available to investors at the time that they made decisions.

C. the data base being used is the same one as other analysts used so the screening is not adding new information or testing new outcomes.

Explanation: LOS: Reading 35-d

Look-ahead bias refers to using financial data that has been restated so the data may not have been available to investors at the time they made decisions.

26. Under US GAAP a company which has grown by acquisition and not recognized impairment of goodwill will, compared to a similar company that has grown internally, tend to report:

    A. lower net income.

*B. higher net income.

    C. identical net income.

Explanation: LOS: Reading 35-e

The company which has grown internally will have expensed items such as research, advertising etc. so the company that has grown by acquisition tends to report higher net income.

Study Session 11:   Corporate Finance

This study session covers the principles that corporations use to make their investing and financing decisions. Capital budgeting is the process of making decisions about which long-term projects the corporation should accept for investment, and which it should reject. Both the expected return of a project and the financing cost should be taken into account. The cost of capital, or the rate of return required for a project, must be developed using economically sound methods. Corporate managers are concerned with liquidity and solvency, and use financial statements to evaluate performance as well as to develop and communicate future plans.

The final reading in this study session is on corporate governance practices, which can expose the firm to a heightened risk of ethical lapses. Although these practices may not be inherently unethical, they create the potential for conflicts of interest to develop between shareholders and managers, and the extent of that conflict affects the firm's valuation.

Corporate managers are concerned with liquidity and solvency, and use financial statements to evaluate performance as well as to develop and communicate future plans. The final reading in this study session is on corporate governance practices, which can expose the firm to a heightened risk of ethical lapses. Although these practices may not be inherently unethical, they create the potential for conflicts of interest to develop between shareholders and managers, and the extent of that conflict affects the firm's valuation.

Reading Assignments

Reading 35:   Capital Budgeting
      by John D. Stowe, CFA and Jacques R. Gagné, CFA
Reading 36:   Cost of Capital
      by Yves Courtois, CFA, Gene C. Lai, and Pamela Peterson Drake, CFA
Reading 37:   Measures of Leverage
      by Pamela Peterson Drake, CFA, Raj Aggarwal, CFA, Cynthia Harrington, CFA, and
      Adam Kobor, CFA
Reading 38:   Dividends and Share Repurchases: Basics
      by George H. Troughton, CFA and Gregory Noronha, CFA
Reading 39:   Working Capital Management
      by Edgar A. Norton, Jr., CFA, Kenneth L. Parkinson, and Pamela Peterson Drake, CFA
Reading 40:   The Corporate Governance of Listed Companies:
      A Manual for Investors
      by Kurt Schacht, CFA, James C. Allen, CFA, and Matthew Orsagh, CFA, CIPM

1. A proposed project is expected to increase shareholders' wealth if:

	Profitability index	**Cost of capital versus internal rate of return**
A.	Less than 1.	Cost of capital is lower.
B.	Less than 1.	Cost of capital is *higher*.
C.	Greater than 1.	Cost of capital is lower.

2. Uncommitted lines of credit are an attractive source of short-term financing for a company because:

   A. banks do not require a commitment fee.

   B. banks make a firm promise that funds will be available if required.

   C. they are strong legal agreements that can be effective for a number of years.

1. A proposed project is expected to increase shareholders' wealth if:

	Profitability index	Cost of capital versus internal rate of return
A.	Less than 1.	Cost of capital is lower.
B.	Less than 1.	Cost of capital is *higher*.
*C.	**Greater than 1.**	**Cost of capital is lower.**

Explanation: LOS: Reading 35-d
The profitability index must be greater than one; this indicates the NPV is positive. The internal rate of return must be *higher* than the cost of capital if the project is going to increase stockholders' wealth.

---

2. Uncommitted lines of credit are an attractive source of short-term financing for a company because:

*A. banks do not require a commitment fee.

    B. banks make a firm promise that funds will be available if required.

    C. they are strong legal agreements that can be effective for a number of years.

Explanation: LOS: Reading 39-g
The main advantage of uncommitted lines is that they do not require any compensation, such as a commitment fees, other than the interest payment. The disadvantage is that a bank can withdraw the use of the line at any point in time.

3. South Corporation's target capital structure is 50% debt, 10% preferred stock and 40% common equity. If the before-tax costs of debt, preferred stock and common equity are 10%, 11% and 14% respectively and the marginal tax rate is 40% the weighted *average* cost of capital is *closest* to:

    A. 9.3%.

    B. 9.7%.

    C. 10.3%.

---

4. In calculating the cost of preferred stock:

    A. the after-tax cost should be used since the preferred dividends are paid from pre-tax profits.

    B. the cost should be adjusted for flotation costs since it is the cost of issuing new preferred stock in the current market.

    C. if the stock has no maturity date we can apply a perpetuity formula to find the discount factor which is the cost of the preferred stock.

3. South Corporation's target capital structure is 50% debt, 10% preferred stock and 40% common equity. If the before-tax costs of debt, preferred stock and common equity are 10%, 11% and 14% respectively and the marginal tax rate is 40% the weighted *average* cost of capital is *closest* to:

    A. 9.3%.

*B. 9.7%.

    C. 10.3%.

Explanation: LOS: Reading 36-a

$$WACC = w_d k_d (1-T) + w_{ps} k_{ps} + w_e k_e$$
$$= (0.50 \times 10\% \times 0.6) + (0.10 \times 11\%) + (0.40 \times 14\%) = 9.7\%$$

4. In calculating the cost of preferred stock:

    A. the after-tax cost should be used since the preferred dividends are paid from pre-tax profits.

    B. the cost should be adjusted for flotation costs since it is the cost of issuing new preferred stock in the current market.

    C. if the stock has no maturity date we can apply a perpetuity formula to find the discount factor which is the cost of the preferred stock.

Explanation: LOS: Reading 36-b

Preferred stock is valued using a perpetuity formula so C is correct. The dividend is not tax-deductible and flotation cost should be reflected in cash flows as they are a one-off expense.

5. Which one of the following is *least likely* to be considered good corporate governance of a listed company?

A. Appropriate controls and procedures are in place covering management's activities in running the day-to-day operations of the company.

B. The board and its committees are structured to act independently from management and other parties that might influence the management.

C. All shareowners have the same right to participate in the governance of the company, with founding shareowners normally given the right to veto certain resolutions.

---

6. A company has trade credit which is 2/10, net 30. The company pays on the 20th day. The effective borrowing cost of not paying on the 10th day is *closest* to:

A. 44.6%.

B. 106.0%.

C. 109.0%.

5. Which one of the following is *least likely* to be considered good corporate governance of a listed company?

A. Appropriate controls and procedures are in place covering management's activities in running the day-to-day operations of the company.

B. The board and its committees are structured to act independently from management and other parties that might influence the management.

*C. All shareowners have the same right to participate in the governance of the company, with founding shareowners normally given the right to veto certain resolutions.

Explanation: LOS: Reading 40-g
In a listed company, all shareowners should have equal rights to participate in the governance of the company. Differentiating between economic and voting rights should be avoided.

---

6. A company has trade credit which is 2/10, net 30. The company pays on the 20th day. The effective borrowing cost of not paying on the 10th day is *closest* to:

A. 44.6%.

B. 106.0%.

*C. 109.0%.

Explanation: LOS: Reading 39-d
The cost of trade credit is calculated as the implicit rate of return which is represented by the trade discount offer.

$$\text{Cost} = \left(1 + \frac{0.02}{1-0.02}\right)^{365/20} - 1 = 109\%$$

7. A company has trade credit with its suppliers and receives a discount if it pays within a specified number of days. It works out the cost of trade credit is 50% if it pays on the net day. If the company's short term cost of funds is 18% then the company should pay:

   A. on the net day.

   B. on the day of purchase.

   C. on the last day of the discount period

8. Which of the following is *least likely* to be a pull on liquidity for a company?

   A. paying vendors early.

   B. low liquidity positions.

   C. uncollected receivables.

7. A company has trade credit with its suppliers and receives a discount if it pays within a specified number of days. It works out the cost of trade credit is 50% if it pays on the net day. If the company's short term cost of funds is 18% then the company should pay:

   A. on the net day.

   B. on the day of purchase.

*C. on the last day of the discount period

Explanation: LOS: Reading 39-d

The discount offers a *higher* return for the company compared to its borrowing rate so it should take advantage of the discount offered and pay on the last day of the discount period. Losing the discount is more costly than delaying payment to the net day.

---

8. Which of the following is *least likely* to be a pull on liquidity for a company?

   A. paying vendors early.

   B. low liquidity positions.

*C. uncollected receivables.

Explanation: LOS: Reading 39-a

A pull on liquidity refers to payments that are made too early or when credit availability is limited forcing the company to pay out funds before they receive money from sales or other sources. Uncollected receivables or not a pull, but a drag, on liquidity.

9. A company is offered two projects with the net cash flows, in $ million, from each project as shown below. The cost of project A is $2 million and the cost of project B is $10 million. The cost of capital for project A is 10% and for project B is 12%. Which of the projects should be accepted for inclusion in the capital budget?

End of year	Project A	Project B
1	1.1	2.0
2	0.8	4.0
3	0.4	7.0

A. Both projects should be rejected.

B. Both projects should be accepted.

C. A should be accepted and B rejected.

10. Which of the following is *most accurate* with respect to dividend payment procedures?

A. The ex-dividend date is after the holder-of-record date.

B. The ex-dividend date is before the holder-of-record date.

C. The ex-dividend date is the same as the holder-of-record date.

9. A company is offered two projects with the net cash flows, in $ million, from each project as shown below. The cost of project A is $2 million and the cost of project B is $10 million. The cost of capital for project A is 10% and for project B is 12%. Which of the projects should be accepted for inclusion in the capital budget?

End of year	Project A	Project B
1	1.1	2.0
2	0.8	4.0
3	0.4	7.0

*A. Both projects should be rejected.

   B. Both projects should be accepted.

   C. A should be accepted and B rejected.

Explanation: LOS: Reading 35-d

The present value of the cash flows for project A, discounted at 10%, is $1.96 million (1.00 + 0.66 + 0.30) which is less than the cost, therefore the project should be rejected.

The present value of the cash flows for project B, discounted at 12%, is $9.96 million (1.79 + 3.19 + 4.98) which is less than the cost; therefore the project should be rejected.

---

10. Which of the following is *most accurate* with respect to dividend payment procedures in the US? The ex-dividend date is?

   A. after the holder-of-record date.

*B. before the holder-of-record date.

   C. the same as the holder-of-record date.

Explanation: LOS: Reading 38-b

The ex-dividend date is the date that a holder of the stock is no longer entitled to the dividend; in the US this is two days before the holder-of-record date. On the holder-of-record date whoever is a registered stockholder will receive the dividend.

11. North Company has a common stock price of $72. The latest reported earnings per share were $4.80 and dividends per share were $1.60. The return on equity is 8%. The cost of equity is *closest* to:

A. 7.46%.

B. 7.55%.

C. 7.67%.

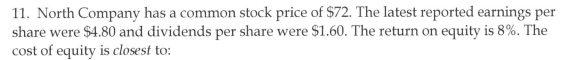

12. A firm is looking at borrowing for two months and could issue $500,000 nominal of commercial paper at 7.5%. Dealer's commission would be 0.25% and backup line costs would be 0.3% based on the $500,000 issued. The cost of borrowing is *closest* to:

A. 7.85%

B. 8.05%.

C. 8.15%

11. North Company has a common stock price of $72. The latest reported earnings per share were $4.80 and dividends per share were $1.60. The return on equity is 8%. The cost of equity is *closest* to:

    A. 7.46%.

    B. 7.55%.

*C. 7.67%.

Explanation: LOS: Reading 36-h

The growth rate is the earnings retention rate multiplied by the ROE, this is 5.33%.

Next year's dividends will be $1.60 x 1.0533 = $1.685

$$k_e = \frac{D_1}{P} + g = \frac{\$1.685}{\$72} + 5.33\% = 7.67\%$$

---

12. A firm is looking at borrowing for two months and could issue $500,000 nominal of commercial paper at 7.5%. Dealer's commission would be 0.25% and backup line costs would be 0.3% based on the $500,000 issued. The cost of borrowing is *closest* to:

    A. 7.85%

    B. 8.05%.

*C. 8.15%

Explanation: LOS: Reading 39-g

cost = (interest + dealer's commission + back-up costs)/net proceeds x 12

$$= \frac{[(0.075 + 0.0025 + 0.003) \times \$500{,}000 \times 2/12]}{\$500{,}000 - (0.075 \times \$500{,}000 \times 2/12)} \times 6 = 0.0805/0.9875 = 8.15\%$$

13. Islington Corporation provides you with the following information:

Income Statement $ million		Balance Sheet Average over period			$ million
Sales	298	Cash	50	Accounts Payable	80
COGS	(200)	Accounts Receivable	60	Accrued Expenses	65
Gross Profit	98	Inventory	100	Long-term Debt	150
SGA Expenses	(60)	Property, P & E	375		
Op. Profit	38	Depreciation	(85)	Common Stock	140
Interest expense	(6)			Retained Earnings	65
Tax	(13)				
Net Income	**19**	**Total Assets**	**500**	**Total Liabilities & Equity**	**500**

The quick ratio is *closest* to:

A. 0.34.

B. 0.63.

C. 0.76.

13. Islington Corporation provides you with the following information:

Income Statement $ million		Balance Sheet Average over period $ million			
Sales	298	Cash	50	Accounts Payable	80
COGS	(200)	Accounts Receivable	60	Accrued Expenses	65
Gross Profit	98	Inventory	100	Long-term Debt	150
SGA Expenses	(60)	Property, P & E	375		
Op. Profit	38	Depreciation	(85)	Common Stock	140
Interest expense	(6)			Retained Earnings	65
Tax	(13)				
Net Income	**19**	**Total Assets**	**500**	**Total Liabilities & Equity**	**500**

The quick ratio is *closest* to:

    A. 0.34.

    B. 0.63.

*C. 0.76.

Explanation: LOS: Reading 39-a

Quick ratio   = (cash + marketable securities + receivables)/current liabilities

                 = (50 + 60)/145

                 = 0.76

14. Islington Corporation provides you with the following information:

Income Statement $ million		Balance Sheet Average over period			$ million
Sales	298	Cash	50	Accounts Payable	80
COGS	(200)	Accounts Receivable	60	Accrued Expenses	65
Gross Profit	98	Inventory	100	Long-term Debt	150
SGA Expenses	(60)	Property, P & E	375		
Op. Profit	38	Depreciation	(85)	Common Stock	140
Interest expense	(6)			Retained Earnings	65
Tax	(13)				
Net Income	**19**	**Total Assets**	**500**	**Total Liabilities & Equity**	**500**

The *average* receivables collection period for Islington Corporation is *closest* to:

A. 5.0 days.

B. 73.5 days.

C. 109.5 days.

14. Islington Corporation provides you with the following information:

Income Statement $ million		Balance Sheet Average over period			$ million
Sales	298	Cash	50	Accounts Payable	80
COGS	(200)	Accounts Receivable	60	Accrued Expenses	65
Gross Profit	98	Inventory	100	Long-term Debt	150
SGA Expenses	(60)	Property, P & E	375		
Op. Profit	38	Depreciation	(85)	Common Stock	140
Interest expense	(6)			Retained Earnings	65
Tax	(13)				
Net Income	**19**	**Total Assets**	**500**	**Total Liabilities & Equity**	**500**

The *average* receivables collection period for Islington Corporation is *closest* to:

   A. 5.0 days.

*B. 73.5 days.

   C. 109.5 days.

Explanation: LOS: Reading 39-a

Receivables turnover   = credit sales/*average* receivables

$$= 298/60$$

$$= 4.966$$

Average receivables collection period

$$= 365/\text{receivables turnover}$$

$$= 73.5 \text{ days}$$

15. A company is currently financed using debt and equity. The market value of debt is $25 million and the market value of equity is $40 million. The company has recently announced that it will reduce the proportion of debt financing so the debt to equity ratio is 45%. The current after-tax cost of debt and equity are 8% and 12% respectively. Using the current capital structure and target capital structure, the company's cost of capital are *closest* to:

	Current	Target
A.	7.4%	10.2%
B.	10.5%	10.2%
C.	10.5%	10.8%

16. The case that the board chair also holds the title of chief executive, from the corporate governance point of view, is:

A. I. unacceptable because it is universally prohibited in all jurisdictions.

B. II. acceptable, because the effectiveness of the chief executive would be enhanced by his or her position as the chairperson of the board.

C. III. unacceptable because combining the two positions may reduce the ability and willingness of independent board members to exercise their independent judgment.

15. A company is currently financed using debt and equity. The market value of debt is $25 million and the market value of equity is $40 million. The company has recently announced that it will reduce the proportion of debt financing so the debt to equity ratio is 45%. The current after-tax cost of debt and equity are 8% and 12% respectively. Using the current capital structure and target capital structure, the company's cost of capital are *closest* to:

	Current	Target
A.	7.4%	10.2%
B.	10.5%	10.2%
*C.	**10.5%**	**10.8%**

Explanation: LOS: Reading 36-c

The current cost of capital is given by:

$$\frac{25 \times 8\% + 12\%}{65} = \mathbf{10.28\%}$$

A debt to equity ratio of 45% indicates the target weighting of debt is 45/145 = 31%

The target cost of capital is:

$(0.31 \times 8\%) + (0.69 \times 12\%) = 10.76\%$

16. The case that the board chair also holds the title of chief executive, from the corporate governance point of view, is:

A. I. unacceptable because it is universally prohibited in all jurisdictions.

B. II. acceptable, because the effectiveness of the chief executive would be enhanced by his or her position as the chairperson of the board.

*C. III. unacceptable because combining the two positions may reduce the ability and willingness of independent board members to exercise their independent judgment.

Explanation: LOS: Reading 40-c

Choice I. is incorrect because there are some jurisdictions that allow the combining of the two positions.

Choice II. is incorrect because it is not the effectiveness of the chief executive that is being questioned.

The main issue is whether the board's independence would be compromised.

17. The cost of a project is $150 million and it will be depreciated using the straight line method over 5 years with a zero salvage value. The following net income is anticipated.

Year	Net Income ($ million)
1	4
2	20
3	22
4	20
5	– 5

The *average* accounting rate of return (AAR) of the project is *closest* to

    A. 8.1%

    B. 12.2%

    C. 16.3%

17. The cost of a project is $150 million and it will be depreciated using the straight line method over 5 years with a zero salvage value. The following net income is anticipated.

Year	Net Income
	($ million)
1	4
2	20
3	22
4	20
5	– 5

The *average* accounting rate of return (AAR) of the project is *closest* to

    A. 8.1%

    B. 12.2%

*C. 16.3%

Explanation: LOS: Reading 35-d

Average book value is ($150 million + $0million)/2 = $75 million

Average net income is $(4 + 20 + 22 + 20 – 5)million/5 = $12.2 million

AAR   =   *Average* net income

    Average book value

  = $12.2 million

    $75 million

  =   16.3%

18. National Telecoms Corporation provides the following 2013 information:

Income Statement $ million		Balance Sheet Average over period $ million			
Sales	1050	Cash	90	Accounts Payable	50
COGS	(780)	Accounts Receivable	170	Notes payable	125
Gross Profit	270	Inventory	200	Long term debt	300
SGA exp.	(150)	Property, P & E	650		
Op. Profit	120	Depreciation	(430)	Common Stock	150
Interest exp.	(45)			Retained Earnings	55
Tax	(25)				
Net Income	50	Total Assets	680	Total Liabilities & Equity	680

Dividends Paid 12

*Inventory is unchanged over the 2012 period

National Telecoms Corporation's net operating cycle in 2014 is *closest* to:

  A. 58 days.

  B. 130 days.

  C. 153 days.

18. National Telecoms Corporation provides the following 2014 information:

Income Statement		Balance Sheet			
$ million		Average over period $ million			
Sales	1050	Cash	90	Accounts Payable	50
COGS	(780)	Accounts Receivable	170	Notes payable	125
Gross Profit	270	Inventory	200	Long term debt	300
SGA exp.	(150)	Property, P & E	650		
Op. Profit	120	Depreciation	(430)	Common Stock	150
Interest exp.	(45)			Retained Earnings	55
Tax	(25)				
Net Income	50	Total Assets	680	Total Liabilities & Equity	680
Dividends Paid	12				

*Inventory is unchanged over the 2013 period

National Telecoms Corporation's net operating cycle in 2014 is *closest* to:

   A. 58 days.

   B. 130 days.

*C. 153 days.

Explanation: LOS: Reading 39-a

number of days of receivables = 365/

annual receivables turnover =365/(1050/170) = 59 days

number of days of inventory = 365/

inventory turnover = 365/(780/200) = 94

days operating cycle = number of days of receivables
 + number of days of inventory = 153 days

19. A company has a target capital structure of 70% debt and 30% equity. If the company raises equity of less than $10 million then its cost of equity is 12%, if the new equity issued is above $10 million its cost of equity is 14%. The first break point in the cost of capital raised due to the change in the cost of equity is *closest* to:

   A. $10.00 million.

   B. $14.29 million.

   C. $33.33 million.

20. Which of the following is *least likely* to be a reason why a firm would carry out a stock repurchase program?

   A. It believes that the shares are undervalued.

   B. There is a large block of stock overhanging the market.

   C. The firm wants to increase the proportion of equity in its capital structure.

19. A company has a target capital structure of 70% debt and 30% equity. If the company raises equity of less than $10 million then its cost of equity is 12%, if the new equity issued is above $10 million its cost of equity is 14%. The first break point in the cost of capital raised due to the change in the cost of equity is *closest* to:

A. $10.00 million.

B. $14.29 million.

*C. $33.33 million.

Explanation: LOS: Reading 36-k

Break point

= amount of capital at which cost of equity changes/proportion of equity in new capital = $10 million/0.30

= $33.33 million.

20. Which of the following is *least likely* to be a reason why a firm would carry out a stock repurchase program?

A. It believes that the shares are undervalued.

B. There is a large block of stock overhanging the market.

*C. The firm wants to increase the proportion of equity in its capital structure.

Explanation: LOS: Reading 38-c

Repurchasing equity will reduce the proportion of equity in the capital structure.

21. Which of the following statements is *most accurate* concerning the different methods for evaluating projects?

A. The IRR method can give multiple answers if there are nonconventional cash flows.

B. The IRR method is preferred since it assumes reinvestment at the project's cost of capital.

C. The *average* accounting rate of return is attractive because it does not need a present value calculation.

22. In order to secure short-term funding a company factors its accounts receivable. This means that:

A. receivables are being used as collateral for a loan.

B. it pays over any receivables collected to the factor in return for short-term funding.

C. sells the receivables to the factor who takes responsibility for collecting the receivables.

21. Which of the following statements is *most accurate* concerning the different methods for evaluating projects?

*A. The IRR method can give multiple answers if there are nonconventional cash flows.

B. The IRR method is preferred since it assumes reinvestment at the project's cost of capital.

C. The *average* accounting rate of return is attractive because it does not need a present value calculation.

Explanation: LOS: Reading 40-c

When a project has nonconventional cash flows (such as more than one cash inflow over the project's life) the IRR method can give more than one solution, or multiple IRRs. The IRR method discounts back at the IRR, andthe lack of adjustment for time value of money is a disadvantage of the AAR method.

---

22. In order to secure short-term funding a company factors its accounts receivable. This means that:

A. receivables are being used as collateral for a loan.

B. it pays over any receivables collected to the factor in return for short-term funding.

*C. sells the receivables to the factor who takes responsibility for collecting the receivables.

Explanation: LOS: Reading 39-g

When a company factors its accounts receivables it sells its receivables to the factor and transfers credit granting and collection to the factor. This is different to when receivables are used as collateral for a loan which is an assignment of the accounts receivable.

23. The cost of a project is $150 million and the following cash flows are anticipated, the cost of capital is 10%.

Year	Net Cash Flow ($ million)
0	-150
1	25
2	50
3	55
4	40
5	60
Total	

The implied decision to accept or reject the project, and the Profitability Index (PI) is *closest* to:

Accept/reject	PI
A. Reject	0.13
B. Reject	0.53
C. Accept	1.13

23. The cost of a project is $150 million and the following cash flows are anticipated, the cost of capital is 10%.

Year	Net Cash Flow ($ million)
0	-150
1	25
2	50
3	55
4	40
5	60
Total	

The implied decision to accept or reject the project, and the Profitability Index (PI) is *closest* to:

Accept/reject	PI
A. Reject	0.13
B. Reject	0.53
*C. Accept	1.13

Explanation: C LOS: Reading 35-d

First of all calculate the present values of the cash flows:

Year	Net Cash Flow ($ million)	Discounted Cash Flow ($ million)	Net
0	-150	-150.0	
1	25	22.7	
2	50	41.3	
3	55	41.3	
4	40	27.3	
5	60	37.3	
Total		19.9	

PI   = PV of future cash flows/Initial investment

= 1 + NPV/ Initial investment

= 1 + 19.9/150

= 1.13

This is greater than 1, so the project is expected to add to shareholder value.

24. It is recommended that flotation costs when a firm issues new equity are:

A. ignored.

B. incorporated in the calculation for a firm's cost of capital.

C. treated as a cash outflow at the time of the issue of the new equity. .

_____

25. A company prohibits itself from offering shares at discounted prices to management, board members and other insiders prior to a public offering of its securities. This practice is:

A. preferred by investors because it demonstrates that the company aligns itself with the investors' interests.

B. not preferred by the capital markets regulatory body because it might encourage an opportunity for insiders' trading.

C. not preferred from a corporate governance point of view because it might encourage the executives to give compensation to themselves from short-term share transactions.

24. It is recommended that flotation costs when a firm issues new equity are:

   A. ignored.

   B. incorporated in the calculation for a firm's cost of capital.

*C. treated as a cash outflow at the time of the issue of the new equity. .

Explanation: LOS: Reading 36-1
The cost of raising new equity is usually much higher than that of raising new debt so it should not be ignored. It is preferable to treat flotation costs as an initial cash outflow as opposed to adjusting the cost of capital and therefore the discount factor applied to all future cash flows.

25. A company prohibits itself from offering shares at discounted prices to management, board members and other insiders prior to a public offering of its securities. This practice is:

*A. preferred by investors because it demonstrates that the company aligns itself with the investors' interests.

  B. not preferred by the capital markets regulatory body because it might encourage an opportunity for insiders' trading.

  C. not preferred from a corporate governance point of view because it might encourage the executives to give compensation to themselves from short-term share transactions.

Explanation: LOS: Reading 40-g

This is a preferred practice from a corporate governance point of view, which indicates it is beneficial for the long-term interests of the investors.

Study Session 12: Portfolio Management

As the first discussion within the CFA curriculum on portfolio management, this study session provides the critical framework and context for subsequent Level I study sessions covering equities, fixed income, derivatives, and alternative investments. Furthermore, this study session provides the underlying theories and tools for portfolio management at Levels II and III.

The first reading discusses the asset allocation decision and the portfolio management process—they are an integrated set of steps undertaken in a consistent manner to create and maintain an appropriate portfolio (combination of assets) to meet clients' stated goals. The last two readings focus on the design of a portfolio and introduces the capital asset pricing model (CAPM), a centerpiece of modern financial economics that relates the risk of an asset to its expected return.

Reading Assignments

Reading 41:. Portfolio Management: An Overview
    by Robert M. Conroy, CFA and Alistair Byrne, CFA
Reading 42:. Portfolio Risk and Return: Part I
    by Vijay Singal, CFA
Reading 43:. Portfolio Risk and Return: Part II
    by Vijay Singal, CFA
Reading 44:. Basics of Portfolio Planning and Construction
    by Alistair Byrne, CFA and Frank E. Smudde.

1. Which of the following is *least likely* to be part of the portfolio management process?

     A. Preparing a client policy statement.

     B. Evaluating investment performance

*C. Advertising the manager's performance record.

---

2. In capital market theory, systematic risk is:

     A. total risk.

     B. market risk.

     C. diversifiable risk.

1. Which of the following is *least likely* to be part of the portfolio management process?

    A. Preparing a client policy statement.

    B. Evaluating investment performance

*C. Advertising the manager's performance record.

Explanation: LOS: Reading 41-d

The portfolio management process consists of four steps: construct the policy statement, forecast future economic and market trends, construct the portfolio and the continual monitoring and evaluation of performance.

---

2. In capital market theory, systematic risk is:

    A. total risk.

*B. market risk.

    C. diversifiable risk.

Explanation: LOS: Reading 43-c

"Diversifiable Risk" refer to unsystematic risk and "Total Risk" includes systematic and unsystematic risk.

3. A doctor is in her late twenties with no dependents, but at present she has her savings invested in bank deposits and is not familiar with security markets. She is *most likely* to have a:

  A. low ability to take risk and low willingness to take risk.

  B. low ability to take risk and high willingness to take risk.

  C. high ability to take risk and low willingness to take risk.

4. An investor policy statement is important because it:

  A. clarifies the investors' objectives.

  B. provides the investor with the portfolio manager's market outlook.

  C. provides details on the stocks that will be purchased for the portfolio.

3. A doctor is in her late twenties with no dependents, but at present she has her savings invested in bank deposits and is not familiar with security markets. She is *most likely* to have a:

  A. low ability to take risk and low willingness to take risk.

  B. low ability to take risk and high willingness to take risk.

  *C. high ability to take risk and low willingness to take risk.

Explanation: LOS: Reading 44-d

On the basis of the information supplied in the question the doctor would be reasonably wealthy with a long time horizon suggesting she has the ability to take risk, but given her cautious stance to investing up to now it suggests she may be less willing to take risk.

---

4. An investor policy statement is important because it:

*A. clarifies the investors' objectives.

  B. provides the investor with the portfolio manager's market outlook.

  C. provides details on the stocks that will be purchased for the portfolio.

Explanation: LOS: Reading 44-a

A policy statement helps the investor specify realistic goals and in setting the goals become more aware of the risks of investing. It is a valuable way of communicating with the portfolio manager. It also helps set the benchmark against which performance can be measured.

5. The optimal portfolio for an investor is represented by the point where the:

    A. investor utility curves intersect each other.

    B. security market line is tangent to the efficient frontier.

    C. investor utility curve is tangent to the efficient frontier.

---

6. Over very long time periods US market data suggest that:

    A. riskier assets tend to generate higher returns.

    B. Treasury bills have performed better than government bonds.

    C. the equity risk premium measured relative to Treasury bonds has disappeared.

5. The optimal portfolio for an investor is represented by the point where the:

    A. investor utility curves intersect each other.

    B. security market line is tangent to the efficient frontier.

*C. investor utility curve is tangent to the efficient frontier.

Explanation: LOS: Reading 42-g

The utility curves represent the trade-off between risk and return. The optimal portfolio will be where the highest utility curve touches the efficient frontier.

6. Over very long time periods US market data suggest that:

*A. riskier assets tend to generate higher returns.

    B. Treasury bills have performed better than government bonds.

    C. the equity risk premium measured relative to Treasury bonds has disappeared.

Explanation: LOS: Reading 42-b

The data in the text is for the period 1926-2008 and shows that equities have been the riskiest asset and produced the highest returns, followed by bonds and then cash (Treasury bills).

7. The beta of an asset:

    A. I. lies between -1 and 1.

    B. II. is 1 if the asset is the market portfolio.

    C. III. is the covariance of the asset with the market.

---

8. Which of the following is *least likely* to be a step in the investment process?

    A. Asset allocation.

    B. Monitoring the portfolio.

    C. Submitting regulatory reports to the appropriate authority.

7. The beta of an asset:

   A. I. lies between -1 and 1.

*B. II. is 1 if the asset is the market portfolio.

   C. III. is the covariance of the asset with the market.

Explanation: LOS: Reading 43-e

I. is not correct since beta does not lie in any fixed range.

II. is not correct, it is a measure of systematic risk.

III. is not correct because beta is the covariance divided by the variance of the market.

By definition the beta of the market itself is one.

---

8. Which of the following is *least likely* to be a step in the investment process?

   A. Asset allocation.

   B. Monitoring the portfolio.

*C. Submitting regulatory reports to the appropriate authority.

Explanation: LOS: Reading 41-c

The portfolio management process consists of three steps: the planning step, the execution step and the feedback step. Asset allocation is part of the execution step and monitoring is part of the feedback step. Submitting regulatory reports is not part of the investment decision-making process so C is the best answer.

9. The stock analyst in your firm recommends that you buy shares in Mayfair Corp. The current share price is $26 and she forecasts that a year from now the share price will have risen to $30. There is no dividend payment expected. You note that the beta of the stock is 0.8, the expected market return over the next year is 15% and the risk-free rate is 5%. On the basis of the analyst's forecast, Mayfair Corp.'s stock is:

A. overvalued.

B. undervalued.

C. correctly valued.

---

10. If a stock lies above the security market line (SML) this would indicate that the stock:

A. is overvalued.

B. is undervalued.

C. has a *higher* expected return than the market.

9. The stock analyst in your firm recommends that you buy shares in Mayfair Corp. The current share price is $26 and she forecasts that a year from now the share price will have risen to $30. There is no dividend payment expected. You note that the beta of the stock is 0.8, the expected market return over the next year is 15% and the risk-free rate is 5%. On the basis of the analyst's forecast, Mayfair Corp.'s stock is:

    A. overvalued.

*B. undervalued.

    C. correctly valued.

Explanation: LOS: Reading 43-g

Using CAPM the estimated return is:

$$R_x = R_f + \beta[E(R_m) - R_f] = 5\% + 0.8(15\% - 5\%) = 13\%$$

The analyst is forecasting a return of 15.4% so the stock looks undervalued.

---

10. If a stock lies above the security market line (SML) this would indicate that the stock:

    A. is overvalued.

*B. is undervalued.

    C. has a *higher* expected return than the market.

Explanation: LOS: Reading 43-g

The stock is undervalued because the expected rate of return is *higher* than the required rate of return to compensate for its beta risk.

11. A client's investment policy statement says that the target return is to outperform LIBOR by 2 percent, this is a:

A. income requirement.

B. relative return objective.

C. absolute return objective.

---

12. A portfolio is 70% invested in an index fund and 30% in a risk-free asset. The index fund has a variance of returns of 0.0027; the variance for the total portfolio is *closest* to:

A. 0.0013.

B. 0.0019.

C. 0.0027.

11. A client's investment policy statement says that the target return is to outperform LIBOR by 2 percent, this is a:

    A. income requirement.

*B. relative return objective.

    C. absolute return objective.

Explanation: LOS: Reading 44-c

The objective is to outperform LIBOR so this is a relative return objective.

---

12. A portfolio is 70% invested in an index fund and 30% in a risk-free asset. The index fund has a variance of returns of 0.0027, the variance for the total portfolio is *closest* to:

*A. 0.0013.

    B. 0.0019.

    C. 0.0027.

Explanation: LOS: Reading 43-b

The variance and standard deviation of the risk-free asset are zero. Therefore the variance of the portfolio is:

$$RRFR = \frac{(1 + NRFR)}{(1 + Exp.\,rate\,of\,inflation\,)} - 1$$

$$NRFR = \frac{1 + RRFR}{(1 + inf\,.)} - 1 = (1.05)(1.03) - 1 = 8.15\%$$

13. In capital market theory the Market Portfolio can be *least accurate*ly described as:

   A. the portfolio where systematic risk has been completely diversified away.

   B. it is the point where the Capital Market Line touches the efficient frontier.

   C. the portfolio which contains all risky assets in proportion to their market value.

14. If an investor has flat indifference curves it is likely to indicates that the investor:

   A. is aggressive.

   B. is conservative.

   C. has a long time horizon.

13. In capital market theory the Market Portfolio can be *least accurate*ly described as:

*A. the portfolio where systematic risk has been completely diversified away.

   B. it is the point where the Capital Market Line touches the efficient frontier.

   C. the portfolio which contains all risky assets in proportion to their market value.

Explanation: LOS: Reading 43-b

"the portfolio where systematic risk" is not correct

   – it is the unsystematic risk that can be diversified away.

---

14. If an investor has flat indifference curves it is likely to indicates that the investor:

   A. is aggressive.

*B. is conservative.

   C. has a long time horizon.

Explanation: LOS: Reading 42-d

A flat utility or indifference curve shows that the investor is happy to be compensated for taking a small amount of additional risk by receiving a small additional return, indicating he has a high tolerance for risk.

15. A US based investment manager is concerned that the volatility of an international equity fund he is managing is too high. Which of the following would be an appropriate course of action?

A. Sell the international holdings and only hold US stocks.

B. Consider investing in markets which have a low correlation with the existing assets in the portfolio.

C. Sell small capitalization stocks and concentrate the portfolio in a small number of big market capitalization stocks.

16. Portfolio monitoring is part of which step in the portfolio management process?

A. The planning step.

B. The feedback step.

C. The execution step.

15. A US based investment manager is concerned that the volatility of an international equity fund he is managing is too high. Which of the following would be an appropriate course of action?

    A. Sell the international holdings and only hold US stocks.

*B. Consider investing in markets which have a low correlation with the existing assets in the portfolio.

    C. Sell small capitalization stocks and concentrate the portfolio in a small number of big market capitalization stocks.

Explanation: LOS: Reading 41-a

In order to reduce volatility, which is the standard deviation of returns, the manager could include assets which have a low correlation with the existing assets in the portfolio.

---

16. Portfolio monitoring is part of which step in the portfolio management process?

    A. The planning step.

*B. The feedback step.

    C. The execution step.

Explanation: LOS: Reading 41-d

The feedback step is the third step and includes Portfolio monitoring and rebalancing, and performance measurement and reporting.

17. Which of the following will usually have a short-time horizon with respect to their investments?

    A. Pensions funds.

    B. Life insurance companies.

    C. Non-life insurance companies.

---

18. In a rapidly rising market, a stock with a beta of 0.5 is expected, relative to the market performance, to:

Performance	Direction
A. outperform	Same
B. outperform	Opposite
C. underperform	Same

17. Which of the following will usually have a short-time horizon with respect to their investments?

A. Pensions funds.

B. Life insurance companies.

*C. Non-life insurance companies.

Explanation: LOS: Reading 41-b

Life insurance companies and pension funds will tend to have long time horizons representing the time between premiums and contributions are collected and subsequently paid out. Non-life insurance (fire, theft etc.) will need to keep most of their funds liquid and have a short time horizon.

18. In a rapidly rising market, a stock with a beta of 0.5 is expected, relative to the market performance, to:

Performance	Direction
A. outperform	Same
B. outperform	Opposite
*C. underperform	Same

Explanation: LOS: Reading 34-e

A low beta means the stock will move by less than the market if the market moves upwards by more than the risk-free rate. The positive beta means it will move in the same direction as the market.

19. The efficient frontier represents portfolios that:

   A. offer the highest return for a given level of total risk.

   B. offer the highest return for a given level of systematic risk.

   C. are equally attractive to an investor with a specified level of total risk tolerance.

---

20. A portfolio is invested equally between two assets, the assets have standard deviations of 4% and 8%, and the correlation between the two assets is 0.3. The standard deviation of the combined portfolio is *closest* to:

   A. 4.98%.

   B. 6.64%.

   C. 24.80%.

19. The efficient frontier represents portfolios that:

*A. offer the highest return for a given level of total risk.

    B. offer the highest return for a given level of systematic risk.

    C. are equally attractive to an investor with a specified level of total risk tolerance.

Explanation: LOS: Reading 42-g

The efficient frontier represents the portfolios which offer the highest return for any given level of risk.

---

20. A portfolio is invested equally between two assets, the assets have standard deviations of 4% and 8%, and the correlation between the two assets is 0.3. The standard deviation of the combined portfolio is *closest* to:

*A. 4.98%.

    B. 6.64%.

    C. 24.80%.

Explanation: LOS: Reading 42-e

$$\sigma_{port}^2 = w_1^2\sigma_1^2 + w_2^2\sigma_2^2 + 2r_{12}w_1w_2\sigma_1\sigma_2$$

$$= (0.5)^2(0.04)^2 + (0.5)^2(0.08)^2 + 2(0.3)(0.5)(0.04)(0.5)(0.08)$$

$$= 0.0004 + 0.0016 + 0.00048$$

$$= 0.00248$$

$$\sigma = 0.0498$$

where:

        σ_i =   standard deviation of returns of asset i

        σ_j =   standard deviation of returns of asset j

        w_i =   weighting of asset i in the portfolio

        r_{ij} =   correlation between the returns of assets i and j

21. Which of the following is a least accurate description of an assumption of the capital asset pricing model (CAPM)?

   A. All investors have the same time horizon.

   B. Investors can borrow or lend at the risk-free rate.

   C. Investors are not able to correctly anticipate inflation.

---

22. The expected return from a market is 12% and the risk-free rate is 5% and a stock has a beta of 0.5. The required rate of return from the stock is:

   A. 6.0%.

   B. 8.5%.

   C. 11.0%.

21. Which of the following is a least accurate description of an assumption of the capital asset pricing model (CAPM)?

    A. All investors have the same time horizon.

    B. Investors can borrow or lend at the risk-free rate.

*C. Investors are not able to correctly anticipate inflation.

Explanation: LOS: Reading 43-f

Capital Market Theory makes the assumption that there is no inflation or change in interest rates, or any inflation is fully anticipated.

---

22. The expected return from a market is 12% and the risk-free rate is 5% and a stock has a beta of 0.5. The required rate of return from the stock is:

    A. 6.0%.

*B. 8.5%.

    C. 11.0%.

Explanation: LOS: Reading 43-g

Using CAPM we can calculate the required return from the stock:

$$R_x = R_f + \beta[E(R_m) - R_f] = 5\% + 0.5(12\% - 5\%) = 8.5\%$$

23. The beta of a stock can be computed from the:

    A. relative volatility of the stock returns to the market returns.

    B. correlation of the stock with the market and the market return.

    C. covariance of the stock with the market and the variance of the market returns.

---

24. (Two assets have zero correlation. If a portfolio is invested with 30% in the first asset that has a variance of 12, and 70% in the second asset that has a variance of 8, the variance of the combined portfolio is closest to:

    A. 2.2.

    B. 5.0.

    C. 6.7.

---

25. The investment objective of an endowment fund is *most likely* to include:

    A. outperform an index of international equities.

    B. maintain the real value of the fund in the long term.

    C. minimize risk in order to achieve and stable nominal rate of return.

23. The beta of a stock can be computed from the:

    A. relative volatility of the stock returns to the market returns.

    B. correlation of the stock with the market and the market return.

*C. covariance of the stock with the market and the variance of the market returns.

Explanation: LOS: Reading 43-e

The beta of an asset is the covariance of the assets returns with market returns divided by the variance of the market returns.

---

24. Two assets have zero correlation. If a portfolio is invested with 30% in the first asset that has a variance of 12, and 70% in the second asset that has a variance of 8, the variance of the combined portfolio is closest to:

    A. 2.2.

*B. 5.0.

    C. 6.7.

Explanation: LOS: Reading 42-e

Variance is given by:

$$\sigma^2_{port} = w_1^2\sigma_1^2 + w_2^2\sigma_2^2 + 2r_{12}w_1w_2\sigma_1\sigma_2$$
$$= (0.3)^2 12 + (0.7)^2 8$$
$$= 1.08 + 3.92$$
$$= 5$$

where:

    σ_i =   standard deviation of returns of asset i

    wi   =   weighting of asset i in the portfolio

    rij   =   correlation between the returns of assets i and j

25. The investment objective of an endowment fund is *most likely* to include:

    A. outperform an index of international equities.

*B. maintain the real value of the fund in the long term.

    C. minimize risk in order to achieve and stable nominal rate of return.

Explanation: LOS: Reading 41-b

An endowment fund typically has two objectives:

Maintain the real value of the investments and generate funds to meet objectives which are often paying scholarships etc.

Study Session 13: Equity Investments: Market Organization, Market Indices, and Market Efficiency

This study session addresses how securities are bought and sold and what constitutes a well-functioning securities market. The reading on market indexes gives an understanding of how indexes are constructed and calculated and the biases inherent in each of the weighting schemes used. Some of the most interesting and important work in the investment field during the past several decades revolves around the efficient market hypothesis (EMH) and its implications for active versus passive equity portfolio management. The readings on this subject provide an understanding of the EMH and the seemingly persistent anomalies to the theory, an understanding that is necessary to judge the value of fundamental or technical security analysis.

Reading Assignments

Reading 45: Market Organization and Structure
    by Larry Harris
Reading 46: Security Market Indices
    by Paul D. Kaplan, CFA and Dorothy C. Kelly, CFA
Reading 47: Market Efficiency
    by W. Sean Cleary, CFA, Howard J. Atkinson, CFA, and Pamela Peterson Drake, CFA

1. An index calculated using the freely floating shares is *most likely* to be:

Index construction	Shares included
A. price-weighted index	authorized shares
B. price-weighted index	fully paid-up shares
C. value-weighted index	shares held by independent investors

2. Which of the following statements regarding the Dow Jones Industrial *Average* (DJIA) is *least accurate*?

   A. The daily performance of the indices is similar to other New York Stock Exchange indexes.

   B. The DJIA is an equal-weighted index and therefore each of the 30 stocks carries an equal weight.

   C. Since the DJIA only includes 30 stocks it will only represent the performance of the larger, mature companies listed on the New York Stock Exchange.

1. An index calculated using the freely floating shares is *most likely* to be:

   Index construction   Shares included

   A. price-weighted index   authorized shares

   B. price-weighted index   fully paid-up shares

   *C. value-weighted index   shares held by independent investors

Explanation: LOS: Reading 46-d

It is only a value-weighted, not price-weighted index, which is affected by the number of shares included in the calculation. The shares in the free float are the ones that are held independently, and not by insiders. Insiders are likely to be long term investors, so their shares are not available for trading in the market.

---

2. Which of the following statements regarding the Dow Jones Industrial *Average* (DJIA) is *least accurate*?

   A. The daily performance of the indices is similar to other New York Stock Exchange indexes.

*B. The DJIA is an unweighted index and therefore each of the 30 stocks carries an equal weight.

   C. Since the DJIA only includes 30 stocks it will only represent the performance of the larger, mature companies listed on the New York Stock Exchange.

Explanation: LOS: Reading 46-d

The DJIA is a price-weighted index and it is the arithmetic average of the prices of the shares in the index, i.e. a high-priced share will have a larger influence on the index than a low priced share. The other NYSE indices are value-weighted. Although on a daily basis the difference in moves between the indices is small, over the long term the indices are not comparable.

3. A bond market index is *most likely* to be constructed as:

   A. an equal-weighted total return index.

   B. a price-weighted capital-only index.

   C. a market–weighted total return index.

---

4. The Efficient Market Hypothesis and the tests done to prove the Hypothesis imply doing which of the following is the least useful for portfolio managers?

   A. Momentum effects

   B. Minimizing total transaction costs.

   C. Overweighting small, value shares for long-term investors.

3. A bond market index is *most likely* to be constructed as:

    A. an equal-weighted total return index.

    B. a price-weighted capital-only index.

*C. a market–weighted total return index.

Explanation: LOS: Reading 46-i

A bond market index is usually constructed based on the market value of the issues and the capital gain plus income are included, although capital-only indices are available.

4. The Efficient Market Hypothesis and the tests done to prove the Hypothesis imply doing which of the following is the least useful for portfolio managers?

*A. Using technical analysis.

    B. Minimizing total transaction costs.

    C. Focusing on analyzing neglected companies.

Explanation: LOS: Reading 47-c

The weak-form of the Efficient Market Hypothesis implies that technical analysis based on past trading data does not have any value.

5. Which of the following supports the semistrong-form of the Efficient Market Hypothesis?

    A. The neglected firm effect.

    B. The performance of stocks with a low price/book value ratio.

    C. The performance of stocks that have announced a change in accounting methods.

---

6. A corporation looking to raise funds may decide to do a private placement because:

    A. it will reduce issuing costs.

    B. it will avoid using an investment bank.

    C. the issue can be sold at a *higher* price than if it was sold in a public offering.

5. Which of the following supports the semistrong-form of the Efficient Market Hypothesis?

    A. Momentum effects

    B. The performance of stocks with a low price/book value ratio.

*C. The performance of stocks that have announced a change in accounting methods.

Explanation: LOS: Reading 47-f

Momentum effects and the outperformance of low price/book value stocks are both anomalies of the semistrong-form of the EMH. The performance of stocks that have announced a change in accounting methods supports the semistrong-form of the EMH. Studies find that analysts look at the true value of companies rather than the effects of a change in the way financial performance is reported.

---

6. A corporation looking to raise funds may decide to do a private placement because:

*A. it will reduce issuing costs.

    B. it will avoid using an investment bank.

    C. the issue can be sold at a *higher* price than if it was sold in a public offering.

Explanation: LOS: Reading 45-b

A private placement will have lower issue costs, mainly since the requirement for lengthy registration documentation is reduced. However the pricing will be lower than for a public offer since the purchasers will need to be compensated for the lack of liquidity in the secondary market.

7. When a stock in the Dow Jones Industrial *Average* has a stock split this will lead to:

   A. the divisor increasing.

   B. the divisor decreasing.

   C. the divisor increasing if the stock is a high-priced stock and falling if it is a low-priced stock.

8. A short seller of a stock will generally:

   A. I. sell the stock when the price is rising.

   B. II. deposit collateral when he borrows stock.

   C. III. benefit from the price fall when a stock goes ex-dividend.

7. When a stock in the Dow Jones Industrial *Average* has a stock split this will lead to the divisor:

    A. increasing.

*B. decreasing.

    C. increasing if the stock is a high-priced stock and falling if it is a low-priced stock.

Explanation: LOS: Reading 46-d

When there is a stock split the stock price will fall, there is no immediate impact on the index so the divisor must also decrease.

---

8. A short seller of a stock will generally:

    A. sell the stock when the price is rising.

*B. deposit collateral when he borrows stock.

    C. benefit from the price fall when a stock goes ex-dividend.

Explanation: LOS: Reading 45-e

A is not correct since he is anticipating falls in prices in the future so current prices could be rising or falling.

C is not correct since he must pay the dividends to the lender of the stock. Usually the lender of stock will require collateral as protection against the borrower failing to return the stock.

9. The over-the-counter (OTC) market refers to trading in shares that:

    A. are not listed on an exchange.

    B. may or may not be listed on an exchange.

    C. are quoted using order-driven pricing mechanisms.

---

10. An investor calls a broker on the first day of the month to find out the price of ABC Inc.'s shares and is quoted $103 bid – 103½ ask. The shares are very liquid. The share price then moves to $98 – 98½ before rising to $115 –115¾ at the end of the month. If the investor had (i) placed a market order to buy the shares on the first day and then sold them on the last day (ii) a limit order to buy at $100 and sell at the end of the month, his profit before transaction costs would be *closest* to:

    A. (i) 11.11%   (ii) 15.00%.

    B. (i) 11.11%   (ii) 15.75%.

    C. (i) 12.39%   (ii) 15.00%.

9. The over-the-counter (OTC) market refers to trading in shares that:

    A. are not listed on an exchange.

*B. may or may not be listed on an exchange.

    C. are quoted using order-driven pricing mechanisms.

Explanation: LOS: Reading 45-i

The OTC market includes the trading of all shares that are not listed on an exchange and the trading of listed shares outside an exchange. The OTC markets are quote-driven, not order-driven markets.

---

10. An investor calls a broker on the first day of the month to find out the price of ABC Inc.'s shares and is quoted $103 bid – 103½ ask. The shares are very liquid. The share price then moves to $98 – 98½ before rising to $115 –115¾ at the end of the month. If the investor had (i) placed a market order to buy the shares on the first day and then sold them on the last day (ii) a limit order to buy at $100 and sell at the end of the month, his profit before transaction costs would be *closest* to:

*A. (i) 11.11%   **(ii) 15.00%.**

    B. (i) 11.11%   (ii) 15.75%.

    C. (i) 12.39%   (ii) 15.00%.

Explanation: LOS: Reading 45-g

(i) If it is a market order he will pay the ask price to buy the shares, i.e. $103 ½ and he will sell at the bid price of $115 making a profit of 11.11%.

(ii) A limit order to buy at $100 will be executed and he will sell at $115 giving a profit of 15%.

11. An informationally efficient market is one where:

    A. information is available on a timely basis to all investors.

    B. security prices adjust slowly to the arrival of new information giving investors time to take advantage of positive news.

    C. security prices adjust rapidly to the arrival of new information and therefore security prices reflect all information about the security.

---

12. Buying on margin means that:

    A. I. if the margin requirement is 60%, the investor may borrow 60% of the cost of buying shares, allowing him to leverage his transaction.

    B. II. the returns from buying on margin will only be *higher* than paying in full for shares when the share price moves significantly up or down.

    C. III. if an investor has bought shares on margin and the share price rises he will have made a more attractive return on his investment than if he had fully paid for the shares.

11. An informationally efficient market is one where:

   A. information is available on a timely basis to all investors.

   B. security prices adjust slowly to the arrival of new information giving investors time to take advantage of positive news.

*C. security prices adjust rapidly to the arrival of new information and therefore security prices reflect all information about the security.

Explanation: LOS: Reading 47-a
An informationally efficient market is one where security prices adjust very rapidly to the arrival of new information.

---

12. Buying on margin means that:

   A. I. if the margin requirement is 60%, the investor may borrow 60% of the cost of buying shares, allowing him to leverage his transaction.

   B. II. the returns from buying on margin will only be *higher* than paying in full for shares when the share price moves significantly up or down.

*C. III. if an investor has bought shares on margin and the share price rises he will have made a more attractive return on his investment than if he had fully paid for the shares.

Explanation: LOS: Reading 45-f
I. is not true since if the margin requirement is 60% the investor can only borrow 40%.

II. is not true since if the share moves down the losses will be *higher* if the investor has bought on margin.

III. is true due to the leverage effect.

13. A call market refers to:

A. a market where trades are done by open outcry.

B. a market where it is attempted to match all the bids and asks at a specified time.

C. a market where all the trading is done by computer rather than on a trading floor.

---

14. In an order-driven system with order precedence hierarchy there are three buy orders as below:

Order	Limit Price	Time Placed	
Order A	$63.45	10.36 am	Displayed
Order B	$63.60	10.34 am	Hidden
Order C	$63.60	10.36 am	Displayed

Which order will usually be executed first?

A. Order A.

B. Order B.

C. Order C.

13. A call market refers to:

    A. a market where trades are done by open outcry.

*B. a market where it is attempted to match all the bids and asks at a specified time.

    C. a market where all the trading is done by computer rather than on a trading floor.

Explanation: LOS: Reading 45-j

In a call market all the bids and asks for a stock are collected and a stock price that will *best* match buyers and sellers is decided.

---

14. In an order-driven system with order precedence hierarchy there are three buy orders as below:

Order	Limit Price	Time Placed	
Order A	$63.45	10.36 am	Displayed
Order B	$63.60	10.34 am	Hidden
Order C	$63.60	10.36 am	Displayed

Which order will usually be executed first?

    A. Order A.

*B. Order B.

    C. Order C.

Explanation: LOS: Reading 45-i

The first rule is price priority, so for a buy order the highest price is executed first (B or C), the next rule is usually which order was placed first (B), and the next gives preference to displayed over hidden orders.

15. The quotations for the price of Brown and Co. are given by 3 dealers as shown below:

	Bid	Ask
Dealer 1	17 ¾	18 1/4
Dealer 2	17 ½	18
Dealer 3	17 5/8	18

If Dealer 3 has excess inventory of Brown and Co. stock, changing his quote to which of the following would be the most effective in reducing his inventory?

 A. 17 5/8 - 18.

 B. 17 1/4 - 18 1/4.

 C. 17 1/4 - 17 3/4.

16. Followers of behavioral finance believe:

 A. cognitive biases in investor behavior can explain pricing anomalies.

 B. investor psychology explains why investors do not differentiate between upside and downside risk.

 C. investors are irrational which means certain investors will be able to persistently outperform the market.

15. The quotations for the price of Brown and Co. are given by 3 dealers as shown below:

	Bid	Ask
Dealer 1	17 3/4	18 1/4
Dealer 2	17 1/2	18
Dealer 3	17 5/8	18

If Dealer 3 has excess inventory of Brown and Co. stock, changing his quote to which of the following would be the most effective in reducing his inventory?

   A. 17 5/8 - 18.

   B. 17 1/4 - 18 1/4.

*C. 17 1/4 - 17 3/4.

Explanation: LOS: Reading 45-g

Moving the ask price lower than the other dealers will mean the dealer is able to sell stock, and moving the bid price lower will mean he is unlikely to have to buy stock, until the other dealers move their prices.

---

16. Followers of behavioral finance believe:

*A. cognitive biases in investor behavior can explain pricing anomalies.

   B. investor psychology explains why investors do not differentiate between upside and downside risk.

   C. investors are irrational which means certain investors will be able to persistently outperform the market.

Explanation: LOS: Reading 47-g

Behavioral finance explores the links between investor psychology and market behavior and looks at cognitive biases that can explain pricing anomalies so A is correct. Investors weigh downside risk more heavily than upside risk and despite investors' irrationality there is scant evidence that investors can persistently outperform the market so B and C are not correct.

17. A call market is one in which:

   A. dealers are making markets in stocks.

   B. stock prices are determined by auction.

   C. individual stocks are traded at specified times.

18. A market anomaly is best described as:

   A. a price move that reflects a factor that is specific to the individual stock.

   B. a short-term random movement in a stock price giving an opportunity to make a profit.

   C. a persistent deviation between the actual return for a stock and the return expected due to relevant information in the market.

17. A call market is one in which:

    A. dealers are making markets in stocks.

    B. stock prices are determined by auction.

*C. individual stocks are traded at specified times.

Explanation: LOS: Reading 45-c

In a call market the exchange usually sets the price and all trades are executed at a specified time at this price.

The A and B choices are types of continuous market.

---

18. A market anomaly is best described as:

    A. a price move that reflects a factor that is specific to the individual stock.

    B. a short-term random movement in a stock price giving an opportunity to make a profit.

*C. a persistent deviation between the actual return for a stock and the return expected due to relevant information in the market.

Explanation: LOS: Reading 47-f

An anomaly is a persistent rather than a random move in the price of a stock which does not reflect information in the market.

19. If a market is perfectly efficient and a portfolio manager does not have superior analysts then the portfolio manager should:

A. only hold cash.

B. select a portfolio of securities at random.

C. diversify away unsystematic risk and adjust the systematic risk of each portfolio to meet clients' objectives.

20. Which of the following is *least likely* to be a reason why we should be skeptical of claims by analysts to have discovered an anomaly?

A. Data mining.

B. Limited capital of arbitrageurs.

C. Dependence on the testing period selected.

19. If a market is perfectly efficient the implication is that a portfolio manager should:

A. only hold cash.

B. select a portfolio of securities at random.

*C. diversify away unsystematic risk and adjust the systematic risk of each portfolio to meet clients' objectives.

Explanation: LOS: Reading 47-e

Portfolio managers should construct a portfolio which has the appropriate risk profile and minimize costs.

---

20. Which of the following is *least likely* to be a reason why we should be skeptical of claims by analysts to have discovered an anomaly?

A. Data mining.

*B. Limited capital of arbitrageurs.

C. Dependence on the testing period selected.

Explanation: LOS: Reading 47-f

Limited capital can constrain the ability of arbitrageurs to take advantage of anomalies, but it is not a reason to be skeptical that they exist.

21. If an investor buys 1,000 shares at $50 and the initial margin is 60% and the maintenance margin is 30%, he/she will receive the first margin call when the stock price falls below:

   A. $14.00.

   B. $21.00.

   C. $28.57.

22. If there are the same constituent stocks included in a price-weighted index and a value-weighted index and the price-weighted index performs better than the value-weighted index it could be explained by:

   A. there were a large number of stock splits.

   B. there were a small number of stock splits.

   C. high-priced stocks generally performed better than low-priced stocks.

21. If an investor buys 1,000 shares at $50 and the initial margin is 60% and the maintenance margin is 30%, he/she will receive the first margin call when the stock price falls below:

    A. $14.00.

    B. $21.00.

*C. $28.57.

Explanation: LOS: Reading 45-f

The amount borrowed would be $20,000. We need to calculate when the value of the equity equals 30% of the total value of the stock. This is given by:

$1,000P - \$20,000 = 0.30(1,000P)$

$P = \$28.57$

---

22. If there are the same constituent stocks included in a price-weighted index and a value-weighted index and the price-weighted index performs better than the value-weighted index it could be explained by:

    A. there were a large number of stock splits.

    B. there were a small number of stock splits.

*C. high-priced stocks generally performed better than low-priced stocks.

Explanation: LOS: Reading 46-e

Stock splits, since they are more commonly done by successful companies, will tend to have a downward bias on the price-weighted index. High priced stocks are more heavily weighted in the price-weighted index so if they perform well it will lead to the price-weighted index outperforming the value-weighted index.

23. Rebalancing of an index will occur most frequently for:

A. a price-weighted index.

B. an equal-weighted index.

C. a market-capitalization weighted index.

---

24. A market-capitalization weighted index is made up of two stocks, X and Y, and the following data is provided:

| Stock | December 31st 2013 | | December 31st 2014 | |
	Price	Shares outstanding	Price	Shares outstanding
X	$25	10,000	$15	20,000*
Y	$50	6,000	$65	6,000

* after a 2 for 1 stock split

The base index is set at 100 on December 31st 2013. The index on December 31st 2014 is *closest* to:

A.   98.18.

B.   125.45.

C.   126.67.

---

25. The initial margin requirement for a stock purchase is:

A. the market value of the stock less the amount borrowed.

B. the market value of the stock less the amount paid in cash.

C. the percentage of the transaction value that must be paid for in cash.

23. Rebalancing of an index will occur most frequently for:

    A. a price-weighted index.

*B. an equal-weighted index.

    C. a market-capitalization weighted index.

Explanation: LOS: Reading 46-f

A price weighted index should not need rebalancing since as prices move the weightings automatically move. Market-capitalization weights will only need to be rebalanced if there is a merger or other relevant corporate action whereas in an equal-weighted indices will need to be rebalanced frequently since stocks weightings will move as prices move. If there was no rebalancing the best performing stocks would increase their weights and vice versa.

24. A market-capitalization weighted index is made up of two stocks, X and Y, and the following data is provided:

Stock	December 31st 2013		December 31st 2014	
	Price	Shares outstanding	Price	Shares outstanding
X	$25	10,000	$15	20,000*
Y	$50	6,000	$65	6,000

* after a 2 for 1 stock split

The base index is set at 100 on December 31st 2013. The index on December 31st 2014 is *closest* to:

    A.   98.18.

*B.   125.45.

    C.   126.67.

Explanation: LOS: Reading 46-e

Total market value on Dec. 31st 2013 is ($25 x 10,000) + ($50 x 6,000) = $550,000

Total market value on Dec. 31st 2014 is ($15 x 20,000) + ($65 x 6,000) = $690,000

The index = ($690,000/$550,000) x100 = 125.45

25. The initial margin requirement for a stock purchase is:

    A. the market value of the stock less the amount borrowed.

    B. the market value of the stock less the amount paid in cash.

*C. the percentage of the transaction value that must be paid for in cash.

Explanation: LOS: Reading 45-f

The initial margin is simply the percentage or proportion of the transaction value that must be paid for in cash, rather than borrowed.

Study Session 14: Equity: Analysis and Valuation

This study session focuses on industry and company analysis and describes the tools used in forming an opinion about investing in a particular stock or group of stocks. This study session begins with the essential tools of equity valuation: the discounted cash flow technique and the relative valuation approach. These techniques provide the means to estimate reasonable price for a stock. The readings on industry analysis are an important element in the valuation process, providing the top–down context crucial to estimating a company's potential. Also addressed is estimating a company's earnings per share by forecasting sales and profit margins. The last reading in this study session focuses on price multiples, one of the most familiar and widely used tools in estimating the value of a company, and introduces the application of four commonly used price multiples to valuation.

Reading Assignments

Reading 48: Overview of Equity Securities
    by Ryan C. Fuhrmann, CFA and Asjeet S. Lamba, CFA
Reading 49: Introduction to Industry and Company Analysis
    by Patrick W. Dorsey, CFA, Anthony M. Fiore, CFA, and Ian Rossa O'Reilly, CFA
Reading 50: Equity Valuation: Concepts and Basic Tools
    by John J. Nagorniak, CFA and Stephen E. Wilcox, CFA

1. When using book value as a tool for valuing a company an analyst should consider
    A. excluding all intangible items.
    B. adjusting for off-balance-sheet assets and liabilities.
    C. looking at the book value at the midpoint of the business cycle.

2. An analyst forecasts that a company will pay a dividend of $2.30 next year, $2.60 in the following year and dividends will grow at 5% thereafter. If an investor's required rate of return is 12%, the value of the company is *closest* to:
    A. $33.73.
    B. $35.21.
    C. $42.04.

1. When using book value as a tool for valuing a company an analyst should consider

   A. excluding all intangible items.

*B. adjusting for off-balance-sheet assets and liabilities.

   C. looking at the book value at the midpoint of the business cycle.

Explanation: LOS: Reading 50-j

Certain intangibles should be excluded but others may have an economic value and could be sold (e.g. patents) and these would often not be excluded. Book value is a cumulative number so it is not customary to adjust for cyclical effects.

Adjusting book value for off-balance-sheet assets and liabilities would bring it closer to a fair value calculation so B is the best answer

---

2. An analyst forecasts that a company will pay a dividend of $2.30 next year, $2.60 in the following year and dividends will grow at 5% thereafter. If an investor's required rate of return is 12%, the value of the company is *closest* to:

   A. $33.73.

*B. $35.21.

   C. $42.04.

Explanation: LOS: Reading 50-e

Discount back the first two years' dividends at 12% to get $2.05 and $2.07.

Thereafter apply the DDM to give value of shares at the end of the second year as $2.73/(0.12 - 0.05) = \$39$, which discounts back to $31.09.

The value of the company = $2.05 + $2.07 + $31.09 = $35.21

3. Which of the following is *least likely* to be a reason why price/cash flow is considered a useful valuation method?

    A. It is consistently calculated by analysts.

    B. Cash flow is a good indicator of financial strength of a company.

    C. Cash flow is less subject to distortion due to accounting methods than earnings.

---

4. When a German investor buys a US dollar-denominated GDR sponsored by an American company and the US dollar depreciates against the euro the investor will:

    A. tend to see the value of the GDR depreciate in euro terms.

    B. tend to see the value of the GDR appreciate in euro terms.

    C. see no change in the value of the GDR in euro terms due to the movement in exchange rates.

3. Which of the following is *least likely* to be a reason why price/cash flow is considered a useful valuation method?

*A. It is consistently calculated by analysts.

   B. Cash flow is a good indicator of financial strength of a company.

   C. Cash flow is less subject to distortion due to accounting methods than earnings.

Explanation: LOS: Reading 50-h
Analysts use different definitions of cash flow, although free cash flow is probably the most appropriate.

---

4. When a German investor buys a US dollar-denominated GDR sponsored by an American company and the US dollar depreciates against the euro the investor will:

*A. tend to see the value of the GDR depreciate in euro terms.

   B. tend to see the value of the GDR appreciate in euro terms.

   C. see no change in the value of the GDR in euro terms due to the movement in exchange rates.

Explanation: LOS: Reading 48-f
A depository receipt does not offer protection against foreign exchange rate risk so the depreciation in the dollar will reduce the value of the GDR in euro terms.

5. An analyst calculates the price to sales ratio for a company and finds it is significantly less than the market *average*, this could be explained by:

    A. sales per share are *higher* than for the *average* company.

    B. the company has a low profit margin relative to the *average* for the market.

    C. the company has exhibited rapid sales growth relative to the market *average*.

6. If an investor's required rate of return is 12% and a company's stock price is $45.00, the next dividend is estimated to be $3.60 and the growth rate of dividends is a constant 4.5%, then the stock is:

    A. overvalued.

    B. undervalued.

    C. fairly valued.

5. An analyst calculates the price to sales ratio for a company and finds it is significantly less than the market *average*, this could be explained by:

    A. sales per share are *higher* than for the *average* company.

*B. the company has a low profit margin relative to the *average* for the market.

    C. the company has exhibited rapid sales growth relative to the market *average*.

Explanation: LOS: Reading 50-h

P/S is the same as P/E multiplied by the profit margin, so a low profit margin could explain a low P/S ratio. High sales per share are not going to necessarily lead to a low P/S ratio.

---

6. If an investor's required rate of return is 12% and a company's stock price is $45.00, the next dividend is estimated to be $3.60 and the growth rate of dividends is a constant 4.5%, then the stock is:

    A. overvalued.

*B. undervalued.

    C. fairly valued.

Explanation: LOS: Reading 50-e

The stock price using the DDM should be $3.6/(0.12 - 0.045) = \$48$, if the price is $45 the stock is undervalued.

7. A firm in the US a company which is in the auto sector is *most likely* to be:

   A. a cyclical company.

   B. a defensive company.

   C. a non-cyclical company.

---

8. The infinite period dividend discount model assumes:

   A. the company is a high growth company.

   B. dividends will grow at a constant rate indefinitely.

   C. investors required rate of return is less than the growth rate in dividends.

7. A firm in the US a company which is in the auto sector is *most likely* to be:

*A. a cyclical company.

    B. a defensive company.

    C. a non-cyclical company.

Explanation: LOS: Reading 49-c

Since auto purchases can often be delayed in a slow economic environment the auto sector is a cyclical industry. .

---

8. The infinite period dividend discount model assumes:

    A. the company is a high growth company.

*B. dividends will grow at a constant rate indefinitely.

    C. investors required rate of return is less than the growth rate in dividends.

Explanation: LOS: Reading 50-e

High growth companies will not be able to sustain an above average rate of growth indefinitely, so A is not correct. Investors required rate of return must be more than the growth rate in dividends so C is not correct.

9. An analyst forecasts a company will pay dividends of $2 in the first year, $3 in the second year and $3.50 in the third year. After the third year dividends are forecast to grow at 4% per annum. If an investor's required rate of return is 12% the value of the stock is *closest* to:

  A. $36.56.

  B. $37.81.

  C. $39.05

10. An example of a fundamentals-based P/E is when the P/E is based on:

  A. historical multiples.

  B. the law of one price.

  C. the Gordon growth model

9. An analyst forecasts a company will pay dividends of $2 in the first year, $3 in the second year and $3.50 in the third year. After the third year dividends are forecast to grow at 4% per annum. If an investor's required rate of return is 12% the value of the stock is *closest* to:

   A. $36.56.

   B. $37.81.

*C. $39.05

Explanation: LOS: Reading 50-e

First, calculate the value of the stock at the end of year three,

$$\text{Value} = \frac{D_4}{(k-g)} = \frac{\$3.50(1.04)}{(0.12-0.04)} = \$45.50$$

The value of the stock today is the sum of the present values of the first three years' dividends plus the present value of the end-year-three value.

$$\text{Value} = \frac{D_1}{(1+k)} + \frac{D_2}{(1+k)^2} + \frac{P+D_3}{(1+k)^3}$$

$$= \frac{\$2}{(1.12)} + \frac{\$3}{(1.12)^2} + \frac{\$45.50+\$3.50}{(1.12)^3} = \$39.05$$

10. An example of a fundamentals-based P/E is when the P/E is based on:

   A. historical multiples.

   B. the law of one price.

*C. the Gordon growth model

Explanation: LOS: Reading 50-g

A fundamentals-based P/E is often related to future prospects using a discounted cash flow model such as the Gordon growth model.

11. When a board of directors is being elected statutory voting rights gives shareholders the right to:

    A. one vote per share that they own.

    B. vote only of they hold founder shares.

    C. allocate votes based on the number of shares they own multiplied by the number of candidates.

12. The first step for an analyst in constructing a list of peer group companies will usually be:

    A. reviewing commercial industry classification systems.

    B. examining the sources of demand for different companies.

    C. examining the companies' revenue and profit breakdowns.

11. When a board of directors is being elected statutory voting rights gives shareholders the right to:

*A. one vote per share that they own.

    B. vote only of they hold founder shares.

    C. allocate votes based on the number of shares they own multiplied by the number of candidates.

Explanation: LOS: Reading 48-d

Statutory voting rights simply means one share has one vote. C refers to cumulative voting rights.

---

12. The first step for an analyst in constructing a list of peer group companies will usually be:

*A. reviewing commercial industry classification systems.

    B. examining the sources of demand for different companies.

    C. examining the companies' revenue and profit breakdowns.

Explanation: LOS: Reading 49-d

If available the first step will usually be to look at the commercial classification systems before reviewing each company's activities.

13. The branded pharmaceutical industry in the US is *most likely* to have:

   A. low concentration and industry stability.

   B. high concentration and growth industry.

   C. a positive demographic influence and mature industry.

14. The restaurant industry in the US is:

   A. fragmented with weak pricing power.

   B. fragmented with strong pricing power.

   C. concentrated with strong pricing power.

13. The branded pharmaceutical industry in the US is *most likely* to have:

    A. low concentration and industry stability.

    B. high concentration and growth industry.

*C. a positive demographic influence and mature industry.

Explanation: LOS: Reading 49-i

This is a concentrated industry with a small number of companies dominating the industry; it is stable and helped by the demographics of an aging population which increases demand. It is in the mature stage of the industry cycle.

---

14. The restaurant industry in the US is:

*A. fragmented with weak pricing power.

    B. fragmented with strong pricing power.

    C. concentrated with strong pricing power.

Explanation: LOS: Reading 49-h

The restaurant business has numerous participants and is highly competitive so A is correct.

15. Which of the following is *most likely* to lead to a company's P/E multiple being higher than the market P/E multiple?

   A. The company has a high beta.

   B. The risk of the company's earnings is *higher* than the market.

   C. High earnings growth rates for the company relative to the market.

---

16. If a firm pays out 30% of its earnings as dividends, its return on equity is 12%, and its return on capital is 8%, then the long-term dividend growth rate is *closest* to:

   A. 3.6%.

   B. 5.6%.

   C. 8.4%.

15. Which of the following is *most likely* to lead to a company's P/E multiple being higher than the market P/E multiple?

    A. The company has a high beta.

    B. The risk of the company's earnings is higher than the market.

*C. High earnings growth rates for the company relative to the market.

Explanation: LOS: Reading 50-e

A high beta would lead to a high required rate of return and therefore a lower P/E so A is not correct.

Higher risk means a higher required rate of return, and therefore a lower P/E multiple so B is not correct.

High growth generally leads to a high P/E, so C is the correct answer.

16. If a firm pays out 30% of its earnings as dividends, its return on equity is 12%, and its return on capital is 8%, then the long-term dividend growth rate is *closest* to:

    A. 3.6%.

    B. 5.6%.

*C. 8.4%.

Explanation: LOS: Reading 50-f

Growth = Earnings Retention Rate x Return on Equity = 0.7 x 12% = 8.4%

17. Which of the following is *least likely* to be an adjustment made to book value in order to make it better reflect the value of shareholders' investment?

  A. Use tangible book value rather than total book value.

  B. Adjust book value for off-balance-sheet assets and liabilities.

  C. Use historic *average* of past book values over a business cycle.

18. If a company has an earnings retention ratio of 70%, earnings are growing at 8% per annum and investors' required rate of return is 10%, the P/E of the stock is *closest* to:

  A. 5.6.

  B. 11.0.

  C. 15.0.

17. Which of the following is *least likely* to be an adjustment made to book value in order to make it better reflect the value of shareholders' investment?

    A. Use tangible book value rather than total book value.

    B. Adjust book value for off-balance-sheet assets and liabilities.

*C. Use historic *average* of past book values over a business cycle.**

Explanation: LOS: Reading 50-j
Since book value is a cumulative number, reflecting retained earnings, it is a more stable number than one year earnings, so it is less likely that an *average* historic figure would be used.

---

18. If a company has an earnings retention ratio of 70%, earnings are growing at 8% per annum and investors' required rate of return is 10%, the P/E of the stock is *closest* to:

    A. 5.6.

    B. 11.0.

*C. 15.0.**

Explanation: LOS: Reading 50-e

$$P/E = (D_1/E_1)/(k - g)$$

where:

k = required rate of return

D_1/E_1 = expected dividend payout ratio

g = expected growth rate of dividends

$$P/E = 0.30/(0.10 - 0.02) = 15.0$$

19. An analyst forecasts that a company will pay a dividend of $3.50 for the next three years and dividends will grow at 4% thereafter. If investors' required rate of return is 8%, the value of the company is closest to:

A. $64.19.

B. $81.26.

C. $100.02.

20. Which of the following is *least likely* to be a reason for using a price/sales (P/S) ratio to value a company?

A. Sales are generally more stable than earnings per share.

B. Sales numbers are less subject to accounting manipulation.

C. P/S valuation methods can be used comparing companies with different cost structures.

19. An analyst forecasts that a company will pay a dividend of $3.50 for the next three years and dividends will grow at 4% thereafter. If investors' required rate of return is 8%, the value of the company is closest to:

    A. $64.19.

*B. $81.26.

    C. $100.02.

Explanation: LOS: Reading 50-e

Discount back the first three years' dividends at 8% to get $3.24, $3.00 and $2.78.

Thereafter apply the DDM to give value of the shares at the end of the third year as $3.50(1.04)/(0.08 - 0.04) = 91 which discounts back to $72.24.

The value of the company = $3.24 + $3.00 + $2.78 + $72.24 = $81.26

---

20. Which of the following is *least likely* to be a reason for using a price/sales (P/S) ratio to value a company?

    A. Sales are generally more stable than earnings per share.

    B. Sales numbers are less subject to accounting manipulation.

*C. P/S valuation methods can be used comparing companies with different cost structures.

Explanation: LOS: Reading 50-h

P/S is not a good method for comparing companies with different cost structures because it doesn't take into account a company's profitability. It is generally only useful for comparing companies operating in the same industry.

21. A company has a dividend retention ratio of 60%, dividends are expected to grow by 3% per annum and the investors' required rate of return is 8%. The theoretical price earnings ratio is:

A. 5.0.

B. 8.0.

C. 12.5.

22. Convertible preference shares allow the holders to convert to:

A. common shares.

B. cumulative preference shares.

C. participating preference shares.

21. A company has a dividend retention ratio of 60%, dividends are expected to grow by 3% per annum and the investors' required rate of return is 8%. The theoretical price earnings ratio is:

   A. 5.0.

*B. 8.0.

   C. 12.5.

Explanation: LOS: Reading 50-h

$$P/E = D/[E(k - g)] = 0.4/(0.08 - 0.03) = 8.0$$

---

22. Convertible preference shares allow the holders to convert to:

*A. common shares.

   B. cumulative preference shares.

   C. participating preference shares.

Explanation: LOS: Reading 4b-b

Convertible preference shares allow the holder to convert to common shares.

23. Which of the following would tend to increase a firm's long-term growth rate?

A. Increasing its profit margin.

B. Reducing its financial leverage.

C. Increasing the dividend payout ratio.

---

24. Which of the following would be *most likely* to be a result of cyclical change in the US economy?

A. Rising consumer confidence leading to a surge in housing sales.

B. A rise in the minimum wage increasing costs for fast-food outlets.

C. Increasing demand for residential nursing care as the population ages.

---

25. Which of the following is one of the reasons why price to book value is a useful valuation measure?

A. It can be used to value loss-making companies.

B. It is useful for comparing the value of stocks across industries.

C. Book value is not usually distorted by the accounting methods used.

23. Which of the following would tend to increase a firm's long-term growth rate?

*A. Increasing its profit margin.

   B. Reducing its financial leverage.

   C. Increasing the dividend payout ratio.

Explanation: LOS: Reading 50-e

The growth rate is earnings retention rate x ROE.

ROE is asset turnover x profit margin x financial leverage.

Therefore increasing the profit margin is the only choice which increases, rather than decreases, the growth rate.

---

24. Which of the following would be *most likely* to be a result of cyclical change in the US economy?

*A. Rising consumer confidence leading to a surge in housing sales.

B. A rise in the minimum wage increasing costs for fast-food outlets.

C. Increasing demand for residential nursing care as the population ages.

Explanation: LOS: Reading 49-c

Rising consumer confidence leading to a surge in housing sales would usually be the result of a cyclical move in the economy. The other choices reflect longer-term structural changes in the economy, so A is the best answer.

25. Which of the following is one of the reasons why price to book value is a useful valuation measure?

*A. It can be used to value loss-making companies.

B. It is useful for comparing the value of stocks across industries.

C. Book value is not usually distorted by the accounting methods used.

Explanation: LOS: Reading 50-j

Loss making companies cannot be valued using current P/E and will often also have negative cash flow so P/B, which is based on book value representing cumulative earnings and paid up capital, is a method that can usually be applied.

Study Session 15:   Fixed Income: Analysis and Valuation

This study session presents the foundation for fixed income investments, one of the largest and fastest growing segments of global financial markets. It begins with an introduction to the basic features and characteristics of fixed income securities and the associated risks. The session then builds by describing the primary issuers, sectors, and types of bonds. Finally, the study session concludes with an introduction to yields and spreads and the effect of monetary policy on financial markets. These readings combined are the primary building blocks for mastering the analysis, valuation, and management of fixed income securities.

Reading Assignments

Reading 51:. Fixed-Income Securities: Defining Elements
    by Moorad Choudhry, PhD, and Stephen E. Wilcox, PhD, CFA
Reading 52:. Fixed-Income Markets: Issuance, Trading, and Funding
    by Moorad Choudhry, PhD, Steven V. Mann, PhD, and Lavone F. Whitmer, CFA
Reading 53:. Introduction to Fixed-Income Valuation
    by James F. Adams, PhD, CFA, and Donald J. Smith, PhD
Reading 54:. Introduction to Asset-Backed Securities
    by Frank J. Fabozzi, CFA.

1. A bond will trade at a premium if:

   A. it is a zero-coupon bond.

   B. market interest rates are *lower* than the coupon rate.

   C. market interest rates are *higher* than the coupon rate.

---

2. The Z-spread is:

   A. the option-adjusted spread if a bond has embedded options.

   B. the adjustment to the option-adjusted spread as volatility changes.

   C. the spread earned on a bond over the Treasury spot rate curve if it is held to maturity.

1. A bond will trade at a premium if:

A. it is a zero-coupon bond.

*B. market interest rates are *lower* than the coupon rate.

C. market interest rates are *higher* than the coupon rate.

Explanation: LOS: Reading 53-b

When market interest rates are below the coupon rate the bondholders will demand a lower rate than the coupon rate so the bond price will be set higher than its par value.

---

2. The Z-spread is:

A. the option-adjusted spread if a bond has embedded options.

B. the adjustment to the option-adjusted spread as volatility changes.

*C. the spread earned on a bond over the Treasury spot rate curve if it is held to maturity.

Explanation: LOS: Reading 53-i

The Z-spread, also called zero volatility or static spread, is the spread that must be added to the Treasury spot rate to give a discount rate which will make the discounted cash flows from a bond equal to its price. The option-adjusted spread is the Z spread minus the option value in basis points per year.

3. The yield to worst for a callable bond is the:

    A. yield assuming the bond is called at the lowest possible call price.

    B. yield assuming that the bond is called at the first possible call date.

    C. lowest of the yield to maturity and yields to call, calculated using all possible call dates.

---

4. The current yield of a bond is:

    A. always lower than the yield to maturity, if there are no embedded options.

    B. always higher than the yield to maturity, if there are no embedded options.

    C. lower than the yield to maturity, if the bond is trading at a discount to maturity value.

3. The yield to worst for a callable bond is the:

    A. yield assuming the bond is called at the lowest possible call price.

    B. yield assuming that the bond is called at the first possible call date.

*C. lowest of the yield to maturity and yields to call, calculated using all possible call dates.

Explanation: LOS: Reading 53-f

The yield to worst for a callable bond is the lowest yield that an investor could receive so it is the lowest of the yield to maturity and all possible yields to call.

---

4. The current yield of a bond is:

    A. always lower than the yield to maturity, if there are no embedded options.

    B. always higher than the yield to maturity, if there are no embedded options.

*C. lower than the yield to maturity, if the bond is trading at a discount to maturity value.

Explanation: LOS: Reading 53-f

The current yield is the annual coupon divided by the market price of the bond. It does not include the capital gain or loss on the bond so if the bond is at a discount the current yield will be lower than the yield to maturity and vice versa.

5. The flat or clean price of a bond is the agreed bond price:

    A. without accrued interest.

    B. plus the accrued interest due to the seller of the bond.

    C. for the bond less the accrued interest due to the buyer of the bond.

---

6. Which of the following is *least likely* to be an example of embedded options that might be granted to the issuer of a bond?

    A. A floor on a floater.

    B. The right to call the issue.

    C. An accelerated sinking fund provision.

5. The flat or clean price of a bond is the agreed bond price:

*A. without accrued interest.

    B. plus the accrued interest due to the seller of the bond.

    C. for the bond less the accrued interest due to the buyer of the bond.

Explanation: LOS: Reading 53-d

The clean price of a bond is the quoted price of a bond where the accrued interest is excluded.

---

6. Which of the following is *least likely* to be an example of embedded options that might be granted to the issuer of a bond?

*A. A floor on a floater.

    B. The right to call the issue.

    C. An accelerated sinking fund provision.

Explanation: LOS: Reading 51-e

A floor on a floater is a benefit to the holder of the bond if interest rates fall, not to the issuer.

7. Which of the following is *least likely* to be an example of embedded options that might be granted to bondholders?

    A. A cap on a floater.

    B. A floor on a floater.

    C. Conversion privileges.

---

8. Which of the following is an example of a negative covenant?

    A. The issuer must submit periodic statements to the bond trustee.

    B. Mortgage holders are not permitted to prepay mortgages ahead of the scheduled date.

    C. The issuer cannot secure any of its assets to a new debt issue without giving equal treatment to the existing debt holders.

7. Which of the following is *least likely* to be an example of embedded options that might be granted to bondholders?

*A. A cap on a floater.

   B. A floor on a floater.

   C. Conversion privileges.

Explanation: LOS: Reading 51-e

A cap on a floater is a benefit to the issuer if interest rates rise, not to the bondholders.

---

8. Which of the following is an example of a negative covenant?

   A. The issuer must submit periodic statements to the bond trustee.

   B. Mortgage holders are not permitted to prepay mortgages ahead of the scheduled date.

*C. The issuer cannot secure any of its assets to a new debt issue without giving equal treatment to the existing debt holders.

Explanation: LOS: Reading 51-c

A negative covenant is a restriction on the issuer to protect investors in the bond. An example is when unsecured debt holders are protected from the assets of the issuer being given as collateral in a subsequent debt issue.

9. When the issuer of a bond agrees to retire a certain proportion of a bond issue each year, this is an example of a:

    A. a refundable bond.

    B. a prepayment option.

    C. a sinking fund provision.

---

10. The yield-to-maturity calculation assumes that coupon payments can be reinvested at the:

    A. coupon rate.

    B. current yield.

    C. yield to maturity.

9. When the issuer of a bond agrees to retire a certain proportion of a bond issue each year, this is an example of a:

    A. a refundable bond.

    B. a prepayment option.

*C. a sinking fund provision.

Explanation: LOS: Reading 51-e

A sinking fund provision allows the issuer of a bond to retire a certain proportion of a bond issue each year.

---

10. The yield-to-maturity calculation assumes that coupon payments can be reinvested at the:

    A. coupon rate.

    B. current yield.

*C. yield to maturity.

Explanation: LOS: Reading 53-b

The yield to maturity will only be realized if the following assumptions hold:

1. The bond is held to maturity.

2. The coupon payments can be reinvested at a yield equivalent to the yield to maturity.

11. Which of the following statements is the *least accurate* regarding callable bonds?

    A. The issuer's obligation of paying interest ends at the call date.

    B. A callable bond is more likely to be called after interest rates have fallen.

    C. A callable bond will generally be issued at a lower coupon rate than a non-callable bond with the same terms.

12. Liquidity risk in bond markets can be measured by:

    A. price volatility.

    B. the bid-ask spread.

    C. the slope of the yield curve.

11. Which of the following statements is the *least accurate* regarding callable bonds?

   A. The issuer's obligation of paying interest ends at the call date.

   B. A callable bond is more likely to be called after interest rates have fallen.

*C. A callable bond will generally be issued at a lower coupon rate than a non-callable bond with the same terms.

Explanation: LOS: Reading 51-f

A callable bond will normally be offered at a *higher* coupon rate to compensate the investor for the possibility that the bond might be called in prior to maturity.

---

12. Liquidity risk in bond markets can be measured by:

   A. price volatility.

*B. the bid-ask spread.

   C. the slope of the yield curve.

Explanation: LOS: Reading 52-d

The bid-ask spread quoted by dealers reflects the liquidity of an issue.

13. Which one of the following is the *least likely* to be an example of a securitized bond?

   A. Covered bond.

   B. Treasury bond.

   C. Mortgage-backed security.

---

14. An option-free bond has a remaining life of three years and carries an 8% annual coupon rate payable annually and has a yield to maturity of 9%. If the one- and two-year spot rates are 6.0% and 6.5% (annual basis), respectively, then the three-year spot rate is *closest* to:

   A. 7.0%.

   B. 8.1%.

   C. 9.2%.

13. Which one of the following is the *least likely* to be an example of a securitized bond?

    A. Covered bond.

*B. Treasury bond.

    C. Mortgage-backed security..

Explanation: LOS: Reading 51-a

Treasury bonds are sovereign debt and not structured with securitization techniques, such as the use of bankruptcy-remote special purpose vehicles.

---

14. An option-free bond has a remaining life of three years and carries an 8% annual coupon rate payable annually and has a yield to maturity of 9%. If the one- and two-year spot rates are 6.0% and 6.5% (annual basis), respectively, then the three-year spot rate is *closest* to:

    A. 7.0%.

    B. 8.1%.

*C. 9.2%.

Explanation: LOS: Reading 55-f

    The following relationship must hold, where the three-year spot rate is z:

    $8/(1.09)+8/(1.09)^2+108/(1.09)^3=8/(1.06)+8/(1.065)^2+108/(1+z)^3$

    $97.47 = 14.60+108/(1+z)^3$

    $(1+z)^3 = 108/82.87$

    $1+z = (1.3032)^{1/3}$

    $z = 9.23\%$

15. If the yield spread of a bond has widened it means that:

    A. it is a high-grade bond.

    B. the bond price has risen relative to that of an equivalent Treasury bond issue.

    C. the bond price has declined relative to that of an equivalent Treasury bond issue.

16. Medium-term notes (MTNs) differ from corporate bonds since:

    A. MTNs have a maximum maturity of 10 years.

    B. MTNs are not rated by any of the major credit rating organizations.

    C. MTNs are offered to investors on a continuous basis by the issuer or its agent.

15. If the yield spread of a bond has widened it means that:

   A. it is a high-grade bond.

   B. the bond price has risen relative to that of an equivalent Treasury bond issue.

*C. the bond price has declined relative to that of an equivalent Treasury bond issue.

Explanation: LOS: Reading 53-i

The yield spread is the difference between the yield on the bond and the yield on a Treasury bond. If the spread has widened it means that the yield demanded by an investor in the bond has increased, so the price has fallen, relative to a Treasury bond.

---

16. Medium-term notes (MTNs) differ from corporate bonds since:

   A. MTNs have a maximum maturity of 10 years.

   B. MTNs are not rated by any of the major credit rating organizations.

*C. MTNs are offered to investors on a continuous basis by the issuer or its agent.

Explanation: LOS: Reading 52-f

The unique feature of MTNs is that they are offered to investors on a continuous basis by the issuer or its agent.

17. Which of the following statements is least accurate?

A. The yields of on-the-run issues are generally lower than off-the-run issues.

B. The financing rates (repo rates) of on-the-run issues are generally lower than off-the-run issues.

C. The interest rate risks of on-the-run and off-the-run issues with the same maturity are identical.

18. Which of the following embedded options is increasingly valuable to an investor in a rising interest rate environment?

A. Put option.

B. Call option.

C. Interest rate cap.

17. Which of the following statements is least accurate?

    A. The yields of on-the-run issues are generally lower than off-the-run issues.

    B. The financing rates (repo rates) of on-the-run issues are generally lower than off-the-run issues.

*C. The interest rate risks of on-the-run and off-the-run issues with the same maturity are identical.

Explanation: LOS: Reading 52-e

Interest Rate Risks is false because bonds with identical maturities may not have identical coupon rates, hence the durations may differ.

---

18. Which of the following embedded options is increasingly valuable to an investor in a rising interest rate environment?

*A. Put option.

    B. Call option.

    C. Interest rate cap.

Explanation: LOS: Reading 51-f

From the investor perspective, a put option is beneficial when interest rates rise. The investor benefits from being able to sell back the bond at a specified price that is *higher* than the prevailing market price.

19. The legal entity that is used in asset securitization for bankruptcy remoteness is:

    A. an indenture trustee.

    B. an investment bank.

    C. a special purpose vehicle.

---

20. The following data is collected:

Years to maturity	Spot rate (Semiannual bond basis)
0.5	5.75%
1.0	6.25%
1.5	7.00%
2.0	7.25%

Based on the above data, the six-month implied forward rate one and a half years from now is *closest* to:

    A. 4.00%.

    B. 6.25%.

    C. 8.00%.

19. The legal entity that is used in asset securitization for bankruptcy remoteness is:

A. an indenture trustee.

B. an investment bank.

*C. a special purpose vehicle.

Explanation: LOS: Reading 51-d

A special purpose vehicle is the legal entity that the assets are sold to, so the assets used as collateral are separate from the firm that is requiring funding.

---

20. The following data is collected:

Years to maturity	Spot rate (Semiannual bond basis)
0.5	5.75%
1.0	6.25%
1.5	7.00%
2.0	7.25%

Based on the above data, the six-month implied forward rate one and a half years from now is *closest* to:

A. 4.00%.

B. 6.25%.

*C. 8.00%.

Explanation: LOS: Reading 53-h

$$_1f_3 = [(1+ 0.03625)^4/(1 + 0.035)^3] - 1$$

$$= 4.0\%$$

The forward rate is $4.0\% \times 2 = 8.0\%$

21. If the semiannual bond-equivalent yield on a bond which pays semiannual coupons is 5%, the effective annual yield is *closest* to:

    A. 4.94%.

    B. 5.06%.

    C. 5.51%.

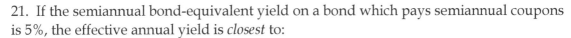

22. A sinking fund provision refers to when:

    A. an issuer is required to retire a pre-specified portion of a bond each year.

    B. an issuer has made an arrangement to buy back a bond at par in the case of deterioration in the quality of collateral for a bond.

    C. an investor has the right to sell the bonds back to the issuer prior to maturity if the market price has fallen below a prespecified level.

21. If the semiannual bond-equivalent yield on a bond which pays semiannual coupons is 5%, the effective annual yield is *closest* to:

  A. 4.94%.

*B. 5.06%.

  C. 5.51%.

Explanation: LOS: Reading 53-f

Effective annual yield = $(1 + \text{bond-equivalent yield}/2)^2 - 1 = 5.06\%$

---

22. A sinking fund provision refers to when:

*A. an issuer is required to retire a pre-specified portion of a bond each year.

  B. an issuer has made an arrangement to buy back a bond at par in the case of deterioration in the quality of collateral for a bond.

  C. an investor has the right to sell the bonds back to the issuer prior to maturity if the market price has fallen below a prespecified level.

Explanation: LOS: Reading 51-f

A sinking fund requirement is usually put in place to reduce credit risk because the issuer has to retire a portion of the bond issue prior to maturity, either by buying bonds in the market or providing cash for the trustee to call bonds using a lottery system.

23. The following information is given:

Issue	Yield
10-year on-the-run Treasury 6% coupon	6.15%
10-year ABG Corporation Series J 5% coupon	7.85%
10-year IBN Limited 8% coupon	8.00%

The yield spread between IBN Limited and ABG Corporation bonds is:

A. 3.000%.

B. 3 basis points.

C. 15 basis points.

24. The following data has been provided:

Years to maturity	Spot rate (Semiannual bond basis)
0.5	8.75%
1.0	6.25%
1.5	5.00%

The six-month forward rate one year from now is *closest* to:

A. 1.26%.

B. 2.52%.

C. 3.78%.

23. The following information is given:

Issue	Yield
10-year on-the-run Treasury 6% coupon	6.15%
10-year ABG Corporation Series J 5% coupon	7.85%
10-year IBN Limited 8% coupon	8.00%

The yield spread between IBN Limited and ABG Corporation bonds is:

   A. 3.000%.

   B. 3 basis points.

*C. 15 basis points.

Explanation: LOS: Reading 53-i

The absolute yield spread = 8.0% - 7.85% = 0.15% or 15 basis points.

Do not use the coupon rates.

---

24. The following data has been provided:

Years to maturity	Spot rate (Semiannual bond basis)
0.5	8.75%
1.0	6.25%
1.5	5.00%

The six-month forward rate one year from now is *closest* to:

   A. 1.26%.

*B. 2.52%.

   C. 3.78%.

Explanation: LOS: Reading 53-h

$$_1f_2 = [(1+ 0.025)^3/(1 + 0.03125)^2] - 1 = 1.26\%$$

The forward rate is 1.26% x 2 = 2.52%

25. A foreign bond is

    A. traded in a national bond market.

    B. traded outside the jurisdiction of any one country.

    C. issued in a different currency to that of the country it is traded in.

---

26. A capital-indexed bond is a bond where:

    A. there is no coupon but the principal increases with inflation.

    B. only the principal, not the coupon, payment increases with inflation.

    C. there is a fixed coupon rate applied to a principal that increases with inflation.

25. A foreign bond is

*A. traded in a national bond market.

    B. traded outside the jurisdiction of any one country.

    C. issued in a different currency to that of the country it is traded in.

Explanation: LOS: Reading 51-b.

A foreign bond is traded in a domestic market, but it is a foreign bond because the issuer is incorporated in a different country.

---

26. A capital-indexed bond is a bond where:

    A. there is no coupon but the principal increases with inflation.

    B. only the principal, not the coupon, payment increases with inflation.

*C. there is a fixed coupon rate applied to a principal that increases with inflation.

Explanation: LOS: Reading 51-e.

The coupon rate is fixed, but it is applied to an inflation-adjusted principal, so both coupon payment and principal reflect increases in inflation.

27. From the equity markets, central banks find it most useful to derive information on:

    A. future economic activity.

    B. international trade activity.

    C. market expectations of interest rates.

---

28. A bond has a yield of 7.50% and the on-the-run Treasury yield is 6.55%.

The yield spread and yield ratio are:

	Relative yield spread	**Yield ratio**
A.	12.67%	0.873
B.	14.50%	0.873
C.	14.50%	1.145

---

29. Which a firm issues bonds that are nonrefundable this means that:

    A. the bonds can be called but the investor cannot be offered a replacement bond with a similar yield.

    B. an investor cannot exercise an embedded put option whilst they are in a prespecified nonrefunding period.

    C. the bonds cannot be redeemed using proceeds of another debt issue that has provided a lower cost source of funds.

27. From the equity markets, central banks find it most useful to derive information on:

*A. future economic activity.

    B. international trade activity.

    C. market expectations of interest rates.

Explanation: LOS: Reading 51-e.

Equity markets provide information on anticipated economic activity.

---

28. A bond has a yield of 7.50% and the on-the-run Treasury yield is 6.55%. The yield spread and yield ratio are:

	Relative yield spread	Yield ratio
A.	12.67%	0.873
B.	14.50%	0.873
*C.	**14.50%**	**1.145**

Explanation: LOS: Reading 55-c

The market practice is to measure the spread and ratio against Treasuries.

Relative yield spread:

    = (Yield on Bond A - Yield on Treasury)/Yield on Treasury

    = (7.5% - 6.55%)/6.55% = 14.50%

Yield ratio:

    = Yield on Bond A/Yield on Treasury

    = 1.145

29. Which a firm issues bonds that are nonrefundable this means that:

    A. the bonds can be called but the investor cannot be offered a replacement bond with a similar yield.

    B. an investor cannot exercise an embedded put option whilst they are in a prespecified nonrefunding period.

    *C. the bonds cannot be redeemed using proceeds of another debt issue that has provided a lower cost source of funds.

Explanation: LOS: Reading 51-e

When a callable bond is issued it may have restrictions on when it can be called, nonrefundable is such a restriction and means that the firm cannot issue a new bond on a lower yield to pay back the original bond holders.

Study Session 16: Fixed Income: Analysis and Valuation

This study session explains tools for valuation and analysis of fixed-income securities and markets. The first reading is an introduction to the valuation of bonds. The other two readings provide additional coverage of valuation-related topics.

Reading Assignments

Reading 55: Understanding Fixed-Income Risk and Return
    by James F. Adams, PhD, CFA, and Donald J. Smith, PhD
Reading 56: Fundamentals of Credit Analysis
    Reference: By Christopher L. Gootkind, CFA

1. The duration of two bonds in a portfolio are 5 and 10 and the bonds are equally weighted in the portfolio. The portfolio duration is *closest* to:

   A. 5.0.

   B. 7.5.

   C. 15.0.

2. After a corporate default which of the following would have the lowest expected recovery rate?

   A. Senior secured bonds.

   B. Senior unsecured bonds.

   C. Senior subordinated bonds.

1. The duration of two bonds in a portfolio are 5 and 10 and the bonds are equally weighted in the portfolio. The portfolio duration is *closest* to:

   A. 5.0.

*B. 7.5.

   C. 15.0.

Explanation: **LOS: Reading 55-e**

The portfolio duration is approximately the weighted average of the durations of the bonds in the portfolio.

$$Dport = (½ \times D1) + (½ \times D2)$$
$$= (½ \times 5) + (½ \times 10)$$
$$= 7.5$$

---

2.   After a corporate default which of the following would have the lowest expected recovery rate?

   A. Senior secured bonds.

   B. Senior unsecured bonds.

*C. Senior subordinated bonds.

Explanation: **LOS: Reading 56-b**

Subordinated bonds will have the lowest ranking.

3.   Which of the following fixed-rate bonds would have the highest convexity?

   A. A 5% coupon bond that matures in 5 years' time.

   B. A 3% coupon bond that matures in 20 years' time.

   C. A 10% coupon bond that matures in 3 years' time.

---

4.   There are two non-callable bonds with equal duration and one has higher positive convexity than the other. If interest rates rise which bond is expected to fall the least?

   A. The one with lower convexity.

   B. The one with higher convexity.

   C. They will fall by equal amounts.

3. Which of the following fixed-rate bonds would have the highest convexity?

   A. A 5% coupon bond that matures in 5 years' time.

*B. A 3% coupon bond that matures in 20 years' time.**

   C. A 10% coupon bond that matures in 3 years' time.

Explanation: **LOS: Reading 55-g**

The longer the time to maturity and the lower the coupon rate are both factors that increase the convexity of a bond.

---

4. There are two non-callable bonds with equal duration and one has higher positive convexity than the other. If interest rates rise which bond is expected to fall the least?

   A. The one with lower convexity.

*B. The one with higher convexity.**

   C. They will fall by equal amounts.

Explanation: **LOS: Reading 55-h**

Convexity reduces the size of the fall in the bond price that is estimated using duration.

5. The *price value of a basis point* is the:

A. absolute change in price of a bond if there is a one basis point change in yield.

B. absolute change in dollar duration of a bond if there is a one hundred basis point change in yield.

C. percentage change in dollar duration of a bond if there is a one hundred basis point change in yield.

---

6. A company is experiencing deterioration in its profitability and the yield to maturity on their 6-year zero coupon bonds has increased from 3.1% to 3.3%. The return impact is *closest* to:

A. -1.2%.

B. -0.012%.

C. +0.012%.

5.   The *price value of a basis point* is the:

*A. absolute change in price of a bond if there is a one basis point change in yield.

    B. absolute change in dollar duration of a bond if there is a one hundred basis point change in yield.

    C. percentage change in dollar duration of a bond if there is a one hundred basis point change in yield.

Explanation: **LOS: Reading 55-f**

The *price value of a basis point* is the absolute change in price of a bond if there is a one basis point change in yield. It is a special case of dollar duration.

---

6.   A company is experiencing deterioration in its profitability and the yield to maturity on their 6-year zero coupon bonds has increased from 3.1% to 3.3%. The return impact is *closest* to:

*A. -1.2%.

    B. -0.012%.

    C. +0.012%.

Explanation: **LOS: Reading 56-i**

The return impact or percentage change in price is approximately

   – Duration x ΔSpread = -6 x 20 basis points =   -1.2%

(The duration of a 6 year zero-coupon bond is 6 years)

7. If the modified duration of a bond portfolio is 5 and the average yield of bonds in the portfolio rises by 100 basis points then:

A. the market value of the portfolio will fall, but by less than 5%.

B. the market value of the portfolio will rise by approximately 5%.

C. we do not have sufficient information to calculate the impact on the market value of the portfolio.

8. A company announces that it is increasing the debt on its balance sheet to finance an expansion of its business, this leads to a downgrading of the bond by credit rating agencies and an overnight widening in yield spreads of 25 bps. The bond's duration is 6. The impact of the announcement is a fall in the bond price which is *closest* to a fall of:

A. 0.25%.

B. 1.50%.

C. 2.50%.

7.   If the modified duration of a bond portfolio is 5 and the average yield of bonds in the portfolio rises by 100 basis points then:

   A. the market value of the portfolio will fall, but by less than 5%.

   B. the market value of the portfolio will rise by approximately 5%.

*C. we do not have sufficient information to calculate the impact on the market value of the portfolio.

Explanation: **LOS: Reading 55-h**

The yield of each bond in the portfolio must rise by 100 basis points, namely there should be a parallel shift in the yield curve, for the portfolio duration to be an indicator of the price move of the total portfolio. We need to know information on whether there was a parallel shift in the yield curve or the curve changed shape (e.g. steepened or flattened), so C is the correct answer.

8.   A company announces that it is increasing the debt on its balance sheet to finance an expansion of its business, this leads to a downgrading of the bond by credit rating agencies and an overnight widening in yield spreads of 25 bps. The bond's duration is 6. The impact of the announcement is a fall in the bond price which is *closest* to a fall of:

   A. 0.25%.

*B. 1.50%.

   C. 2.50%.

Explanation: **LOS: Reading 56-j**

$$\% \text{ change in price} = -D \times \Delta y \times 100$$
$$= -6 \times (0.0025) \times 100$$
$$= -1.5$$

9. The Macaulay duration of a semiannual bond with a 12% coupon is 6.0 and the yield to maturity is 8%. The modified duration is *closest* to:

    A. 5.66.

    B. 5.77.

    C. 6.24.

10. If the liquidity of a bond deteriorates relative to comparable benchmark bonds it is *likely* that the yield spread will:

    A. widen.

    B. narrow.

    C. remain unchanged.

9. The Macaulay duration of a semiannual bond with a 12% coupon is 6.0 and the yield to maturity is 8%. The modified duration is *closest* to:

    A. 5.66.

*B. 5.77.

    C. 6.24.

Explanation: **LOS: Reading 55-b**

Semiannual bonds mean k = 2

Modified duration   = Macaulay duration/$[(1 + yield/k)]$

                       = 6.0/(1.04)

                       = 5.77

---

10. If the liquidity of a bond deteriorates relative to comparable benchmark bonds it is *likely* that the yield spread will:

*A. widen.

    B. narrow.

    C. remain unchanged.

Explanation: **LOS: Reading 56-h**

The yield spread reflects credit risk and liquidity risk. Investors will generally require a higher yield to compensate them for holding an illiquid bond so the spread will widen.

11. Which of the following companyies is *most likely* to be able to service its debt in an economic recession?

    A. a steel company.

    B. an auto manufacturer.

    C. a health care company.

---

12. The Macaulay duration of a bond tends to be lower for a bond if its coupon rate and yield to maturity are:

Coupon rate	Yield to maturity
A. Lower	Lower
B. Lower	Higher
C. Higher	Higher

11. Which of the following companyies is *most likely* to be able to service its debt in an economic recession?

    A. a steel company.

    B. an auto manufacturer.

*C. a health care company.

Explanation: **LOS: Reading 56-g**

A health care company is generally considered non-cyclical, whereas an auto manufacturer and steel company are more cyclical. Cyclical companies have more volatile cash flows and are therefore generally considered to have higher credit risk.

---

12. The Macaulay duration of a bond tends to be lower for a bond if its coupon rate and yield to maturity are:

Coupon rate	Yield to maturity
A. Lower	Lower
B. Lower	Higher
*C. Higher	Higher

Explanation: **LOS: Reading 55-d**

High coupon rates and high yields to maturity will tend to lower duration.

13. The appropriate duration measure to use for a high coupon callable bond is:

   A. effective duration.

   B. modified duration.

   C. Macaulay duration.

---

14. When investors hold bonds which have the same seniority of ranking in a company's capital structure but different maturity dates, which investors will have first claim in the event of default?

   A. Holders of long-term bonds will have first claim.

   B. Holders of short-term bonds will have first claim.

   C. Neither have first claim; holders of short-term and long-term bonds are treated equally.

13. The appropriate duration measure to use for a high coupon callable bond is:

*A. effective duration.

    B. modified duration.

    C. Macaulay duration.

Explanation: **LOS: Reading 55-b**

In a callable bond, the cash flows might change as interest rates change. The most appropriate duration measure is effective duration.

---

14. When investors hold bonds which have the same seniority of ranking in a company's capital structure but different maturity dates, which investors will have first claim in the event of default?

    A. Holders of long-term bonds will have first claim.

    B. Holders of short-term bonds will have first claim.

*C. Neither have first claim; holders of short-term and long-term bonds are treated equally.

Explanation: **LOS: Reading 56-b**

The time to maturity is not relevant, all maturities will be treated equally if they have the same seniority ranking, they are ranked 'pari passu'.

15. A non-callable bond has:

    A. positive convexity throughout the yield range.

    B. negative convexity throughout the yield range.

    C. negative convexity at low yields and positive convexity at high yields.

---

16. A downgrade in a credit rating of a bond tends to

    A. lag a widening in the credit spread of the bond.

    B. lead to a widening in the credit spread of the bond.

    C. lead to a narrowing in the credit spread of the bond.

15. A non-callable bond has:

*A. positive convexity throughout the yield range.

   B. negative convexity throughout the yield range.

   C. negative convexity at low yields and positive convexity at high yields.

Explanation: **LOS: Reading 55-g**

The presence of embedded options, such as a call option in a bond, would make the convexity negative in certain yield ranges. Non-callable bonds have positive convexity throughout the yield range.

---

16. A downgrade in a credit rating of a bond tends to

*A. lag a widening in the credit spread of the bond.

   B. lead to a widening in the credit spread of the bond.

   C. lead to a narrowing in the credit spread of the bond.

Explanation: **LOS: Reading 56-d**

The credit rating agencies tend to lag the market, with the market reacting more quickly to a deterioration in an issuer's prospects by marking the price of their bonds down and therefore widening the credit spread.

17. In credit analysis the capacity of the issuer refers to:

   A. the market share of the issuing company.

   B. the ability of the issuer to service its debt.

   C. the confidence in the issuing company management's character.

---

18. Given the following information on a bond:

   Duration   =   7.5670.

   Convexity =   82.1870.

   Yields fall by: 250 basis points.

The total estimated price change in percentage terms is *closest* to:

   A. 7.57%.

   B. 18.92%.

   C. 21.49%.

17. In credit analysis the capacity of the issuer refers to:

A. the market share of the issuing company.

*B. the ability of the issuer to service its debt.

C. the confidence in the issuing company management's character.

Explanation: **LOS: Reading 56-e**

Capacity simply refers to the ability to make its debt repayments on time.

---

18. Given the following information on a bond:

Duration   =   7.5670.

Convexity =   82.1870.

Yields fall by: 250 basis points.

The total estimated price change in percentage terms is *closest* to:

A. 7.57%.

B. 18.92%.

*C. 21.49%.

Explanation: **LOS: Reading 55-h**

Estimated change using duration	$7.5670\% \times 0.025 \times 100$	= 18.9175
Convexity adjustment:	$\frac{1}{2} \times 82.1870 \times (0.025)^2 \times 100$	= 2.5684
Total estimated percentage price change		= 21.4858

19. Which of the following is *least likely* to be a characteristic of bonds with positive convexity?

A. For a large change in yields, the percentage price decrease is greater than the percentage price increase.

B. For a small change in yields, the percentage changes are roughly the same, whether the yield increases or decreases.

C. For a large change in yields, the percentage price change is not the same for an increase in yields as it is for a decrease in yields.

---

20. A bond is priced at 90. If the yield declines by 25 basis points the price rises to 94.8 and if the yield rises by 25 basis points the price falls to 84.9. The approximate modified duration is *closest* to:

A. 9.9.

B. 22.0.

C. 44.0.

19. Which of the following is *least likely* to be a characteristic of bonds with positive convexity?

*A. For a large change in yields, the percentage price decrease is greater than the percentage price increase.

   B. For a small change in yields, the percentage changes are roughly the same, whether the yield increases or decreases.

   C. For a large change in yields, the percentage price change is not the same for an increase in yields as it is for a decrease in yields.

Explanation: **LOS: Reading 55-h**

For a large change in yields, the percentage price increase is greater than the percentage price decrease, when a bond has positive convexity.

---

20. A bond is priced at 90. If the yield declines by 25 basis points the price rises to 94.8 and if the yield rises by 25 basis points the price falls to 84.9. The approximate modified duration is *closest* to:

   A. 9.9.

*B. 22.0.

   C. 44.0.

Explanation: **LOS: Reading 55-b**

   The duration formula is:

$$\frac{\text{price if yields decline} - \text{price if yields rise}}{2 \times (\text{initial price}) \times (\text{change in yield in decimals})}$$

   $= (94.8 - 84.9)/(2 \times 90 \times 0.0025) = 22.0$

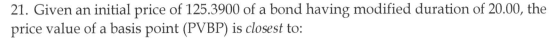

21. Given an initial price of 125.3900 of a bond having modified duration of 20.00, the price value of a basis point (PVBP) is *closest* to:

  A. $0.2509.

  B. $6.27.

  C. $25.09.

22. Using the weighted average of the Macaulay durations of bonds in a portfolio in order to calculate the Macaulay duration of a portfolio is only accurate when:

  A. the yield curve is flat.

  B. they are all zero coupon bonds.

  C. there are no embedded options in the bonds.

470 Study Session 16:

21. Given an initial price of 125.3900 of a bond having modified duration of 20.00, the price value of a basis point (PVBP) is *closest* to:

*A. $0.2509.

   B. $6.27.

   C. $25.09.

Explanation: **LOS: Reading 55-f**

The price value of a basis point (PVBP), is simply a special case of money duration, it is the absolute value of the change in the price of a bond for a 1 basis point change in yield. It is given by

$20.00 \times 0.0001 \times 125.39 = \$0.2509$

---

22. Using the weighted average of the Macaulay durations of bonds in a portfolio in order to calculate the Macaulay duration of a portfolio is only accurate when:

*A. the yield curve is flat.

   B. they are all zero coupon bonds.

   C. there are no embedded options in the bonds.

Explanation: **LOS: Reading 55-e**

The weighted-average duration is only an approximation of the accurate measure of portfolio duration which takes into account the aggregated cash flows of the individual bonds. The approximation is only accurate if the yield of the bonds is the same, i.e. the yield curve is flat.

23. When interest rates change, it is observed that the price of a callable bond with a coupon of 5% moves as follows:

Rates down 50 basis points	Rates up 50 basis points
Price + 5%	Price - 3%

The bond is likely to have

	Convexity	Yield
A.	Positive	Less than 5%
B.	Positive	More than 5%
C.	Negative	More than 5%

---

24. Coverage ratios in credit analysis refer to:

A. the ability of the issuer to make its interest payments.

C. the cash flow available to repay the principal on maturity of the debt.

B. the value of the issuer's tangible assets as a multiple of the debt in the balance sheet.

23. When interest rates change, it is observed that the price of a callable bond with a coupon of 5% moves as follows:

Rates down 50 basis points	Rates up 50 basis points
Price + 5%	Price - 3%

The bond is likely to have

Convexity	Yield
A. Positive	Less than 5%
*B. Positive	More than 5%
C. Negative	More than 5%

Explanation: LOS: Reading 55-h

The bond has positive convexity since the gain is more than the loss for an equal move in interest rates. The bond's coupon is probably less than market yields meaning it is unlikely to be called in the near future. As yields fall the bond is more likely to be called and starts to exhibit negative convexity.

---

24. Coverage ratios in credit analysis refer to:

*A. the ability of the issuer to make its interest payments.

C. the cash flow available to repay the principal on maturity of the debt.

B. the value of the issuer's tangible assets as a multiple of the debt in the balance sheet.

Explanation: LOS: Reading 56-g

Coverage ratios refer to the ability to cover interest payments, for example EBIT/interest expense.

25. The main risk for an investor with negative duration gap is:

    A. market price risk.

    B. lower interest rates.

    C. higher interest rates.

---

26. Which of the following is a characteristic of Macaulay duration? Macaulay duration

    A. cannot be used for zero-coupon bonds.

    B. can be used to compute modified duration.

    C. is the same as modified duration when a bond pays annual coupons.

25. The main risk for an investor with negative duration gap is:

    A. market price risk.

*B. lower interest rates.

    C. higher interest rates.

Explanation: **LOS: Reading 55-j**

The duration gap is the Macaulay duration minus the investment horizon. When the investment horizon is larger than Macaulay duration then the main risk is lower interest rates affecting the coupon reinvestment rate.

26. Which of the following is a characteristic of Macaulay duration? Macaulay duration

    A. cannot be used for zero-coupon bonds.

*B. can be used to compute modified duration.

    C. is the same as modified duration when a bond pays annual coupons.

Explanation: **LOS: Reading 55-b**

Macaulay duration can be used to calculate modified duration, but has the same problems as modified duration; it cannot be used for bonds where the cash flows are altered by interest rate moves. Modified duration is less than Macaulay duration, for an annual-pay bond we need to divide Macaulay duration by (1 + yield) to get modified duration.

Study Session 17:   Derivatives:

Derivatives—financial instruments that offer a return based on the return of some underlying asset—have become increasingly important and fundamental in effectively managing financial risk and creating synthetic exposures to asset classes. As in other security markets, arbitrage and market efficiency play a critical role in establishing prices and maintaining parity. This study session builds the conceptual framework for understanding derivative investments (forwards, futures, options, and swaps), derivative markets, and the use of options in risk management.

Reading Assignments

Reading 57:. Derivative Markets and Instruments
   Analysis of Derivatives for the Chartered Financial Analyst® Program, by Don M. Chance, CFA

Reading 58:. Basics of Derivative Pricing and Valuation
   by Don M. Chance, CFA

Reading 59:. Risk Management Applications of Option Strategies
   Reference: Analysis of Derivatives for the Chartered Financial Analyst® Program, by Don M. Chance, CFA

---

1. A company announces the payment of a dividend on its stock. Holders of which type of American-style options would consider exercising early?

    A. Put options only.

    B. Call options only.

    C. Both put and call options.

1. A company announces the payment of a dividend on its stock. Holders of which type of American-style options would consider exercising early?

    A. Put options only.

*B. Call options only.

    C. Both put and call options.

Explanation: LOS: Reading 59-o

The payment of the dividend will lead to a fall in the stock price when it goes ex-dividend. If the time value of the call option is more than the dividend a holder will consider exercising early to collect the dividend. A holder of a put option would benefit from the fall in price so would not exercise early.

5. If a seller of a call option deposits the underlying shares with his broker this is:

A. speculation.

B. a naked call.

C. a covered call.

---

6. The value of a stock is $20 and a trader writes a call option with a value of $3 and an exercise price of $22. The stock price at expiration that will be the trader's breakeven point is:

A. $19.

B. $23.

C. $25.

5. If a seller of a call option deposits the underlying shares with his broker this is:

   A. speculation.

   B. a naked call.

*C. a covered call.

Explanation: LOS: Reading 59-b

A covered call means that the broker has the shares available for delivery if the buyer of the call option decides to exercise his option.

---

6. The value of a stock is $20 and a trader writes a call option with a value of $3 and an exercise price of $22. The stock price at expiration that will be the trader's breakeven point is:

   A. $19.

   B. $23.

*C. $25.

Explanation: LOS: Reading 57-c

$$0 = \text{premium} - \text{maximum } [0, (S_T - X)]$$
$$0 = \$3 - (S - \$22)$$
$$S = \$25$$

7. The *least likely* benefit for an investor if a market includes financial derivatives is:

   A. price discovery.

   B. trading efficiency.

   C. regulatory protection.

8. The convenience yield of an asset is the:

   A. cost of holding the asset.

   B. benefit of holding the asset.

   C. return on the cash held when gaining exposure to an asset using derivatives.

7. The *least likely* benefit for an investor if a market includes financial derivatives is:

   A. price discovery.

   B. trading efficiency.

*C. regulatory protection.

Explanation: LOS: Reading 57-c

Price discovery, ability to hedge risk and market efficiency including low transaction costs are all benefits of derivatives. Although exchange-traded derivatives provide some regulatory protection, OTC derivatives often provide less regulatory protection, although many OTC derivatives are now being regulated.

---

8. The convenience yield of an asset is the:

   A. cost of holding the asset.

*B. benefit of holding the asset.

   C. return on the cash held when gaining exposure to an asset using derivatives.

Explanation: LOS: Reading 58-db

A convenience yield refers to the nonmonetary benefit of holding an asset. An example of this is holding a commodity that is in short supply.

9. A trader writes a European-style call option on a stock. The stock's current price is $24, the option price is $4 and the exercise price is $23. At the expiration of the option the stock price is $30. The profit/loss of the option writer is a:

    A. loss of $3.

    B. loss of $4.

    C. profit of $3.

10. The notional principal in a plain vanilla interest rate swap is:

    A. never paid.

    B. paid at the time that the swap agreement is made.

    C. paid in equal parts when each swap payment is made.

9. A trader writes a European-style call option on a stock. The stock's current price is $24, the option price is $4 and the exercise price is $23. At the expiration of the option the stock price is $30. The profit/loss of the option writer is a:

*A. loss of $3.

 B. loss of $4.

 C. profit of $3.

Explanation: LOS: Reading 59-b

The writer has received the premium of $4 but the loss when the option is exercised is $30 minus $23 giving an overall loss of $3.

10. The notional principal in a plain vanilla interest rate swap is:

*A. never paid.

 B. paid at the time that the swap agreement is made.

 C. paid in equal parts when each swap payment is made.

Explanation: LOS: Reading 57-b

The notional principal is the amount on which the interest payments are calculated and does not change hands in an interest rate swap.

11. The value of a put option at expiry is:

    A. maximum of (i) zero and (ii) exercise price minus stock price.

    B. maximum of (i) zero and (ii) stock price minus exercise price.

    C. maximum of (i) zero and (ii) stock price minus exercise price, minus the option premium.

---

12. The spot price of a share is $100, the risk-free rate is 4%, and the present value of the dividends to be paid on the share over the next six months is $5. The price of a forward on the share that expires in six months' time is *closest* to:

    A. $96.88.

    B. $102.96.

    C. $107.08.

11. The value of a put option at expiry is:

*A. maximum of (i) zero and (ii) exercise price minus stock price.

   B. maximum of (i) zero and (ii) stock price minus exercise price.

   C. maximum of (i) zero and (ii) stock price minus exercise price, minus the option premium.

Explanation: LOS: Reading 60-h

The holder of a put option will exercise the option if the exercise price is above the stock price. In that case he could theoretically buy the stock in the market and sell it at a *higher* price. If the stock price is *higher* than the exercise price he will let the option lapse worthless. The option premium should only be taken into account if the profit/loss on the option is being calculated.

---

12. The spot price of a share is $100, the risk-free rate is 4%, and the present value of the dividends to be paid on the share over the next six months is $5. The price of a forward on the share that expires in six months' time is *closest* to:

*A. $96.88.

   B. $102.96.

   C. $107.08.

Explanation: LOS: Reading 58-d

The forward price is the spot price compounded at the risk-free rate over the life of the contract minus the future value of any dividends.

The forward price is:

$$\$100(1.04)^{1/2} - \$5(1.04)^{1/2} = \$96.88$$

13. When a trader writes a covered call this will often be with the objective of:

A. increasing income.

B. insuring his portfolio value.

C. increasing his gain if the stock price rises above the exercise price plus the premium.

14. An investor believes that the S&P Index is going to decline sharply over the next two years. Which of the following strategies would be consistent with this view?

A. Buy call options on the S&P Index.

B. Write put options on the S&P Index.

C. Enter into a two-year equity swap to receive a fixed payment and pay an equity payment based on the performance of the S&P index.

13. When a trader writes a covered call this will often be with the objective of:

*A. increasing income.

    B. insuring his portfolio value.

    C. increasing his gain if the stock price rises above the exercise price plus the premium.

Explanation: LOS: Reading 59-b

Writing a covered call means that the trader will increase his income by the option premium. If the stock price rises above the exercise price his shares will be called and he will lose the capital gain he would have made if he had not written the option.

---

14. An investor believes that the S&P Index is going to decline sharply over the next two years. Which of the following strategies would be consistent with this view?

    A. Buy call options on the S&P Index.

    B. Write put options on the S&P Index.

*C. Enter into a two-year equity swap to receive a fixed payment and pay an equity payment based on the performance of the S&P index.

Explanation: LOS: Reading 57-c

If the S&P Index falls the investor will receive both the fixed payment and an equity payment so this would be a viable strategy.

15. An investor deposits an initial margin of $20,000 for a futures trade and the next day makes a $2,000 loss on the trade. The next day he makes a further loss of $2,000. If the maintenance requirement is $15,000 then he must deposit a variation margin of:

    A. $1,000.

    B. $4,000.

    C. there is no requirement to pay a variation margin.

16. A trader sells both a call and a put option on a stock with the same exercise price and the same expiration, he will make a profit on the transaction:

    A. if the stock price rises sharply or falls sharply.

    B. only if the stock price falls sharply below the exercise price.

    C. if the stock price remains within a narrow range of the exercise price.

15. An investor deposits an initial margin of $20,000 for a futures trade and the next day makes a $2,000 loss on the trade. The next day he makes a further loss of $2,000. If the maintenance requirement is $15,000 then he must deposit a variation margin of:

   A. $1,000.

   B. $4,000.

*C. there is no requirement to pay a variation margin.

Explanation: LOS: Reading 57-c
The variation margin only needs to be paid if the investor's equity has fallen below the maintenance requirement. This is not the case since the equity is still $16,000 ($20,000 - $2,000 - $2,000).

---

16. A trader sells both a call and a put option on a stock with the same exercise price and the same expiration, he will make a profit on the transaction:

   A. if the stock price rises sharply or falls sharply.

   B. only if the stock price falls sharply below the exercise price.

*C. if the stock price remains within a narrow range of the exercise price.

Explanation: LOS: Reading 59-a
This is a straddle (not explicitly covered in the readings) but the candidate can work out that if the stock price moves up sharply the call option would be exercised, or if it moves down sharply the put option would be exercised. If the move is significant the loss made on either option would be greater than the premium income received. His strategy is profitable if the stock price does not move by more than the combined value of the premiums received away from the exercise price.

17. If put options are used to insure a portfolio which of the following statements is *most accurate*?

A. In the majority of cases the insured portfolio will outperform an equivalent uninsured portfolio.

B. The probability of the insured portfolio achieving high positive gains is less than for the uninsured portfolio.

C. There is a *higher* probability that the insured portfolio will achieve any given positive return than the uninsured portfolio.

18. At expiration the value of a long forward contract is the spot price of the underlying minus the:

A. forward price agreed in the contract.

B. forward price agreed in the contract compounded at the risk-free rate over the life of the contract.

C. forward price agreed in the contract discounted at the risk-free rate over the life of the contract.

17. If put options are used to insure a portfolio which of the following statements is *most accurate?*

A. In the majority of cases the insured portfolio will outperform an equivalent uninsured portfolio.

*B. The probability of the insured portfolio achieving high positive gains is less than for the uninsured portfolio.

C. There is a *higher* probability that the insured portfolio will achieve any given positive return than the uninsured portfolio.

Explanation: LOS: Reading 59-b
Correctly insuring a portfolio using put options should eliminate the possibility of a large loss since the portfolio value will not fall below the exercise price less the premium. But if the return from the assets is positive the uninsured portfolio will outperform the insured portfolio because of the cost of the premium.

---

18. At expiration the value of a long forward contract is the spot price of the underlying minus the:

*A. forward price agreed in the contract.

B. forward price agreed in the contract compounded at the risk-free rate over the life of the contract.

C. forward price agreed in the contract discounted at the risk-free rate over the life of the contract.

Explanation: LOS: Reading 58-c
The value is simply the spot price of the underlying minus the agreed forward price.

19. A corporate treasurer knows that his firm will receive a large cash inflow in 180 days' time. He is concerned that interest rates are going to fall and he wishes to put the money on deposit at 90-day LIBOR on receipt. He should consider taking a:

    A. long position in a Forward Rate Agreement (FRA) based on 90-day LIBOR.

    B. long position in a Forward Rate Agreement (FRA) based on 180-day LIBOR.

    C. short position in a Forward Rate Agreement (FRA) based on 90-day LIBOR.

---

20. An investor buys a call option at a premium of $10 on a stock which has a market price of $60. If the exercise price is $62 the investor will make a:

    A. loss if the stock price rises above the breakeven point of $72.

    B. profit if the stock price rises above the breakeven point of $70.

    C. profit if the stock price rises above the breakeven point of $72.

19. A corporate treasurer knows that his firm will receive a large cash inflow in 180 days' time. He is concerned that interest rates are going to fall and he wishes to put the money on deposit at 90-day LIBOR on receipt. He should consider taking a:

    A. long position in a Forward Rate Agreement (FRA) based on 90-day LIBOR.

    B. long position in a Forward Rate Agreement (FRA) based on 180-day LIBOR.

*C. short position in a Forward Rate Agreement (FRA) based on 90-day LIBOR.

Explanation: LOS: Reading 58-e

A short position will generate a profit if interest rates fall which will offset the loss from placing the cash inflow on deposit at a lower rate. A FRA is used which is a 180-day forward contract based on 90-day LIBOR. He is effectively locking in the rate he will receive in 180 days' time.

20. An investor buys a call option at a premium of $10 on a stock which has a market price of $60. If the exercise price is $62 the investor will make a:

    A. loss if the stock price rises above the breakeven point of $72.

    B. profit if the stock price rises above the breakeven point of $70.

*C. profit if the stock price rises above the breakeven point of $72.

Explanation: LOS: Reading 57-c

Breakeven is when $0 = \text{maximum} [\, 0, (S - X)] - \text{premium}$, when $S = \$72$

21. A trader sells one wheat futures contract, which is for 5,000 bushels of wheat, at $4 per bushel. The trader posts an initial margin of $1,500. If the required maintenance margin is $1,100 the trader would first receive a maintenance margin call at a wheat price *closest* to:

    A. $3.92 per bushel.

    B. $4.08 per bushel.

    C. $5.45 per bushel.

---

22. When stock prices and interest rates are both rising, holding a long futures position is:

    A. less attractive than holding an equivalent long forward position.

    B. more attractive than holding an equivalent long forward position.

    C. has exactly the same payoff as holding an equivalent long forward position.

21. A trader sells one wheat futures contract, which is for 5,000 bushels of wheat, at $4 per bushel. The trader posts an initial margin of $1,500. If the required maintenance margin is $1,100 the trader would first receive a maintenance margin call at a wheat price *closest* to:

    A. $3.92 per bushel.

*B. $4.08 per bushel.

    C. $5.45 per bushel.

Explanation: LOS: Reading 57-c

When he has made a loss of $400 he would receive a margin call, this is equivalent to a price rise of 8 cents, since he sold the contract.

---

22. When stock prices and interest rates are both rising, holding a long futures position is:

    A. less attractive than holding an equivalent long forward position.

*B. more attractive than holding an equivalent long forward position.

    C. has exactly the same payoff as holding an equivalent long forward position.

A. B

Explanation: LOS: Reading 58-f

Futures prices are marked to market daily so when prices are rising the profits can be reinvested at an increasing rate of interest, so in this environment futures are preferable to forwards.

23. Which of the following statements concerning futures and forward contracts is *most accurate*?

    A. Only forward contracts are guaranteed by a clearinghouse.

    B. Forward contracts tend to be more heavily regulated than futures contracts.

    C. A futures contract is a type of forward commitment that has standardized contract terms.

24. If there is no exchange of cash flows at the start of an interest rate swap where one party pays a fixed rate, the other party a floating rate, the initial value of the swap is:

    A. zero.

    B. the notional principal.

    C. the fixed rate multiplied by the notional principal.

23. Which of the following statements concerning futures and forward contracts is *most accurate*?

   A. Only forward contracts are guaranteed by a clearinghouse.

   B. Forward contracts tend to be more heavily regulated than futures contracts.

*C. A futures contract is a type of forward commitment that has standardized contract terms.

Explanation: LOS: Reading 57-a
A futures contract is a type of forward agreement that has standardized contract terms and is traded on a regulated exchange.

---

24. If there is no exchange of cash flows at the start of an interest rate swap where one party pays a fixed rate, the other party a floating rate, the initial value of the swap is:

*A. zero.

   B. the notional principal.

   C. the fixed rate multiplied by the notional principal.

Explanation: LOS: Reading 58-h
The value of the swap will be zero, the present value of each parties expected payments will be the same.

25. Which combination of factors would lead to the highest value of a put option?

Interest rates   Volatility of underlying

A. High   High

B. Low   High

C. High   Low

---

26. A European call option is worth more if:

A. more benefits are paid on the underlying.

B . there is a convenience yield on the underlying.

C. there are more costs incurred holding the underlying.

25. Which combination of factors would lead to the highest value of a put option?

   Interest rates   Volatility of underlying

   A. High   High

*B. **Low   High**

   C. High   Low

Explanation: LOS: Reading 58-k

The higher the volatility of the underlying the higher the value of both puts and calls. Low interest rates make puts relatively more attractive (and high interest rates calls more attractive).

---

26. A European call option is worth more if:

   A. more benefits are paid on the underlying.

   B . there is a convenience yield on the underlying.

*C. **there are more costs incurred holding the underlying.**

Explanation: LOS: Reading 58-k

High costs reduce the attraction of holding the underlying and increase the value of a call option which gives exposure to price movements in the underlying.

The holder of the call option will not receive the benefits (e.g. payments of dividends) and they will reduce the price of the underlying so they reduce the value of the call option. Option holders will also not receive the convenience yield associated with holding the underlying.

27. An investor writes a put option at a premium of $6 on a stock with an exercise price of $62. If the stock price is $70 at expiration the investor will make a profit of:

A. $2.

B. $6.

C. $8.

28. A portfolio insurance strategy for a diversified stock portfolio can be implemented by:

A. buying a put option on the stock index representing the underlying stock portfolio.

B. writing a put option on the stock index representing the underlying stock portfolio.

C. writing a covered call option on the stock index representing the underlying stock portfolio.

27. An investor writes a put option at a premium of $6 on a stock with an exercise price of $62. If the stock price is $70 at expiration the investor will make a profit of:

   A. $2.

*B. $6.

   C. $8.

Explanation: LOS: Reading 59-a

The put option will lapse worthless since the exercise price is lower than the market price, so the investor makes a profit of the premium that he collected.

28. A portfolio insurance strategy for a diversified stock portfolio can be implemented by:

*A. buying a put option on the stock index representing the underlying stock portfolio.

B. writing a put option on the stock index representing the underlying stock portfolio.

C. writing a covered call option on the stock index representing the underlying stock portfolio.

Explanation: LOS: Reading 59-b

In the situation that the stock market index falls, the losses on the underlying portfolio will be offset by the profits on the put option.

Study Session 18: Alternative Investments

Due to diversification benefits and higher expectations of investment returns, investors are increasingly turning to alternative investments. This study session describes the common types of alternative investments, methods for their valuation, unique risks and opportunities associated with them, and the relation between alternative investments and traditional investments. Although finding a single definition of an "alternative" investment is difficult, certain features (e.g., limited liquidity, infrequent valuations, and unique legal structures) are typically associated with alternative investments. This study session discusses these features and how to evaluate their impact on expected returns and investment decisions in more detail. The reading provides an overview of the major categories of alternative investments, including real estate, private equity, venture capital, hedge funds, closely held companies, distressed securities, and commodities. Each one of these categories has several unique characteristics, and the readings discuss valuation methods for illiquid assets (such as direct real estate or closely held companies), performance measures for private equity and venture capital investments, differences between various hedge fund strategies, and implementation vehicles for investments in alternative assets.

Reading Assignments

Reading 60:. Introduction to Alternative Investments
   by Terri Duhon, George Spentzos, CFA, and Scott D. Stewart, CFA

1. The target beta of a market-neutral hedge fund is:

    A. -1.

    B. 0.

    C. 1.

---

2. High water marks in hedge fund fee calculations ensure:

    A. performance fees are only paid when the return exceeds a hurdle rate.

    B. performance fees are repaid by the manager in the event of a negative return.

    C. investors don't pay performance fees for positive returns when the return is a recovery of a previous loss.

1. The target beta of a market-neutral hedge fund is:

  A. -1.

*B. 0.

  C. 1.

Explanation: LOS: Reading 60-d

The objective of a market-neutral fund is to have no net market exposure, so the beta would be close to zero.

---

2. High water marks in hedge fund fee calculations ensure:

  A. performance fees are only paid when the return exceeds a hurdle rate.

  B. performance fees are repaid by the manager in the event of a negative return.

*C. investors don't pay performance fees for positive returns when the return is a recovery of a previous loss.

Explanation: LOS: Reading 60-e

High water marks are established when the net asset value has reached a high point, performance fees are not charged again until after the fund has reached the previous high.

3. Standard deviation may not be an appropriate risk measure for alternative investments because:

A. it will overestimate downside risk.

B. alternative investment returns often exhibit positive skew.

C. alternative investment returns often exhibit a higher than expected probability of extreme losses.

4. Alternative investment strategies typically

A. target beta returns.

B. are passively managed.

C. aim to generate alpha returns.

3. Standard deviation may not be an appropriate risk measure for alternative investments because:

    A. it will overestimate downside risk.

    B. alternative investment returns often exhibit positive skew.

*C. alternative investment returns often exhibit a higher than expected probability of extreme losses.

Explanation: LOS: Reading 60-g

Returns from a commodity portfolio usually include interest or collateral yield. Blocks of constituents may be highly correlated but oil related commodities have often had almost no correlation with agricultural commodities, for example. The major commodity indices are at least partially weighted according to production volumes.

---

4. Alternative investment strategies typically

    A. target beta returns.

    B. are passively managed.

*C. aim to generate alpha returns.

Explanation: LOS: Reading 60-a

Although some alternative strategies are passive (e.g. ETFs) the majority aim to generate alpha returns.

5. The beta of equity hedge funds:

  A. are usually zero.

  B. are close to one.

  C. can be positive or negative.

6. The role of venture capital investors is *least likely* to include:

  A. assisting companies to go public.

  B. assisting the companies that they invest in with strategic planning.

  C. making a market in the shares of their investments that have gone public.

5. The beta of equity hedge funds:

   A. are usually zero.

   B. are close to one.

*C. can be positive or negative.

Explanation: LOS: Reading 60-d

Equity hedge funds can take long or short positions in individual securities or equity markets. Betas can be positive or negative depending on each fund's strategy.

---

6. The role of venture capital investors is *least likely* to include:

   A. assisting companies to go public.

   B. assisting the companies that they invest in with strategic planning.

*C. making a market in the shares of their investments that have gone public.

Explanation: LOS: Reading 60-d

The role of venture capitalists is not just to provide finance but to also work with the management team to develop and expand the business. This would usually include assisting with a company going public as venture capitalists have experience dealing with underwriters and other financial institutions. They would not normally be specialists or market makers.

7. Capital provided to a company that is close to going public is:

　　A. later-stage financing.

　　B. mezzanine financing.

　　C. second-stage financing.

8. Which of the following statements is the *most accurate* description of a characteristic of venture capital investing?

　　A. Liquidity is a feature of venture capital investment.

　　B. Investors often need to make a long-term commitment.

　　C. Entrepreneurs have strong management skills which increase the probability of companies being successful.

7. Capital provided to a company that is close to going public is:

A. later-stage financing.

*B. mezzanine financing.

C. second-stage financing.

Explanation: LOS: Reading 60-d

Mezzanine or bridge financing is given to companies who are planning to go public in the near term.

---

8. Which of the following statements is the *most accurate* description of a characteristic of venture capital investing?

A. Liquidity is a feature of venture capital investment.

*B. Investors often need to make a long-term commitment.

C. Entrepreneurs have strong management skills which increase the probability of companies being successful.

Explanation: LOS: Reading 60-d

Venture capital is illiquid and entrepreneurs often have weak management skills so the venture capitalist can help in providing direction and strategic guidance to the company.

9. A hedge fund manager specializes in taking long positions in companies that are being bid for and taking short positions in the acquiring company. He is *most likely* to be managing a hedge fund that is:

   A. a long/short fund.

   B. an event-driven fund.

   C. a market-neutral fund.

10. Using a Sharpe ratio to measure hedge fund performance may be misleading because:

   A. they are absolute return strategies.

   B. the distribution of hedge funds' returns may be asymmetric.

   C. performance measures using beta as the risk measure are more appropriate.

9. A hedge fund manager specializes in taking long positions in companies that are being bid for and taking short positions in the acquiring company. He is *most likely* to be managing a hedge fund that is:

 A. a long/short fund.

*B. an event-driven fund.

 C. a market-neutral fund.

Explanation: LOS: Reading 60-d

B is the best answer since the long and short positions are being taken as a result of specific events, in this case an acquisition.

---

10. Using a Sharpe ratio to measure hedge fund performance may be misleading because:

 A. they are absolute return strategies.

*B. the distribution of hedge funds' returns may be asymmetric.

 C. performance measures using beta as the risk measure are more appropriate.

Explanation: LOS: Reading 60-g

Returns from hedge funds can be skewed and/or exhibit kurtosis in which case standard deviation is not an appropriate risk measure.

11. In a leveraged buyout (LBO) it is common for the private equity firm:

A. to increase debt in the capital structure of the acquired company.

B. to increase their own borrowing secured by the assets of the acquired company.

C. to buy the debt of the acquired company in order to reduce the leverage of the company.

12. Which of the following is the *least accurate* description of a characteristic of commodity investment, based on historic data?

A. It offers inflation protection.

B. It has low volatility of returns.

C. The returns have low correlations with bond and equity returns.

11. In a leveraged buyout (LBO) it is common for the private equity firm:

*A. to increase debt in the capital structure of the acquired company.**

    B. to increase their own borrowing secured by the assets of the acquired company.

    C. to buy the debt of the acquired company in order to reduce the leverage of the company.

Explanation: LOS: Reading 60-d

Borrowing appears in the acquired company's balance sheet, it is collaterized by the acquired company's assets and interest is paid from the acquired company's cash flows.

---

12. Which of the following is the *least accurate* description of a characteristic of commodity investment, based on historic data?

    A. It offers inflation protection.

*B. It has low volatility of returns.**

    C. The returns have low correlations with bond and equity returns.

Explanation: LOS: Reading 60-d

Historically commodities have exhibited higher volatility than equities.

13. Investors in hedge funds are *least likely* to be motivated by which of the following?

   A. Consistent returns across the different categories of hedge funds.

   B. The low volatility of returns from hedge funds compared to equity returns.

   C. Higher average returns provided by hedge funds compared to other investments.

14. Which of the following statements regarding trade sales of private equity investments is the *most accurate*?

   A. Trade sales can maintain greater confidentiality than most exit strategies.

   B. Trade sales take longer and often incur higher transaction costs than an IPO.

   C. Trade sales are one of the most common method of selling investments to another private equity investor.

13. Investors in hedge funds are *least likely* to be motivated by which of the following?

*A. Consistent returns across the different categories of hedge funds.

   B. The low volatility of returns from hedge funds compared to equity returns.

   C. Higher average returns provided by hedge funds compared to other investments.

Explanation: LOS: Reading 60-d

Different types of hedge funds (e.g. fixed-income arbitrage versus global macro) have quite different performance records.

---

14. Which of the following statements regarding trade sales of private equity investments is the *most accurate*?

*A. Trade sales can maintain greater confidentiality than most exit strategies.

   B. Trade sales take longer and often incur higher transaction costs than an IPO.

   C. Trade sales are one of the most common method of selling investments to another private equity investor.

Explanation: LOS: Reading 60-d

Trade sales refer to a private equity investment being sold to a strategic buyer who is often a competitor. These can be quick, cheap and maintain confidentiality. C refers to a secondary sale.

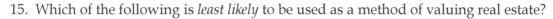

15. Which of the following is *least likely* to be used as a method of valuing real estate?

A. Cost approach.

B. Income approach.

C. Balance sheet approach.

16. There is the potential for the prices of certain hedge funds to be inaccurate because:

A. they use arbitrage strategies.

B. the managers adopt risky strategies.

C. they invest in over-the-counter instruments whose prices are based on estimates.

15. Which of the following is *least likely* to be used as a method of valuing real estate?

     A. Cost approach.

     B. Income approach.

*C. Balance sheet approach.

Explanation: LOS: Reading 60-e

The methods that are covered in the text are the cost approach, sales comparison approach and the income approach.

---

16. There is the potential for the prices of certain hedge funds to be inaccurate because:

     A. they use arbitrage strategies.

     B. the managers adopt risky strategies.

*C. they invest in over-the-counter instruments whose prices are based on estimates.

Explanation: LOS: Reading 60-e

Over the counter instruments do not have market prices and the values are often estimated.

17. Multi-strategy hedge funds offer investors:

A. diversification of strategy only.

B. diversification of manager only.

C. diversification of strategy and manager.

---

18. A clawback provision in a private equity refers to:

A. protecting the general partner by keeping funds in an escrow account to pay future incentive fees.

B. the private equity firms keeps a stake in an investment after an IPO in order to participate in any future growth of the investment.

C incentive fees being held back for potential distribution to limited partners to ensure they receive their initial investment plus their share of profits.

17. Multi-strategy hedge funds offer investors:

*A. diversification of strategy only.

   B. diversification of manager only.

   C. diversification of strategy and manager.

Explanation: LOS: Reading 60-d
Multi-strategy hedge funds invest across a range of strategies but the fund is usually managed by one manager so A is correct.

---

18. A clawback provision in a private equity refers to:

   A. protecting the general partner by keeping funds in an escrow account to pay future incentive fees.

   B. the private equity firms keeps a stake in an investment after an IPO in order to participate in any future growth of the investment.

*C incentive fees being held back for potential distribution to limited partners to ensure they receive their initial investment plus their share of profits.

Explanation: LOS: Reading 60-d
A clawback provision ensures the general partner does not withdraw fees and then, after possible poor performance of investments, there are insufficient funds to repay limited partners. Funds are set aside in an escrow account until limited partners are repaid their initial investment plus their share of any profits.

19. Historically (1990 – 2009) the correlation between commodities (the S&P GSCI Commodity Index) and global equities' returns has generally been:

A. slightly positive.

B. slightly negative.

C. moderately high.

20. Investors in hedge funds which hold illiquid assets:

A. can be protected by long notice periods for investors who wish to redeem their investments.

B. require short notice periods to redeem their investments to avoid being locked into a fund.

C. expect the hedge fund managers to buy illiquid holdings for their own account to ensure redemption requests can be met promptly.

19. Historically (1990 – 2009) the correlation between commodities (the S&P GSCI Commodity Index) and global equities' returns has generally been:

*A. slightly positive.

B. slightly negative.

C. moderately high.

Explanation: LOS: Reading 60-d

Between 1990 and 2009 the correlation was 0.160, commodities also have very low correlation to bonds over this period (0.133).

---

20. Investors in hedge funds which hold illiquid assets:

*A. can be protected by long notice periods for investors who wish to redeem their investments.

B. require short notice periods to redeem their investments to avoid being locked into a fund.

C. expect the hedge fund managers to buy illiquid holdings for their own account to ensure redemption requests can be met promptly.

Explanation: LOS: Reading 60-d

Short notice periods can force the manager to sell holdings in a declining market, if they are illiquid this will force down prices to the detriment of investors in the fund.

21. The general partner of a private equity fund generally receives a management fee based on:

   A. invested capital.

   B. committed capital.

   C. the performance of the investments.

22. Private equity firms usually charge management fees on:

   A. invested capital.

   B. committed capital.

   C. assets under management.

21. The general partner of a private equity fund generally receives a management fee based on:

    A. invested capital.

*B. committed capital.

    C. the performance of the investments.

Explanation: LOS: Reading 60-d

The general partner's management fee is typically 1 to 3% of committed capital. An additional incentive fee is paid based on the investment return exceeding the amount invested by the limited partners or a prespecified target return.

---

22. Private equity firms usually charge management fees on:

*A. invested capital.

    B. committed capital.

    C. assets under management.

Explanation: LOS: Reading 60-d

The fees are charged on committed capital, even if this money is not drawn down and invested.

23. The roll yield for an investor who has taken short positions in commodity futures:

A. is positive when producers are dominating the futures market.

B. is negative when the commodity futures market is in contango.

C. will be higher when the commodity futures market is in contango rather than backwardation.

---

24. A property which is considered a lower risk investment than another property investment, assuming they both generate the same net operating income, will be likely to have a:

Capitalization rate Valuation

A. lower lower

B. lower higher

C. higher lower

23. The roll yield for an investor who has taken short positions in commodity futures:

    A. is positive when producers are dominating the futures market.

    B. is negative when the commodity futures market is in contango.

*C. will be higher when the commodity futures market is in contango rather than backwardation.

Explanation: LOS: Reading 67-b

For a short futures position the roll yield is positive when the futures price is above the spot price i.e. when the market is in contango. When producers dominate the futures price will tend to be below the spot price.

---

24. A property which is considered a lower risk investment than another property investment, assuming they both generate the same net operating income, will be likely to have a:

      Capitalization rate Valuation

    A. lower lower

*B. lower higher

    C. higher lower

Explanation: LOS: Reading 60-e

The capitalization rate reflects the investors' required rate of return from the property, a low risk project will tend to have a low capitalization rate and therefore, for equal net operating income, a higher value.

25. An investor is considering purchasing an office building as an investment, and the following information has been collected. The figures are on an annual basis.

Gross potential rental income	$1,000,000
Estimated vacancy and collection losses	5%
Insurance and taxes	$80,000
Utilities	$30,000
Repairs and maintenance	$60,000
Depreciation	$70,000
Interest on proposed financing	$90,000

The net operating income (NOI) per annum is *closest* to

   A. $690,000.

   B. $710,000.

   C. $780,000.

26. Investing in a hedge fund is *least likely* to be attractive because:

   A. the volatility of returns is lower than that of a fund investing in equities.

   B. the fund will provide greater transparency than a traditional mutual fund.

   C. the return from the fund is likely to have an imperfect correlation with listed stocks and bonds.

25. An investor is considering purchasing an office building as an investment, and the following information has been collected. The figures are on an annual basis.

Gross potential rental income	$1,000,000
Estimated vacancy and collection losses	5%
Insurance and taxes	$80,000
Utilities	$30,000
Repairs and maintenance	$60,000
Depreciation	$70,000
Interest on proposed financing	$90,000

The net operating income (NOI) per annum is *closest* to

    A. $690,000.

    B. $710,000.

*C. $780,000.

Explanation: LOS: Reading 60-e

NOI = gross potential rental income minus expenses

= $1,000,000 – (0.05 x $1,000,000) - $80,000 - $30,000 - $60,000

= $780,000

Note the expenses for this calculation do not include depreciation (it is assumed that repairs will maintain the building in good condition indefinitely) and interest expense.

26. Investing in a hedge fund is *least likely* to be attractive because:

   A. the volatility of returns is lower than that of a fund investing in equities.

*B. the fund will provide greater transparency than a traditional mutual fund.

   C. the return from the fund is likely to have an imperfect correlation with listed stocks and bonds.

Explanation: LOS: Reading 60-d

The most common legal structure is limited partnership (in the US) or an offshore corporation. The legal structure gives the fund managers not only the freedom to implement a variety of strategies but there are less stringent disclosure requirements than for traditional funds. Lack of transparency of hedge funds can be a major drawback for investors.

Download Instructions

The Financial Exams version 4.0

Chartered Financial Analyst (CFA) Level 1 Volume 2 Practice Exam

System Requirements: Windows 95 & 98, Windows NT, Windows 2000/XP, Windows Server 2003 and Windows Server 2010 with a minimum of 60 MB hard disk space and 64 MB RAM

Financial Exams will help you accomplish your CFA Certifications. This state of art software program is designed to cut your study time in half, and get you to a passing knowledge level in the easiest and shortest amount of time possible. The program will adapt to you personally, and then lay out a prioritized study plan that will visually show you your progress on a day to day basis. When the software has recognized that you are at a passing level in each objective category, you're ready to sit for the exam. It's really that easy!

Installation Instructions:

Visit: http://www.financialexams.com

To obtain the FE practice exam simply visit the engine download link.

FinancialExams CFA Level I Volume 2 Mock Exam and Engine Download *

To download the software Click on the link or copy the link to your browser

http://www.financialExams.com/Downloads/CFA2015/ CFA2015B550L1.zip

When the computer prompts you to open or save, choose "save this file to disk."

Select the location for the download file CFA2015B550L1.zip

Your license keys may be found in the download files.

Visit: http://www.financialexams.com

contact Bruce@financialexams.com for Download and Installation Instructions:

Please use Exam Wise Volume 2 Workbook as the Subject.

Starting FinancialExams To start the program the next time (if it doesn't start automatically), select FinancialExams from the Program's menu. Assistance with running and using FE is available under the Help menu.

Content Downloads and Financial Forums
Call 281-992-3131
www.financialexams.com
www.cfaexams.com

Good Luck with your certification!
Your Book Registration Number EW2015-550L1B

Lightning Source UK Ltd.
Milton Keynes UK
UKOW07f1903160915

258766UK00012B/479/P